新编国际贸易函电

主编　张干周　郭社森

编者　（按姓氏音序排列）

曹晓明　郭社森　李　贞

薛　媛　张干周　周　映

ZHEJIANG UNIVERSITY PRESS

浙江大学出版社

图书在版编目（CIP）数据

　　新编国际贸易函电 / 张干周，郭社森主编. — 杭州：
浙江大学出版社，2015.10
　　ISBN 978-7-308-15006-4

　　Ⅰ．①新… Ⅱ．①张… ②郭… Ⅲ．①国际贸易－英
语－电报信函－写作－高等学校－教材 Ⅳ．①H315

　　中国版本图书馆CIP数据核字(2015)第194287号

新编国际贸易函电
Correspondence in International Trade (New Version)
张干周　郭社森　主编

责任编辑	曾熙（zxpeggy@zju.edu.cn）	
封面设计	春天书装	
出版发行	浙江大学出版社	
	（杭州市天目山路148号　　邮政编码　310007）	
	（网址：http://www.zjupress.com）	
排　　版	杭州林智广告有限公司	
印　　刷	杭州杭新印务有限公司	
开　　本	787mm×1092mm　1/16	
印　　张	16.75	
字　　数	500千	
版 印 次	2015年10月第1版　2015年10月第1次印刷	
书　　号	ISBN 978-7-308-15006-4	
定　　价	35.00元

前　言

　　2006年，浙江大学出版社策划并组织全省高校一线教师编写了一套实用性强、适合于培养应用技术型高级人才需求的教材，《国际贸易函电》便是该套教材中的一本，教材出版以来，作为培养国际贸易应用型人才的全英文教材，历经几次印刷，在全国许多高校使用。

　　随着我国经济的快速发展，对外开放和交流进一步深入，对外贸易稳步增长；同时，随着现代网络和通信技术的快速发展，对外贸易开始由传统的贸易形式向多样化的贸易形式转变，网络电商、微商的发展更是高歌猛进，面对新的发展形势，为了适应市场发展的需求，我们组织了长期从事一线教学的教师，通过与外贸企业工作人员的沟通和交流，结合新形势下国际贸易行业对外贸人才的要求，组织对《国际贸易函电》进行了全面彻底的修订，重新编写了这本《新编国际贸易函电》教材。

　　本教材是一本融英语语言知识、英语写作知识和国际贸易知识于一体的语言应用教程，同时也是一本职业技能提高教程。本教材旨在帮助学生了解贸易业务的各个环节，学习和掌握英语在各业务环节中的应用。《新编国际贸易概述》共有18章，重点涵盖了国际贸易业务磋商过程中各个环节的往来函电，涉及商务写作概述、资信调查、建立业务关系、询价与回复、报价与促销、还盘、订货与回复、支付、包装、装运、货运单证、保险、投诉与处理、代理、会展、招标与投标、签订合同、电子商务等。

　　国际贸易既有货物贸易，也有服务贸易。目前，我国许多企业在国际市场上，在对外承包大型工程项目方面越来越活跃，承包的项目也越来越多，为此，我们在教材中增加了会展、招投标的内容。同时，随着国际贸易形式的多样化，本教材也涵盖了电子商务等方面的E-mail函电的写作内容。

　　本教材的主要特点是突出了知识性、应用性、职业性。为了便于课堂教学和自学，帮助学习者更好地了解、掌握和运用国际贸易函电的相关知识，本教材通过实例系统地讲解了国际贸易函电的格式和写作技巧，每一章都列明该章节的学习目标，安排有案例分析、背景介绍、样信、写作模板、关键词汇和短语、实用句型结构等几个部分。为了便于读者学习、操练和检测，巩固和拓展相关知识，每一章的最后都配有课后练习，增加了补充阅读材料，教材的后面附有参考答案。使用本教材时，需要熟读范文，掌握各种文体格式的要求，结合写作模板，勤加练习，这样就一定能够为国际贸易函电的写作奠定坚实的基础。

　　本教材作者在编写过程中吸取众家之长，搜集了许多有关函电的具体实例，参阅了许多国际贸易和国际商务函电写作方面的资料，咨询了部分外贸公司从业人员，在此特表示衷心的感谢。

　　本书编写分工分别为：周映负责第一章，郭社森和张干周共同负责第二、十三、十四、十五、十六、十七章，曹晓明负责第四、五、六、十八章，李贞负责第十、十一、十二章，薛媛负责第三、七、八、九章，全书由张干周负责通稿工作。

　　由于编者的水平有限，书中错误或不妥之处肯定不少，敬请广大读者和专家批评指正。

编者于杭州

2015年8月

Contents
目录

Chapter 1
Overview of Business Writings
商务写作概述

1. Learning Objectives

By the end of this chapter, you will be able to do the following:

· Understand the essentials of business letter writing.

· Get to know the principles of business letter writing.

· Know the structure of business letters.

· Know the format of business letters.

2. Case Study

Compare the following two letters, suppose you were a sales manager in an export company, when you receive the following two letters from separate companies simultaneously, which one would you prefer to keep in contact and make quotation?

Letter 1

Dear Charles Smith,

We have received your letter dated at an early date. We are interested on the woman shirts you mentioned.

It will be grateful for you to send 5 samples with various sizes (XS, S, M, L, XL) in pink. We will ask for quotation by airmail if the samples could be satisfied.

The bank of your city will give you any information about credit.

We insist on a prompt answer to our letter.

Yours friendly,
[Signature]

Letter 2

Dear Charles Smith,

We have received your letter dated on Sept. 16th, 2014. We are interested in the woman shirts you mentioned.

I should be grateful to you if you could send 5 samples with various sizes (XS, S, M, L, and XL) in pink to us. We will ask you to send a quotation by airmail if the samples could be satisfactory.

You may obtain any infomation, if needed, regarding our credit from the Bank of your city.

> We await your early reply.
>
> Yours friendly,
> [Signature]

Generally, good English is one of the basics for good business letters. Meanwhile, some writing principles are also vital.

3. Introduction

Business writing is very important in foreign trade. Despite increased dependence on technology, such as video-conferencing and voice-mail, telegrams, telexes and cables, the most frequent type of business communication is the written document. Effective business writings will benefit the international trade.

It is estimated that close to 100 million business letters are written each workday. Although it is recognized that the style of modern business letters tends to be something like a piece of conversation by post, many executives prefer a written document to other forms of communication, for it is a formal communication tool. Not only can it serve as a contract, but it provides a permanent record. In this way no one is required to rely on memory. You never know what will happen with a verbal conversation. What is more, improvements in communication technology have also increased the delivery of writing. Obviously, written communications are cheaper than other ways. Beyond time zones, business letters are more effective, especially through e-mail or fax. This is why it is important for learners of business communications to master the skills of writing a good business letter, whose function is to get or to convey business information, to make or to accept an offer, and to keep various businesses moving, especially in companies of foreign concerns.

Good English is one of the bases of good business letters, specially, free from grammatical errors. Thus, a business letter can be challenging to write, because you must consider how to keep your readers' attention. Therefore, every business letter could be considered a sales letter. Simply speaking, writing a business letter is like any other document. First, you must analyze your reader and determine your purpose. Then, gather information, create an outline, write a draft, and revise it. Finally, get to the point quickly and present your information clearly. There are certain essential principles of business writings.

4. Principles of Business Letter Writing

Many times, business letters are adverts for companies, which leave significant impressions to customers. Different criteria for good business letters are provided, for example, the "ABC" principle, which stands for Accurate, Brief and Clear. This book would introduce seven "Cs", i.e. correctness, clarity, conciseness, courtesy, completeness, concreteness and considerateness. These are principles of business letter writing widely accepted.

Correctness

Correctness here not only refers to the correct grammar rules, contents and the forms, but also accuracy in style, language and typing. No excuse can make any errors acceptable in business letters, because it concerns the rights, benefits, responsibilities of both sides. Incorrectness cause inconvenience, disputes, and may destroy the relationship between both sides.

On one hand, to choose the right words, that is, to choose the words that can most closely convey the meaning is one of the ways to improve the readability of your business writings. Try to write free from the slightest possibility of being misunderstood. For the changing international market, the letter is expected to express the writer's commands and principles absolutely, so as to help the receiver to make decisions quickly, rather than wasting time. Of course, flowery words and jargon are not included in the right words. In business letters, the date, specification, price, quantity, discount, commission and figures are very important, for they are usually the central points of disputes.

On the other hand, the right tone is also significant. According to the Merriam-Webster dictionary, tone is the use of accent and inflection to express a mood or emotion. Often, it is not what you say, but how you say it. In writing any letter, it is always a good idea to think about your tone so that you do not risk upsetting the reader. Usually, mistakes with tone can be avoided by using the following techniques:

- Place more emphasis on the reader than yourself.
- Avoid extreme cases of humility, flattery, and modesty.
- Avoid condescension.
- Avoid lecturing.

In a word, in order to eliminate mistakes, the more urgent the matter is, the more carefully the letter should be checked and rechecked.

Clarity

A point that is ambiguous in a letter will cause trouble to both sides, and further exchange of letters for explanation will become inevitable, thus time will be lost. In this way, clarity is often considered to be one of the main writing principles and language features.

To achieve clearness and clarity, you may give your letter a heading if it can help to draw the addressee's attention. You must have a clear idea of what you wish to convey in the letter, such as the purpose, the attitude, and the matter concerned. Only a clear mind can express clearly. While drafting an outline, pay attention to the organization, as it is a key to effective business writing. There is altogether 14 parts in a business letter. A separate paragraph for each point, if necessary number each of them, is a good rule. Thus, the recipient may find each point so clear that it can't be misunderstood. Second, you should study the reader' interest and the level of the reader's understanding, and try to imagine how he will feel about what you write. For this reason, business letter must be clear and easily understood. It is said that more than twenty words in a sentence makes reading harder. Thirdly, avoid making the idea confusing by writing the exact and brief words. The following are some tips:

· Use small and short words instead of big and long-winded words when they are synonyms.

· Use simple words instead of complicated phrases.

· Use short sentences instead of long and prolix sentences.

· Except for emphasis, try to avoid using unnecessary words like adjectives, adverbs and phrases.

· Do not use words hard to understand, such as colloquialism, slang and commercial jargon.

· Do not use words having more than one meaning in a sentence.

Conciseness

Clarity and conciseness often go hand-in-hand. Today businessmen are very busy, so clear and concise letters, without sacrificing completeness, are becoming more and more popular. A concise letter is not always a short one. It is found that a succession of short sentences, however, has a disagreeable jerky effort and the best letters are those which provide a mixture of sentences of varying length. A concise letter should be written in a simple and natural way, directly and to the point. Avoid wordiness, flowery words, redundancies and the over frequent use of such conjunction as "and" "but" "however", etc.

Courtesy

Here, courtesy not only means politeness, but also means thinking about the reader's interest, by expressing your enthusiasm, consideration and friendliness. So while writing, put yourself in your reader's shoes, and find out what really concerns him. An honest and professional manner may gain you cooperative partner.

Firstly, promptness is very important. No one likes to wait endlessly for a reply. So if you cannot respond promptly, write and explain why and when you will write again.

Secondly, a warm and friendly tone is more suitable to letter writing. It helps you keep a friendly relationship with the partner and continue to develop your trade relationship.

Thirdly, as the buyer and the seller have both common and contradictory interests, keep in mind the distinction. While writing, express your principles clearly and shows the position of equality and mutual benefit. Any virtue overdone will bring with it some undesirable effort.

Fourthly, pay special attention to names, titles, and genders. Never make mistake on the spelling of the recipient's name, his job title, or gender. It is a basic way to show your respect and courtesy.

Completeness

In business letters, keep in mind that all the information should be covered to help the reader to understand the purpose. Try your best to answer all the questions and requirements put forward by the readers. Incompleteness will lead to the counterpart's unfavorable impression of your firm. If it is urgent, or if other firms can provide him more detailed information, he may give up the deal. Sometimes, incompleteness will even cause unnecessary disputes and lawsuit. There is a way to verify the completeness of what you write, that is five "Ws" (who, what, where, when and why) and one "h" (how). So try to check and recheck the letter.

Concreteness

It is required to be specific, definite and vivid in business letters in the principle of concreteness. Thus you should try to provide specific facts, figures, time and active verbs. The following example is vague, general and abstract: The goods will be delivered soon. However, it is better to express like this: The goods under you order No.1010 for fans will be delivered this afternoon and will reach you in about 10 days.

Considerateness

Considerateness means you should be considerate of the recipients. Try to lay great emphasis on the "you- attitude" rather than "we-attitude". In business letters, you should always remember the person to whom you are writing and try to write in a way to make the recipients feel comfortable. Pay much attention to the recipients' requests, needs, desires, even their feelings. If you fail to meet your customers' demands, you should provide the reasons and show your concern about them. Positive sentences are preferred instead of negative ones. Meanwhile, never push your reader to do something.

To summarize, while writing business letters, you should try to obey all the seven "Cs" principles. Business letters are related with the success of business, thus a high standard of layout, structural frames, protocols are required. Business letters represent you as well as the company you worked for.

5. Structure of Business Letters

Structure of business letters can be divided into two parts: the essential part and the optional part. The essential part consists of seven components, namely, the letterhead, the date, the inside name and address, the salutation, the body of the letter, the complimentary close and the signature. Your company may have specific requirements that you must use. For instance, a company might have a particular way of presenting a salutation or may use a specific type of letterhead. Because a business letter is an effective way to communicate a message, its format should allow readers to quickly grasp information. This information should stand out as the document is scanned. Remember, a business letter reflects your professionalism. There are altogether 14 items, which are listed in the order that they normally appear:

The Letterhead
The Reference line
The Date

The Inside name and address

The Attention Line

The Salutation

The Subject Heading
The Body

The Complimentary Close
[Signature]

Enclosure Notation
C. C.
Identification Initials
P.S. Notations

Example

Beijing Textiles Imp.& Exp.Corp.
11 Renming Road
Beijing 10005, China
Telephone: 86-10-6252-0620
Fax: 86-10-6252-0620
E-mail: textile@ 126.com

Our Ref. _____
Your Ref. _____

Date: December 12, 2014

Messrs Ronald & Co.
87 Eastcheap
London, E.C. 3, England

Attention: Export Department

Dear Sir,

Sub: <u>Detailed information of cotton bed-sheets</u>

Edward Cullen informs us that your company is exporting all cotton bed-sheets. We are particularly interested in your products, and would like to have more detailed information on all of your commodities, including various ranges of sizes, colors and prices, and also samples of the different qualities of material used.

We are large dealers in textiles in China and believe there is a promising market in our area for moderately priced goods of the kinds mentioned.

Yours faithfully,
[Signature]
(Manager)
Beijing Textiles Imp. & Exp. Corp.

Ref. No.
Enclosures
C. C. our Shanghai Branch Office
P.S. We require payment and discount not less than 200 dozen of individual items.

The Letterhead

In many companies, the letterhead are often printed, containing the company's name, address, postcode, telephone number, fax number, e-mail address, website, the addresses of branches or a logo of the company etc. The letterhead is the point of reference of the writer's company for the recipient. As the first and most obvious part of a company's business letter, the letterhead has a function to convey a favorable impression of the writer's firm. The order should be:

· Name and address of the firm.
· Postcode.
· Telephone numbers.
· Fax numbers.
· E-mail address.
· Website.

If the letterhead stationery is not used, the format of the letterhead shall be:

Weavewell Woolen Co. Ltd.
113 Park Avenue New York,
New York 10007
Tel: 224-4980   Fax: 897877
E-mail: master@gmail.com

If the letterhead stationery is used, the format of the letterhead shall be:

CMC INTERNATIONAL ENGINEERING CO., LTD.

Our Ref.	Page(s) No.	Date:

No.178, Guang'anmen Wai Street, Beijing, China   Post Code: 100055
Tel: 0086-10-62520620   Fax: 0086-10-62520621
Baghdad Office: Al-Andlus Q. - Mahala 611-Zukak 77-House

The Date

Every letter should be dated. Date should be placed two or four spaces below the letterhead. The date is vital, because it plays an important role of evidence of the communication. Remember to write the date in full, in the logical order of day, month, year. For the day, either cardinal numbers (1, 2, 3, 4, etc.) or ordinal numbers (1st, 2nd, 3rd, 4th, etc.) can be used, but cardinal numbers are preferred. The day can also be written after the month, in this way, a comma must be used between the day and the year. The month should not be abbreviated or represented by figures.

· September 6, 2014—American form

· 6th September, 2014—British form

It is unwise to give the day in figure (e.g. 6/9/2014) for the various ways of writing dates in different countries. It may easily cause confusion because in Britain this date would mean 6th October 2014, but in the United States and some other countries it would mean 9th June 2014.

It should be mentioned that sometimes the computer year-month-date sequence is adjusted in the expression of e.g. 20140906.

The Inside Name and Address

The inside name and address of the receiver is typed at the left-hand margin and two to six spaces below the date. But in official (i.e. government) correspondence, it is sometimes placed at the foot, in the bottom left-hand corner. The town should be in capital letters. In order to avoid ambiguity, when you write letters to other countries, always include the name of the country, even if the city mentioned is the country's capital. English addresses may have the following parts (not all addresses have all the parts):

· Name of person addressed

- Title of person addressed
- Name of organization
- Name and number of house
- Name and number of street
- Name of city or town
- Country or state and its post-code
- Name of country

When the receiver is a company, the inside name and address should be written as follows, for example:

The Space Engineering Co. ltd.

858 Mountain Place

LONDON N.W. 34

England

At this point one must pay attention, when the firm is named after one or more persons, e.g.: James, Jone Co., You can write Messrs. James & Co.

When the receiver is an individual in the company, the person's name should be preceded by the courtesy title.

- Mr./Messrs (plural)
- Mrs. — for mistress, used for a married woman
- Miss — for an unmarried woman
- Ms. — for all women, married or unmarried, particularly career women, who strongly object to being addressed as Mrs. or Miss

When the receiver holds special title and official position, such as Professor, Colonel, Marketing Manager, you may use the academic title or the title of a person's position, for example:

Ms. Sarah Davis

Sales Manager

The Acme Shoe Co. Ltd.

21 Sunny Road

Telex System, Inc.

Shenzhen Branch P. O. Box 350

P.R. China

The Salutation

You begin your letter, with the salutation, the polite greeting. To some extent, the salutation settles the form of the complimentary close. The salutation is conventionally placed two lines below the address, and before the body of letter. The function of a salutation is not only showing politeness, but also a double check to the recipient that the message is indeed intended for him. The following are some common usages.

"Dear Madam or Sir" or centered in a line "to whom it may concern:".

If you are not certain whether a man or woman manages the company, you'd better use "Dear Madam or Sir", which often followed by a comma.

"Dear Sir/Dear Madam (Dear Sir/Dear Mesdames)" is often followed by a comma, but not a name.

Americans prefer to use Gentlemen, but it cannot be used in the singular followed by a colon. One may also use "Ladies and Gentlemen".

When use Miss/Mr./Mrs./Ms., a person's surname should always be followed.

The Body of the Letter

The body of a business letter should begin two lines below the subject line, if there is one, or the salutation. It is the actual message of the letter. As mentioned above, the body of the letter should be written according to the seven important principles: correctness, clearness, conciseness, courtesy, completeness, concreteness and considerateness. It should be planned and paragraphed carefully. Usually, the first paragraph refers to the previous correspondence and the last one to future actions and plans. There should be only one topic in each paragraph. The next two questions may help you conceive the letter. What is the purpose of writing the letter? And what is the best way to start writing it? The body of the letter is the most important part, and it deserves our special attention.

For example, in a reply, its date and reference number should be mentioned to remind the reader, e. g. Thank you for your letter 458GW/gp of October 23, 2014.

The Complimentary Close

Like the salutation, the complimentary close is merely a matter of custom and a polite way of bringing a letter to a close. It is placed two lines below the last line of the body of the letter. A comma can be either used or omitted.

· Yours faithfully, / Faithfully yours, — formal in Britain

· Yours truly, / Truly yours, — commonly used in America and Canada

· Yours sincerely, /Sincerely yours, — if you don't know the recipient's gender

· Best wishes/ Best regards/ Yours, — informal used between close friends or persons known to each other.

The Signature

All letters must be signed, because signed letters have authority. You may sign name in ink (a rubber stamp is a form of discourtesy.) and type your name, job title or position below the signature. A typed name makes the signature legible.

If the signature is on behalf of a certain organization or a certain person with special authority, the letter P.P.(per procuration) can be placed before the full name of the organization or the person, for example:

Sincerely yours

P. P. Smart Trading Co. Ltd.

[Signature]

Mr. Dugmore

P.P.J.Fisher

Marketing Manager

The Optional Parts

Here are some optional parts which could be used in an appropriate way. They are the reference line, the attention line, the subject heading, the enclosure notation, the C.C. line, the identification initials, the P.S. notations.

The Reference Line

The reference line includes a file number, the goods type, department code or the initials of the signer of the letter to be followed by the typist's initials and etc. This enables replies to be linked with previous correspondence in business communication and ensures that they reach the right person or department without delay.

(1) Many letterheads provide spaces for references, above the inside address, for example:
Your ref: DNM-023/025

　　　　Our ref.: 007A/GAZ/fsh

(2) The reference may form part of the first paragraph of the reply letter:

　　Dear Sir,

　　　　Thank you for your letter, reference ALM/PS, of 25th September.

(3) Or the reference may be typed as a heading:

　　Dear Sir,

Your Ref: BEF/PS

The Attention Line

If the letter is urgent, and the writer wishes an organization to direct it to a particular member, this phrase is used. It is typed two line-spaces above the salutation, underlined, and sometimes centered over the body of the letter, for example:

The Secretary

The Ajax Electrical Co., Ltd.

Fernhall Drive

REDBRIDGE, Essex IG4 5BN

England

For the attention of Mr. T. Waterhouse

It has many other forms, such as Attention: Plan Department; Attention of Mr. Lin Wei;

Attention Marketing Manager.

The Subject Line

The Purpose of subject line is to invite attention to the topic of the letter, just like a title. It is usually centered over the body of the letter and two lines below the salutation. Make sure to provide an attractive heading to your letter. The following are two examples:

(1) Dear Jack,

Subject: <u>Delay in Delivery of Goods</u>

(2) Dear Karin,

Subject: <u>Letter of Credit No. 7709</u>

The Enclosure Notation

Enclosure refers to the added documents followed two lines below the signature at the bottom left-hand, with a figure and certain kinds indicating the number of enclosures, if there are more than one, for example:

> Enclosure: (1) One check
>   (2) The price list
> Enl: 2 invoices

The C.C. line

If copies of the letter are sent to others and the writer wants the recipient to know that, a copy notation—the C.C. line is placed below the enclosure at the left margin. C.C. stands for "Carbon Copies". It has some forms, for example:

C. C. : Ms. J. Cooper

(Ms. J. Cooper is the person who will receive the copies of the letter.)

cc Mr. Lin Wei

c/c: Mr. B. Leung

Copy to Adam Brown.

If copies of the letter are sent to more than a person, you may list their names in alphabetical order, for example:

> Copies to Adam Brown
>   Lin Wei

The Identification Initials

The identification initials mean the initials of the signer's or the typist's name, if it is written by another one, even the dictator's name. The function is to help the recipient to find out the letter more easily. The forms can be GAZ/fsh , GAZ:fsh, or GAZ/zy/fsh.

The P.S. Notation

A postscript (P.S.) is an emphasis, aiming at drawing the reader's attention. If you forget to mention a point in the body, don't use a postscript, since it is a sign of poor planning; it is advisable to rewrite the letter. As a special device the postscript is placed two lines below at the left margin, it has two functions:

Some executives, to add a personal touch to their typewritten letter, occasionally use a postscript in pen and ink.

For emphatic inclusion, writers of sales letters often withhold one last convincing argument in a postscript, for example:

P.S. I'm going to see you at the Pakistan Trading Company.

Format of Business Letter

Although business letter-writing tends to be a less conventional style, the layout or mechanical structure of a letter, as it is called, still follows a more or less set pattern determined by custom. Thus when writing a business letter, you will convey concrete contents and follow a general format. Modern business letters are usually printed instead of written by the writer his own. Usually speaking, there are three kinds of layouts of business letters: indented style, full block style, and modified block style. Of the three layouts, the indented style is the most formal and conventional. As for the writer, a good plan to make correct practice habitual is to adopt one form of layout and to stick to it.

Indented Style

For the indented style, the first line of a new paragraph should be indented by a four-letter space. It is a traditional British style, and it looks attractive.

                                                              ABC Bottles Pty Ltd.
                                                              Kirra Road, Ashtown 398
                                                              July 23, 1999

Mrs.R.G.Cole
Manager
Mables Pty Ltd.
Canterbury780

Dear Sir or Madam,

    ....
....
....
....

                                                                  Yours Faithfully,
                                                                 [Signature]

Full Block Style

In the full block style, a uniform left margin for each line of the letter should be followed including the date and signature lines etc. Although it is unbalanced and less social, it is the commonest style among the three, for it is business-like and easy to prepare. More than 80% of all business letters are written in the full block style. It is an American style.

```
                                          ABC Bottles Pty Ltd.
                                          Kirra Road, Ashtown 398
                                          June 23,2009


Mrs. R.G. Stevenson
Mana ger
Mables Pty Ltd.
Canterbury 8

Dear Madam,

......................................................................................................
......................................................................................................
......................................................................................................
..................................................................
......................................................................................................
...............................................

Yours Sincerely,
[Signature]
```

Modified Block Style

Almost all addressing lines are placed at the left margin, except the letterhead, date, the complimentary close and signature. This modified blocked style is preferred by older reader and has come to be much more widely used than before. It seems more balanced and more gracious.

```
                                          ABC Bottles Pty Ltd.
                                          Kirra Road, Ashtown 680
                                          June 23, 2009

Mrs. R. G. Stevenson
Manager
Mables Pty Ltd.
Canterbury 8

Dear Madam,
```

....
....
....
....
....
....

Yours Sincerely,
[Signature]

Envelope Addressing

Envelope is used to send some files which are quite formal and important. Accuracy, legible and good appearance are the three important requirements of envelope addressing. The style of envelope address should be the same as the inside address on the letter. Usually no punctuation is used on the envelope. Ordinarily, the return address should be written in the upper left corner of the envelope. The name and address of the receiver should be written above half way down from top to bottom and one third of the way across the envelope from left to right. Type words such as "Avenue" in full, except for No. in post office Box Number. The town and country name should be typed in block capitals. Post notation should be placed in the bottom left-hand corner, like, Registered, Confidential, Via Air Mail, sample of no value, Private, Urgent. Usually speaking, the address of the envelope should be written in the following order:

Name of the addressee
Number and street
City, State, and Zip code
Country
There are usually two forms: full block form, and intended form.

Full Block Form

University of Illinois
Stamp
56 Park Street
CHICAGO,ILLINOIS, USA.

Mr. Bill Stevenson
34 Street John's Square
LONDON EC5
ENGLAND

Via Air Mail/Par Avion

Intended Form

University of Illinois
  56 Park Street
    CHICAGO, ILLINOIS, USA.

                    Mr. Bill Stevenson
                    34 Street John's Square
                    LONDON EC5
                      ENGLAND

Via Air Mail

6. Key Words & Expressions

(1) concise 简洁的，简明的

(2) wordiness 啰嗦，冗长

(3) courtesy 礼貌，殷勤

(4) enclosure 附件

(5) layout 版式

(6) letterhead 信头

(7) salutation 称呼语

(8) full-block 全平头式

(9) indented style 缩进式

(10) left margin 左边的留空

(11) Messrs. (Mr.的复数，用于多个男子姓名前，也可用在公司称号前)

(12) signature 签字

(13) carbon copy (副本)抄送

(14) draw one's attention 提醒某人注意

(15) addressee 收件人

(16) reference 编号

(17) subject line 事由

7. Useful Sentence Patterns

(1) We are particularly interested in your products, and would like to have more detailed information on all of your commodities. 本公司对贵方的产品特别感兴趣，盼能从贵方获得更多商品的详细资料。

(2) We take the liberty of writing to you to enquire for Men's Shirts you advertised in *China Daily*. 冒昧写信给贵方，是想了解贵公司在《中国日报》上刊登的男式衬衫的详细信息。

(3) We are willing to establish trade relations with your company. 我们希望与贵公司建立业务往来。

(4) Please allow us to express our hope of opening an account with you. 我们希望在贵方开立一个账户。

(5) We are in the market for chemicals. 我们要购买化工产品。

(6) We are in the market for Chinese leather shoes and should be obliged if you would send us your best quotation. 我方拟购中国皮鞋，请报最优惠价格为盼。

(7) The articles we require should be durable and the colors should be bright and attractive. 本公司要求的货物务必经久耐用，色彩鲜明，有吸引力。

(8) We deal exclusively in light industrial products. 我们专营轻工业产品。

(9) The export of textiles is our line of business. 出口纺织品是我们的经营范围。

(10) Heavy enquiries witness the quality of our products. 大量询盘证明我们产品质量过硬。

(11) We are one of the leading exporters of Chinese silk goods and are enjoying an excellent reputation through sixty years' business experience. 我公司是中国丝绸产品大出口商之一，具有60年商贸经验，享誉中外。

(12) Our company has been in this line of business for many years and enjoys high international prestige. 我们公司承办这项业务多年，且享有很高的国际声誉。

(13) Our products are of very good quality and our firm is always regarded our customers as the most reliable one. 我们的产品质量好，且深受顾客的信任。

(14) We have extensive sales network for this line of goods, and shall always be ready to cooperate with you in marketing of your products in our market. 我方对此产品有广大的销售网，本公司随时准备与贵方合作，以拓展贵方产品在我方的市场。

(15) We have a long experience in the import and export trade and a wide knowledge of commodities as well as of the best sources of supply of these materials. 本公司在进出口贸易方面历史悠久，经验丰富。对各种货品及其货源十分熟悉。

(16) We have excellent connections in the trade and are fully experienced with the import business for this type of product. 在贸易方面，我们有良好的关系，对此类产品进口业务更具有丰富的经验。

(17) As to our credit and financial standing, we can refer you to the Bank of China and the Chamber of Commerce in Hangzhou. 至于我们的信用和财务状况，请向中国银行和杭州商会了解。

(18) We hope to establish business relations with you and trade with you on the basis of equality and mutual benefit. 我们希望和贵方建立贸易关系，并且在平等、互利的基础上进行贸易。

(19) We have your name and address from the Commercial Counsellor's Office of the Chinese Embassy in Korea. 我们从中国驻韩使馆商务处获悉贵公司的行名。

(20) We assure you of our careful attention to your interests at all times. 我们将随时关注你方的利益。

(21) We should appreciate the opportunity of showing you how efficiently we can serve you. 我们十分珍惜为你方提供高效服务的机会。

(22) We shall be grateful for prompt delivery as the goods are needed urgently. 因为急需货物，如能尽快交货，我们将表示非常感激。

8. Exercises

Exercise 1-1

Direction: Restructure the following information into a complete "Order Letter".

(1) On the only one day before it reached us, a contract was signed with Ethiopia for a total of 480,000 tons.

(2) Therefore, we shall be pleased to inform you in detail as soon as the circumstances become favorable for us to do business in this line.

(3) We wish we could have received your inquiry a little earlier.

(4) Because of this, our Government has decided not to grant export licenses for the commodity for areas other than Ethiopia until December 31, 2014, expecting the shortage which may be caused in the domestic market.

(5) We thank you for your letter of September 11 regarding Ammonium Sulphate, for which you have received inquiries from your customers in East Africa.

Exercise 1-2

Direction: Write a letter according to the following information.

Your company is one of the largest importers of electric goods in New York and has been in this line for over twenty years. You are interested in a company's various types of digital cameras displayed at the Guangzhou Fair in April. Write a letter to the company to ask for a full range of illustrated catalogues and samples, as well as the lowest price CIF New York for the digital cameras.

9. Supplementary Readings

Principles and Styles of Writing Business Letters

Writing an effective business letter is an important skill no matter what type of job you hold. No one formula exists for a perfect Business Letter, but there are some basic guidelines that will assist you, regardless of the form, purpose, and audience of the document. Many executives prefer a written document to other forms of communication, not only can it serve as a contract, but it provides a permanent record. In this way no one is required to rely on memory. You never know what will happen with a verbal conversation. Often a month or two down the road the participants could remember a very different conversation. And also, business communications have become much more casual with the advent of the Internet and email, but there are still times when a formal letter is required. This is why it is important to write a good Business Letter.

Writing Principles

Writing for a business audience is usually quite different than writing in the humanities, social sciences, or other academic disciplines. Business writing strives to be crisp and succinct rather than evocative or creative; it stresses specificity and accuracy. This distinction reflects the unique purpose and considerations involved when writing in a business context.

When you write a business document, you must assume that your audience has limited time in which to read it and is likely to skim. Your readers have an interest in what you say insofar as it affects their working world. They want to know the "bottom line": the point you are making about a situation or problem and how they should respond.

· Neat and Clean

Business letters should be neat and error-free. Some companies mandate a standardized format and font to ensure uniformity of company correspondence. If that's the case at your company, find out if a business letter template is available. Use of a template will make it simple to follow the company format. If your company doesn't use a template, follow basic business letter format. Type the recipient's address at the top left of the page. Skip a line and type the date. Start the letter with Dear Mr., Ms. or Mrs., unless you are very well acquainted with the recipient. Skip a line between each paragraph and close the letter with "Sincerely" followed by your name and title.

· Make Your Point

Use the opening paragraph to briefly explain the purpose of the letter. Your first sentence might read, "A recent review of construction purchase orders revealed several cost overruns," or "We would like to offer you a 15 percent discount on your next printing job." State the purpose clearly and avoid jargon or highly technical language. If a secretary or assistant reads the recipient's mail, you'll want to make sure that person understands the significance of your letter, even if she doesn't have a technical background.

Reread the description of your task (for example, the advertisement of a job opening, instructions for a proposal submission, or assignment prompt for a course). Think about your purpose and what requirements are mentioned or implied in the description of the task. List these requirements. This list can serve as an outline to govern your writing and help you stay focused, so try to make it thorough. Next, identify qualifications, attributes, objectives, or answers that match the requirements you have just listed. Strive to be exact and specific, avoiding vagueness, ambiguity, and platitudes. If there are industry-or field-specific concepts or terminologies that are relevant to the task at hand, use them in a manner that will convey your competence and experience. Avoid any language that your audience may not understand. Your finished piece of writing should indicate how you meet the requirements you've listed and answer any questions raised in the description or prompt.

· Details, Details, Details

Expand upon the first paragraph with more details. You might mention that cost overruns occurred during construction of the building's elevator shafts or note that the 15 percent discount applies to printing jobs costing more than $100. Short, concise letters might be more likely to be read, but make sure you provide enough details so that the recipient fully understands the reason for the letter. Keep in mind that the tone of your letter can affect the way the reader perceives it. The Purdue Online Writing Lab suggests using positive words as much as possible and focusing on what your company can do, rather than what it can't do.

· Focus and Specificity

Business writing should be clear and concise. Take care, however, that your document does not turn out as an endless series of short, choppy sentences. Keep in mind also that "concise" does not have to mean "blunt"—you still need to think about your tone and the audience for whom you are writing. Consider the following examples:

After carefully reviewing this proposal, we have decided to prioritize other projects this quarter.

Nobody liked your project idea, so we are not going to give you any funding.

The first version is a weaker statement, emphasizing facts not directly relevant to its point. The second version provides the information in a simple and direct manner. But you don't need to be an expert on style to know that the first phrasing is diplomatic and respectful (even though it's less concise) as compared with the second version, which is unnecessarily harsh and likely to provoke a negative reaction.

· Pronouns and Active versus Passive Voice

Personal pronouns (like I, we, and you) are important in letters and memos. In such documents, it is perfectly appropriate to refer to yourself as I and to the reader as you. Be careful, however, when you use the pronoun we in a business letter that is written on company stationery, since it commits your company to what you have written. When stating your opinion, use I; when presenting company policy, use we.

The best writers strive to achieve a style that is so clear that their messages cannot be misunderstood. One way to achieve a clear style is to minimize your use of the passive voice. Although the passive voice is sometimes necessary, often it not only makes your writing dull but also can be ambiguous or overly impersonal. Here's an example of the same point stated in passive voice and in the active voice:

PASSIVE: The net benefits of subsidiary divestiture were grossly overestimated.

[Who did the overestimating?]

ACTIVE: The Global Finance Team grossly overestimated the net benefits of subsidiary divestiture.

The second version is clearer and thus preferable.

Of course, there are exceptions to every rule. What if you are the head of the Global Finance Team? You may want to get your message across without calling excessive attention to the fact that the error was your team's fault. The passive voice allows you to gloss over an unflattering point—but you should use it sparingly.

· The End

Finish your letter with a request that asks the recipient to take some kind of action. For example, you might write, "Please provide me with the most recent cost projections by Tuesday," or "Call me to take advantage of your discount." Provide more than one way for the recipient to get in touch with you, such as a telephone number and an email address. Before you sign the letter and put it in the mail, be sure to review it for spelling and grammar errors.

Writing Styles

Generally, there are three acceptable styles of business letters which are block, modified block and semi-block. The three differ most in where the lines begin. In the block style, all lines begin at the left margin. If you choose a modified-block style, begin all of the letter's sections except the return address and closing lines—including your signature—at the left margin; begin the exceptions at the center of your page. The semi-block style is identical to the modified block except you should indent the first line of each paragraph of the letter's body.

· Font, Margins and Spacing

Use 12-point Arial or Times New Roman font to make your letter easy to read. Set 1-inch margins all around regardless of the style you choose to give your letter a professional look. The even space around your letter keeps it looking uncluttered and makes it easier to read. If you are using block style, always skip a line after your return address—or heading—before you include a date. If you are using modified block or semi-modified block, the choice is yours whether to skip a line before the date. In all styles, skip a line between each section of your letter and between paragraphs in the letter's body.

· Sections

Business letters have several sections. The heading includes your return address, the date and the recipient's address. The greeting or salutation is next, followed by the body, the closing and the signature line. Always include your full return address, though you can include your email address and phone and fax numbers if you choose. Include in the heading the recipient's identifying information, such as his department, if you have it. Begin your greeting with "Dear" followed by the person's personal or professional title. Use a colon after the greeting. Close your letter with "Sincerely," followed by a comma. Skip four lines and type your name and title. Sign the letter above your name.

· Considerations

Keep your style consistent throughout the letter. Unless it's necessary for proper composition, do not italicize, bold or underline words. Often these styles are used to emphasize certain words when writing informally, but they lend a lack of professionalism to business writing. Instead of one solid block of text in the body, break it up into several easy-to-read paragraphs. Ask someone to proofread your letter for errors and clarity problems before you send it.

Chapter 2
Credit Standing Investigation
资信调查

1. Learning Objectives

By the end of this chapter, you will be able to do the following:

· Get to know the key words and expressions for dealing with Credit Standing.

· Know the useful sentence patterns in writing Credit Reporting.

· Have a general picture of Credit Standing Investigation.

· Know how to do Credit Standing Investigation.

· Know how to write request and reply letters in respect of Credit Standing.

2. Case Study

国内某贸易公司通过与一家英国中间商谈判，最终与一家法国公司签订了金额数十万美元的销售合同，合同规定在英国接货。合同签订后，该中间商出示法国公司的通知，证明自己公司在英国办公经营，可以代为接货销售。该中国贸易公司基于友好合作的态度和对对方的充分信任，同意了法国公司的要求，与中间商签订了销售代理合同，提货单上写明中间商公司的名称，于是将货物运抵英国，再通过中间商从英国转运至法国销售。货物抵达英国后，"中间商"持提货单将货物提走，但国内贸易公司在货款到期后，未收到相关货款，多次给法国公司打电话、发传真，均未得到答复，而"中间商"也对该中国贸易公司的问讯置之不理。之后，通过调查得知，虽然该法国公司在法国合法注册，但因不缴纳注册费，早在一年前已经被法国公司注册署注销。更严重的是，英国中间商根本不具备独立的法人资格，且在英国的办公地址也是临时租用的场地，在提走货物后，已经退租，该地址已被其他公司占用。

在整个交易过程中，该中国贸易公司在没有经过基本的企业资信调查的情况下，就将客户当成销售代理商，并将货物直接发给对方。结果造成因不清楚客户的真实身份，无法直接起诉、追讨欠款，最终只能自己承担所有损失。

After studying the above case, all the companies have to think carefully about what actions should be taken before signing a contract with another company to do business, home or abroad, and what should be the first step.

3. Introduction

Knowing more about your business prospects, customers and vendors helps you make more confident decisions and set terms that optimize profitability while minimizing risk. From verified business identities and detailed credit history to business owner and corporate linkage, business credit reports from reliable resources, domestically or internationally, about agents, sellers and buyers can give you the deepest level of insight into the validity, financial stability and performance of more businesses.

Key Points of the Credit Standing Report:

The key points of the credit reporting generally should contain the introduction of a company including the place where it gets registered, registration time, registered capital, business scope, capital stock, corporate capacity, legal status to sign a contract, form of business, the number of share holders and their shares, financial conditions, current operating state, marketing channels etc. Besides, you may also obtain some information about its capital credibility from the opening bank, do the fact-finding of the company assets and make a verification of the legal authorization of its signing representatives. All of the above credit information can help you make a proper judgment about the counterpart's performance of contract to be signed.

Approaches to Get Credit Standing Report:

As an important part in the international trade, credit reporting can be done through many different channels, among which the following are the most common ways:

· Banks

In the international practices, credit reporting service is one of the business scopes of banks. In China, such service is generally entrusted to the Bank of China, who will carry out the credit reporting service, free of charge or with a small amount of charge, through its branches abroad or other correspondence banks upon the specific demands. When issuing a credit certification, banks often have to examine the credit status of a corporate including its economic nature, history, branches, key persons in charge, capital, credit, business scope etc.

· Inquiry Agencies

Generally, most Chamber of Commerce, Banking Associations and Trade Associations will accept a commission from foreign companies to undertake the credit reporting service about the local companies, but the credit reporting obtained through such channel should be carefully analyzed and dealt with.

· Institutions Functioning Abroad

The information obtained through such channel is more reliable and valuable because of the actual sources.

· Law Firms or Offices

The law firms or offices should be taken as the first choice for credit reporting service because of their analytical capabilities related to the economic and legal affairs, i.e. they can do the analyses of all the relevant data collected quantitatively and qualitatively, and then make judgment with the legal knowledge they have and draw a proper conclusion, for example, they may help a company confirm the legal qualification of its counterpart to sign a contract, and as such to minimize the risks or avoid the business operating risks.

· Credit Reporting Service Companies

Consumers can also turn to the credit reporting service companies, consultant companies, or management consulting companies for help.

Besides, the business directory, yearbook of companies and any other information published or released by the foreign publishers or governments may also be used as sources for obtaining the credit information of your counterparts.

4. Specimen Letters

Specimen 1
Credit Standing Investigation

Dear Sir,

Subject: Credit Standing

You are kindly requested to give us with the information on credit standing and business operation of Krishna And Krishna Trading and Consulting Co. The company address is Gee Gee Universal, 1st Floor, No.2, Mc Nicholas Road, Chennai. Please be convinced that all the materials and information you provide to us will be kept confidential, for which You will not take any responsibilities.

Best Regards.

Yours truly,
[Signature]

Specimen 2
Credit Information

Dear Sir,

Subject: Credit Information

The under-mentioned firm has lately asked for representing us in the marketing of our products in the India as our sole agent:
Sri Balalaji Agencies
79, Murugesan Nagar,
Kumalankuttai, Tamil Nadu pin-548011
We would be very grateful if you could let us have some information about the financial and business standing of the above firm.

Any information that you may give would be treated in strict confidence and we await your early reply.

Yours faithfully,
[Signature]

Specimen 3
Request to Bank for Credit Information

(CONFIDENTIAL)

Dear Sir,

We have received an order for US$ 150,000 worth of goods from Pacific Household Appliances Co., Ltd, USA. They have given us your bank as a reference. We wish to be informed if they are good enough for this amount and in every way trustworthy. We shall be extremely grateful for any information you would provide us.

We will surely treat as highly confidential any advice you would tell us. We enclose a stamped and addressed envelope for your reply.

Yours faithfully,
[Signature]
General Manager
Hangzhou Star Import & Export Co.
Hangzhou P.R. China

Specimen 4
Reply from Bank

ACCOUNT OF CREDIT

August 20, 2014
Hangzhou Star Import & Export Co.
Hangzhou，P.R. China

Re: Account of Credit of Pacific Household Appliances Co., Ltd.

Please be advised that Mr. J. Smith，President of Pacific Household Appliances Co. Ltd. has established several accounts with our Bank. The regular business account was established in October 1995 and the money market account was established in August 1997. The total balance of deposit at our bank for both accounts is US$905,560.00.

Their accounts have always been in good standing.

Thank you.

Sincerely,
[Signature]

Specimen 5
Request to Customers for Credit Information

Dear Sir:

We will be obliged if you will kindly give us the information about credit standing of Aurobindo Garments Pvt Ltd. in your city. We understand that you have regular transactions with the firm. So we take the liberty to ask you about your views concerning the actual position of the firm so that we may take steps to avoid getting into trouble.

Any information you give will be highly appreciated and kept in strict confidence. We shall be pleased to perform a similar service for you if you should need our services at this end.

We are looking forward to your early reply.

Yours faithfully,
[Signature]

Specimen 6
Credit Investigation with Enclosure

Dear Sir,

We have received a sudden bid from the Coventry Trading Co.,Ltd, 120 Coventry Street, London, with which you are now doing business and the firm gives us your name as a reference.

We shall highly appreciate it if you could inform us of your own experiences with the firm by filling in the blanks of the attached sheet and returning it to us with the enclosed stamped and addressed envelope.

Any information you may give us will be treated as strictly confidential and expenses concerned from this inquiry will be gladly paid by us upon receipt of your bill.

Very truly yours,
[Signature]
(Attached Sheet)
(1) How long have you been in business relations with the firm?
(2) What credit limit have you placed on their account?
(3) What amount is currently outstanding?

Specimen 7
Favorable Reply

Dear Sir,

Subject: The Coventry Trading Co., Ltd.

In reply to your letter of July 15, 2014, we want to inform that we have now received from Barclay Bank of London the information you require.

The Coventry Trading Co., Ltd. was founded in 1955 with a capital of 1,500,000 pounds. Their chief line is in the import and export of textiles. So far, their business suppliers are quite satisfied with them and we consider them good for business engagement up to an amount of 200,000 pounds. For larger transations we suggest payment by sight L/C.

The above information is strictly confidential and is given without any responsibility on this bank.

Truly yours,
[Signature]

Specimen 8
Unfavorable Reply

Dear Sir,

Subject: The Coventry Trading Co.,Ltd.

We have completed our enquiries concerning the company mentioned in your letter of July 15, 2014 and have to inform you to consider carefully the business with them.

In the past two years, the captioned company has been experiencing serious difficulties in finance and delayed in executing their normal payment time and again. It seems to us that the company's difficulties were due to bad management and in paricular to overtrading in too many fields which might not be suitable to them.

We would like to advise you to pay more careful attention to any business engagement with them.

The above-mentioned is our unilateral-conceived opinion and we wish you to make further enquiries on your part.

Yours sincerely,
[Signature]

Specimen 9
Reply of Regret

Dear Sir,

Subject: The Coventry Trading Co.,Ltd.

It is a regretful thing that we are unable to give you any positive information concerning the captioned company in question in your letter dated July 15, 2014.

We definitely had business with them in the past few years, but the amount of our transactionwas not so large that we can not give any reasonable and responsible opinion on the business capability and credit standing.

We suggest you make further enquiries from other firms or credit reporting service agencies.

Yours truly,
[Signature]

5. Writing Templates

Credit Standing Investigation

Dear Sir,

Subject: <u>Credit Standing</u>

    You are kindly requested to give us with the information on credit standing and business operation of _____. The company address is _____. Please be convinced that all the materials and information you provide us will be strictly kept confidential, for which you will not take any responsibilities.

Best Regards.

Yours truly,
[Signature]

Request to Bank for Credit Information

(CONFIDENTIAL)

Dear Sir,

    We have received an order for US $ _____ worth of goods from _____. They have given us your bank as a reference. We wish to be informed if they are good enough for this amount and in every way trustworthy. We shall be extremely grateful for any information you would provide us.
    We will surely treat as highly confidential any advice you would give us. We enclose a stamped and addressed envelope for your reply.

Yours faithfully,
[Signature]

Reply from Bank

ACCOUNT OF CREDIT

To Whom It May Concern

    Please be advised that Mr. _____, President of _____ has established several accounts with our Bank. The regular business account was established in _____ and the money market account was established in _____. The total balance of deposit at our bank for both accounts is US$_____.
    Their accounts have always been in good standing.
    Thank you.

Sincerely,
[Signature]

Favorable Reply

Dear Sir,

Subject: _____

In reply to your letter dated _____, we want to inform that we have now received from _____ (Bank) the information you require.

The _____ (company) was founded in the year of _____ with a capital of US$ _____. Their chief line is in the import and export of _____. So far, their business suppliers are quite satisfied with them and we consider them good for business engagement up to an amount of US$ _____. For larger transations we suggest payment by sight L/C.

The above information is strictly confidential and is given without any responsibility on this bank.

Truly yours,
[Signature]

Unfavorable Reply

Dear Sir,

Subject: _____

We have completed our enquiries concerning the company mentioned in your letter of _____(date) and have to inform you to consider carefully the business with them.

In the past _____ years, the captioned company has experienced serious difficulties in finance and delayed in executing their normal payment. It seems to us that the company's difficulties were due to _____.

We would like to advise you to pay more careful attention to any business relations with them.

The above-mentioned is our personal opinion and we wish you to make further enquiries on your part.

Yours sincerely,
[Signature]

6. Key Words and Expressions

(1) credit standing   资信状况

(2) credit reporting   征信，信用报告

(3) registration time   注册时间

(4) registered capital   注册资本

(5) business scope   经营范围

(6) legal personality   法人资格

(7) form of business   企业类型

(8) financial condition　财务状况

(9) marketing channel　销售渠道

(10) Chamber of Commerce　商会

(11) institutions functioning abroad　驻外机构

(12) law firm　律师事务所

(13) consultant company　顾问公司

(14) money market account　货币市场账户

(15) business account　企业账户，商业账户

(16) credit reporting agencies　征信机构

7. Useful Sentence Patterns

(1) We will be obliged if you will kindly give us the information about credit standing of... 若能提供有关……公司的资信状况，我方将非常感激。

(2) We take the liberty to ask you to give your views concerning the actual position of the firm in order that we may take steps to avoid getting into trouble. 恕我们冒昧请求你方提供有关该公司的实际状况的意见，以便我们避免陷入麻烦境地。

(3) Any information you give will be highly appreciated and kept in strict confidence. 对你方所能提供的任何信息，我们都会非常感激，并严守秘密。

(4) We are awaiting your early reply. 静候你方的早日答复。

(5) The above information is strictly confidential and is given without any responsibility on this bank. 以上信息请严守秘密，且我行不承担任何责任。

(6) We would advise you to pay most careful attention to any business relations with them. 建议你方小心对待与他们的一切业务关系。

(7) We regret our inability to let you know any positive information concerning the firm in question in your letter... 非常遗憾，我们无法给你们提供你方信中所提及公司的任何正面信息。

(8) It is true that we had business with them during the past few years, but the amount of business was not so large that we can not supply any responsible opinion on the business capability and credit standing. 的确，在过去几年间，我们和他们之间曾有过业务联系，但是业务量都不大，因此，有关他们的业务能力和资信情况，我们无法提供任何可靠的意见。

(8) Their accounts have always been in good standing. 其账户信誉一贯良好。

8. Exercises

Exercise 2-1

Direction: Put the following letter into Chinese.

Dear Sir,

With reference to your letter dated September 20, in which the firm mentioned is one of the most responsible dealers of textiles.

The company was established in 1968, and has supplied our firm with quality goods for over 20 years. They have always provided complete satisfaction with in-time delivery, moderate prices and high quality.

We believe that they may be rated as an A-Level company with which you can deal freely. Of course, this is our personal opinion and we assume no responsibility in your proposed business negotiations.

We hope the above is satisfactory and will help you make a proper judgment.

Very truly yours,
[Signature]

Exercise 2-2

Direction: Write an unfavorable reply to a letter you received based upon the following particulars.

(1) You received a letter dated June 17, in which the sender asked for the credit Standing of a firm.

(2) You have done business with the firm in the last two years.

(3) You have experienced a lot of trouble in your business settlements.

(4) The company now owes you US$ 250,400 for purchase of an order a few month ago.

(5) The above account is in the hand of your attorneys for collection.

(6) Ask the receiver to take the information you provide as strictly confidential.

9. Supplementary Reading

Commercial Credit Reporting

Credit is defined as "the quality of being likely to repay debts and being trusted in money matters" in Longman Dictionary, but it does not necessarily require money.

Movements of financial capital are normally dependent on either credit or equity transfers. Credit is in turn dependent on the reputation or credit worthiness of the entity which takes responsibility for the funds.

Commercial credit reporting is the maintenance and reporting of credit histories and risks for commercial companies, which exists to assess risk in extending loans to businesses, insuring businesses, underwriting insurance risk, purchasing businesses, investing in businesses and most of all in shipping goods to business on credit terms. Every country in the world has commercial (or mercantile) credit reporting agencies, if for no other reason than to allow foreign exporters to assess the risk in shipping goods to a wholesaler in that country. They can be large public corporation like Dun & Bradstreet (often referred to as D&B, the company's database contains information on more than 235 million companies across 200 countries worldwide) established in 1841 and headquartered in Short Hills, a community in Millburn, New Jersey, US that provides commercial data to businesses on credit history, business-to-business sales and marketing, counterparty risk exposure, supply chain management, lead scoring and social identity matching. They can also be small one man operations serving a limited number of local and foreign clients in a small country.

Before telephones and the internet, the only way to gather risk information on a business was to visit the business owner at their place of business. Credit reporters would ask the owner for the names of the companies that supplied them on credit terms, what banks they dealt with and detailed questions about number of employees, what was sold, etc. They would then contact these suppliers and banks for reference information. It took days, even weeks, to fulfill a request for a commercial credit report.

Electronic communication and computers changed the gathering of commercial risk information. Credit reports can now be compiled in seconds without human intervention and without a business owners knowledge. Suppliers are now requested to supply frequent aged trial balance down loads on all their accounts receivable to commercial credit reporting agencies. These trade payment experiences are linked together to give a profile of how a business is paying numerous suppliers. Collection agencies supply the credit reporting agencies with information on commercial collection claims they receive which are matched to the trade payment experiences.

Public record information such as, bankruptcy filings, legal suits, lease registrations and judgments are also gathered and added to the files on a particular business. As this flood of information accumulates over many years trends are identified and it becomes like a pulse tracking cash flow within a business. Companies unable to come up with sufficient cash to pay suppliers are quickly identified. Computerized monitoring systems tell suppliers when to restrict credit to unhealthy businesses. These very comprehensive, detailed reports, can with mathematical equations be reduced down to two digit scores that now allow for automated credit approvals and rejections.

Commercial credit is more volatile than consumer credit. Few businesses survive five years in the same form that they were first founded. All businesses are in constant competition with other businesses for clients and markets. The granting of credit by businesses is very much a market driven. Retailers hope that they will have sold the goods they bought at a profit before they are required to pay for these goods that they bought on credit. Retailers who can not get credit from suppliers are at a serious competitive disadvantage if they are required to pay for their inventories in cash on delivery.

Strict laws governing consumer credit reporting agencies rarely include commercial credit reporting agencies. Any complaints about the accuracy or incompleteness of information in a commercial credit report can potentially do harm to the agencies reputation, so they do take complaints seriously.

Chapter 3
Establishing Business Relations
建立业务关系

1. Learning Objectives

By the end of this chapter, you will be able to do the following:

· Know how to obtain the information of the potential partners.
· Understand the basic structure of a letter for establishing business relations.
· Learn how to write letters of such nature and how to reply them.
· Learn to use the proper words, phrases and sentence patterns in writing such letters.

2. Case Study

> Jiangsu SOKOYO Solar Lighting Co., Ltd., as one of the most professional solar LED outdoor lighting manufacturers in China, is a solar lighting solution provider in China. The main products are solar street lights, solar garden lights and small and medium solar generating systems, etc. Since 2008, SOKOYO has introduced over 80,000 reliable and cost-effective solar powered lighting systems in more than 50 countries all over the world. SOKOYO's reliable solar lighting solutions are guaranteed by its experienced engineering team, advanced equipments, strict tests and the sound management system. After years of development, SOKOYO has become one of the leading companies in the line of lighting.
>
> One day, one of its foreign trade clerks saw the following news in *International Business Daily*:

国际商报
国际贸易与经济合作机会国际市场快递

加拿大求购	马来西亚求购
加拿大一公司求购中国的水晶灯	马来西亚一公司求购碳酸钙
阿尔及利亚求购	马来西亚一公司求购天然宝石
阿尔及利亚一公司求购各类服装	马来西亚一公司求购60cm直径,890cm长的钢丝绳
阿尔及利亚一公司求购纺织品	

感兴趣者请与本报联系

> After reading the news, he immediately emailed the newspaper and got the contact details of the Canadian company as follows:
> Mr. Paul Lockwood
> Purchasing Division
> James Brown & Sons
> # 304-310 Jalan Street, Toronto, Canada
> Tel No: (01) 7709910
> Fax No: (01) 7701100
> E-mail: plockwood@jbs.com.cnd

Suppose you are the foreign trade clerk working in SOKOYO. Please write a letter to James Brown & Sons, and express your wish to establish business relations with the company.

3. Introduction

The first step towards a successful transaction is to find the prospective dealers and then establish cooperative relationships with them. You may get lost in modern business world when you have so many channels through which you can obtain the desired names and addresses of the companies to be dealt with. Apart from the search engines on the Internet as mentioned earlier, you can also acquire the information of your potential clients through the following channels:

- Banks offer credible information of exporters/importers though you must pay for it.
- You can join your local Chamber of Commerce — a form of business network. Its main task is to offer business information and opportunities.
- You may get the contact details of a foreign company from the Commercial Counselor's Office in our embassy in that country.
- Various trade shows held home and abroad will offer you a face-to-face chance of communication with your potential partners.
- Advertisements in media tell you the exact supply and demand of a specific company.

Above are only the most common ways to get the information you want. After having the names and address of the company, you may need to determine its creditworthiness. The credit reference from a bank can help you investigate that company, confirming it is known to the bank as a good client. It is reassuring to do business with a reputable partner.

Now it's time for you to send the "First Letter" to your potential client. According to business etiquette, this letter begins by telling the addressee how you obtained his name and address and the intention of establishing business relations with him. A self-introduction is then suggested to show the detailed information of your firm. After that, you need to express your expectation of cooperation and an early reply.

If you have specific purposes, you can directly tell him. For example, you may ask for catalogues and samples as a buyer. Always remember the writing principles we've learnt in Chapter 1 when you compose the "First Letter".

A prompt reply is required to show your sincerity when you receive a letter of this nature.

You can create goodwill by answering in compliance with the requests in the "First Letter". Business relations will be probably established in the process.

4. Specimen Letters

Looking for Business Partner
Specimen 1

Dear Sir,

    We owe the name of your firm to the advertisement in Foreign Trade and have the pleasure of addressing this letter to you in the hope of establishing business relations with you.

    We are specialized in the export of Chinese light industrial products. Our products have enjoyed great popularity in the world markets including Europe and North America. Now we are looking for cooperative opportunities in Africa and you are one of the leading African companies dealing in this line.

    Enclosed you will find a copy of our catalogue for your reference and hope that you would contact us if any item is of interest to you.

Yours faithfully,
[Signature]

Specimen 2

Gentlemen:

Sub: <u>Electric Sewing Machines</u>

    We were much impressed by the various styles and good quality of your goods displayed at the Chinese Economic and Trade Exhibition held in Sri Lanka last July, and we take this opportunity to set up business relationship with you.

    We have been in the line of sewing machines for more than ten years. Now, one of our potential customers intends to purchase a number of electric sewing machines. We would be therefore grateful if you would send us a pro forma invoice for 400 sewing machines with 3 drawers quoting your rock-bottom price. Please enclose the latest catalogue in your reply.

    We look forward to hearing from you as soon as possible.

Yours sincerely,
[Signature]

Specimen 3

Dear Mr. Browns:

    From www.alibaba.com we have learned that you are in the market for chinaware, which just falls within our business scope. We are now writing to you in the hope of entering into business relations with you.

As a leading trading company in Shanghai and backed by nearly 20 years of export experience, we have good connections with some reputable ceramics factories and sufficient supplies and on-time delivery are guaranteed.

To give you a general idea of our products, we enclose a complete set of catalogues showing various products being handled with detailed specifications and means of packing. Quotations and samples will be sent upon receipt of your specific inquiries.

Yours faithfully,
[Signature]

Reply
Specimen 1

Dear Sir,

We are glad to note from your letter of the 1st March that you, as importers of light industrial products, are willing to establish direct business relations with us. This happens to coincide with our desire.

We are one of the leading exporters of first class cotton and are enjoying an excellent reputation through fifty years' business experience. We enclose a copy of our catalogue for your reference and hope that you would contact us if you are satisfied with any item.

Yours faithfully,
[Signature]

Specimen 2

Dear Sir,

We were very pleased to receive your letter of 5th April, in which you express the wish to cooperate with us.

We have various types of bicycles in stock and we shall be pleased to arrange for you to try any type you like. Although costs have been rising since March, we have not yet raised our prices. We therefore advise you to place your order with us at once.

Enclosed is our latest catalogue. Hoping to hear from you soon.

Yours faithfully,
[Signature]

Credit Reference

Dear Sir,

We have newly established business relations with Atlantic Electronic Co., Ltd. USA. They have given us your bank as a reference. We wish to know their creditworthiness and whether they are in every way trustworthy and reliable. We shall be most grateful for any information you give us.

We should of course treat as strictly confidential any advice you tell us. We enclose a stamped and addressed envelope for your reply.

Yours faithfully,
[Signature]

5. Writing Templates

Looking for Business Partner

Dear _____,

We owe the name of your firm to _____ and have the pleasure of addressing this letter to you in the hope of establishing business relations with you.

We are specialized in _____. Our products have enjoyed great popularity in _____. Now we are looking for cooperative opportunities in _____ and you are one of the leading _____ companies dealing in this line.

Enclosed you will find _____ for your reference and hope that you would contact us if any item is of interest to you.

Yours faithfully,
[Signature]

Reply

Dear _____,

We are glad to note from your letter of _____ that you, as _____, are willing to establish direct business relations with us. This happens to coincide with our desire.

We are one of the leading _____ of _____ and are enjoying an excellent reputation through _____ business experience. We enclose _____ for your reference and hope that you would contact us if you are satisfied with any item.

Yours faithfully,
[Signature]

Credit Reference

Dear ____,

　　We have newly established business relations with ____. They have given us your bank as a reference. We wish to know their creditworthiness and whether they are in every way trustworthy and reliable. We shall be most grateful for any information you give us.

　　We should of course treat as strictly confidential any advice you tell us. We enclose a stamped and addressed envelope for your reply.

Yours faithfully,
[Signature]

---

6. Key Words and Expressions

(1) Chambers of Commerce　商会

(2) Commercial Counselor's Office　商务参赞处

(3) creditworthiness　商誉

(4) credit reference　资信证明

(5) reputable　声誉好的

(6) catalogue　目录, 价目表

(7) sample　样品

(8) goodwill　商誉, 信誉

(9) owe ... to　承蒙……

(10) be specialized in　专门从事……的生产

(11) popularity　名声，流行

(12) line　行业，专业；某一类商品

(13) pro forma　形式上的，形式的

(14) in the market for　购买，有……的需求

(15) inquiry　询问，质询，询盘

(16) coincide with　与……一致

(17) in stock　有存货

(18) confidential　机密（文件）

7. Useful Sentence Patterns

(1) We owe your name and address to ... 承蒙……介绍，我们得知了贵公司的名称和地址。

(2) Having obtained / knowing your name and address from... 我们从……获悉了贵公司的名称和地址。

(3) Your name and address have been passed on us by... 我们从……获悉了贵公司的名称和地址。

(4) On the recommendation of ..., we have learned with pleasure your name and address. 经

由……的推荐，我们非常高兴地获悉了贵公司的名称和地址。

(5) Through the courtesy of ... we notice that... 承蒙……介绍，我们发现……

(6) Your name and address has been given to us by... 我们从……获悉了贵公司的名称和地址。

(7) We take the liberty of writing to you with a view of building up / opening business relations with your firm. 我们冒昧地写信给您，以期与贵公司建立业务联系。

(8) We are willing to enter into business relations with you. 我们期待与您建立业务联系。

(9) We approach you for the establishment of / in the hope of establishing trade relations with you. 我们期待与您建立业务联系。

(10) We hope that we may have an opportunity to cooperate / of cooperating with you. 我们希望能有机会与您合作。

(11) Our company handles / deals in / is specialized in ... 我公司经营……业务。

(12) We have been exporter / importer of... for many years. 我公司进口/出口……已经多年。

(13) Our lines are mainly in ... 我公司的主要业务是……

(14) To acquaint you with our business lines, we enclose a copy of... 为了使您了解我们的业务，我们附上……的复印件一份。

(15) Could you be kind enough to send us your catalogue / samples in your reply. 希望您在回复时能给我们寄一份产品目录/一些样品。

(16) To promote business, we are sending you a commodity list / a catalogue / a few samples / export (import) list / latest catalogues and price list covering our... 为了促进双方业务，我们给您寄去包含……产品信息的商品清单/产品目录/几个样品/进口（出口）商品清单/最新产品目录及价目表，涵盖我们的……

(17) We regret to inform you that this particular line of ... is not in the scope / has been represented by ... 我们遗憾地通知您，您所需的……产品不在我们的经营范围之内/已经由……（产品）替代。

(18) We look forward to hearing from you / your early reply / to receiving from you. 我们期待您的回复。

(19) We are anticipating your answer / reply. 我们期待您的回复。

(20) By the courtesy of Mr. Smith, we are given to understand the name and address of your firm. 承蒙史密斯先生的介绍，我们得知贵公司的名称和地址。

(21) We are a leading company with 30 years' experience in exporting light industrial products and are closely connected with manufactures in our country. 我们是一家具有30年轻工业产品出口经验的大公司，与国内制造商关系密切。

(22) We are willing to enter into business relations with your firm on the basis of equality and mutual benefit and exchange what one has for what one needs. 我们愿意在平等互利、互通有无的基础上与贵方建立业务关系。

(23) As to our credit and financial standing, we can refer you to Bank of China or the Chamber of Commerce in Guangzhou. 至于信誉和财务状况，我们请贵公司向中国银行或者广

州商会咨询。

(24) We should be obliged if you would give us an early reply. 贵方如能早日回复，我们将感激不尽。

(25) We are given to understand that you are potential buyers of Chinese Silk, which is within the frame of our business scopes. 据了解，你们是中国丝绸有潜力的买主，而该商品正属于我们的业务经营范围。

8. Exercises

Exercise 3-1

Direction: Put the following sentences into English.

(1) 我们从新加坡驻北京大使馆商务参赞处得知贵公司的名称和地址，并获悉贵公司愿同我们建立业务关系。

(2) 据了解，贵公司是陶瓷工艺品的潜在买主，而陶瓷工艺品正属于我们的经营范围。

(3) 我们相信通过双方的努力，贸易往来定会朝着互利的方向发展。

(4) 因该类商品属于我们的经营范围，我们很高兴与你方直接建立贸易关系。

(5) 随函附上公司概况、业务范围和其他方面的小册子一本，以供参考。

(6) 我方将写信通知你方有关我们的资信情况。

(7) 我们从商会得知贵公司有意购买大量红茶。特致函予你，望能与你们建立业务关系。并随附我们最新的商品目录一份。

(8) 能否让我方大致了解一下你方城市里纺织品的市场价格。

(9) 我们借此机会再次强调，定会尽力随时提供贵方所需的信息。恳请贵方给予信任，并大力支持。

(10) 按照你方9月3日来信要求，兹附上样品及小册子。

Exercise 3-2

Direction: Write a letter based on the following information.

You are an exporter of electrical goods in Hangzhou. Recently you got an email from an Indian company as follows:

Dear Sir,

We saw your supply information on the Internet and shall be pleased to establish business relations with your firm.

We are one of the leading importers of electrical goods in India. We are willing to enter into business relations with your firm on the basis of equality and mutual benefit and exchange what one has for what one needs.

Please enclose your latest catalogue for our reference. Your early reply will be highly appreciated.

Yours faithfully,
[Signature]

Please make a reply to the above letter with what you've learnt in this chapter.

Exercise 3-3

Supplementary task.

Search for an item on www.alibaba.com and get as much information about the suppliers as possible. Suppose you are a foreign trade clerk in an import company. Write a letter to one of the suppliers to establish long-term business relations.

9. Supplementary Readings

Levels of Relationship Marketing

What type of relationships should an organization have with its customers? Is the cost of keeping a relationship worth it? To answer these questions, let's define the three general levels of selling relationships with customers:

Transaction selling: customers are sold to and not contacted again.

Relationship selling: the seller contacts to improve its customers' operations, sales, and profits.

Partnering selling: the seller establishes cooperative relations with its clients.

Most organizations focus solely on the single transaction with each customer. When you go to McDonald's and buy a hamburger, that's it. You never hear from them again unless you return for another purchase. The same thing happens when you go to a movie, rent a video, open a bank checking account, visit the grocery store, or have your clothes cleaned. Each of these examples involves low-priced, low-profit products. Also involved are a large number of customers who are geographically dispersed. This makes it very difficult and quite costly to contact customers. The business is forced to use transactional marketing.

Relationship marketing focuses on the transaction-marketing, the sale-along with follow-up and service after the sale. The seller contacts the customer to ensure satisfaction with the purchase. The Cadillac Division of General Motors contacts each buyer of a new Cadillac to determine the customer's satisfaction with the car. If that person is not satisfied, General Motors works with the retailer selling the car to make sure the customer is happy.

Partnering is a phenomenon of the 1990s. Businesses' growing concern over the competition not only in America but also internationally revitalized their need to work closely with important customers. The familiar 80/20 principle states that 80 percent of sales often come from 20 percent of a company's customers. Organizations now realize the need to identify their most important customers and designate them for their partnering programs. The organization's best salespeople are assigned to sell and serve these customers.

Chapter 4
Inquiries and Replies
询价与回复

1. Learning Objectives

By the end of this chapter, you will be able to do the following:

· Get to know the key words and expressions for writing inquiries and replies.

· Know the useful sentence patterns in writing inquires.

· Know how to write inquires.

· Know how to reply these inquires.

2. Case Study

> Shenzhen Napov Technology Co., Ltd. is an outstanding distributor concerning Mobile Phone Case, Carbon Fiber Case, Carbon Fiber Money Clip, Carbon Fiber Wallet Case, and Bluetooth Selfie Case. Established in 2008, located in Guangdong, China (Mainland), it has 101-200 employees with Total Annual Sales Volume of US$1 Million - US$2.5 Million. Currently, it is intended to seek for an American supplier of iPhone 6 leather case. Its foreign trade clerk visits alibaba.com and gets one Korean supplier' information:
> Company Name: NEWVIT CO., LTD
> Operational Address: Yeongdong-Daero, Gangnam-Gu, Seoul, Republic of Korea
> Website: http://global.newvit.net
> Website on alibaba.com: http://kr1073690459.trustpass.alibaba.com

The foreign trade clerk plans to write an inquiry to this company. What should he/she specifically write? How would the Korean supplier reply?

3. Introduction

If a buyer is interested in certain goods or service, he would make a general inquiry, in which he states clearly all the information he needs: a catalogue, a quotation list, a sample or sample book, etc. In a specific inquiry, he points out what product(s) he wants and relevant information needed.

General inquiries should be written concisely and clearly to the points. When writing such letters, you (as the buyer) should:

· Tell the seller how you get his information and introduce your business.

· Politely raise your request (asking for a catalogue, a quotation list, a sample or sample book, etc.). Appreciate whatever help you may obtain.

· End with a hope to establish long-term relationship.

Of course, inquiries from old customers may be simpler in content, only covering the unclear details, like the specifications of commodity, terms of payment (such as FOB, CIF, etc.), quantity discount, etc.

There is another kind of inquiry asking for the credit, reputation or financial situation of the firm with which you are going to establish business relations. We can obtain such information from business friends, chambers of commerce, inquiry agencies or banks. Although banks could provide more reliable information, they might only give information to their own customers or fellow banks. Thus we could inquire through our own bank to other banks.

In reply to the general inquiries, you (as the seller) should:

· Answer promptly and courteously.

· Repeat the date of the inquiry.

· Give a full answer to the inquiry.

· Offer a substitute if you cannot do as requested.

· End with a hope that the information provided is helpful and a willingness to offer further help.

4. Specimen Letters

Specimen 1
General Inquiry

> Dear Madams or Sirs,
>
> We learn from alibaba.com that you can supply health food, sports nutrition, dietary supplements, etc. We would appreciate so much if you could kindly send us as soon as possible your catalogues, or samples if possible.
>
> Please state clearly in your reply your earliest delivery date, terms of payment, the minimum order quantity and discounts. Prices should be quoted CIF Shanghai.
>
> We hope this will be a good start for a long and profitable business relations.
>
> Yours faithfully,
> [Signature]

Specimen 2
Reply

> Dear Madams or Sirs,
>
> In reply to your letter of February16th, we are now enclosing you our latest price list for our products, together with our illustrated catalogue. We are sending you some samples under

separate cover as well. As you will see in the above list, our products are good in quality and reasonable in price. We believe you will favor us with your valued orders.

We will offer a proper discount according to the quantity ordered. We usually require Letter of Credit payable by sight draft for terms of payment.

Your further inquiries of any kind are always welcome. We are looking forward to your early reply and doing business with you.

Yours faithfully,
[Signature]

Specimen 3
General Inquiry

Dear Madams or Sirs,

Your advertisement in the trade directory has attracted our interest and we are interested in textile products for sales in North American market.

We shall be appreciative if you would send us your latest catalogue and price list. We trust that you will make an effort to give us your earliest delivery time and discounts for regular purchases.

We are looking forward to your early reply.

Yours respectfully,
[Signature]

Specimen 4
Reply

Dear Madams or Sirs,

We welcome you for your inquiry of January 1 and thank you for your interest in our textile products. We have sent you a priced catalogue and labeled samples. From the price list you can see that we have managed to give you the lowest quotation with the increasing price in recent months. We believe you will place an order before further rises in costs after you examine the samples.

Thank you again for you interest in our products. We are looking forward to your order.

Yours sincerely,
[Signature]

Specimen 5
Specific Inquiry

Dear Madams or Sirs,

Thank you for your letter of July 7. We have studied your catalogue and are interested in your air cleaner Model KJF-1000A and KJF-1000B. Please quote us your lowest price, CIF Liverpool and tell us your minimum order quantity.

Furthermore, please tell us the packing, weight, deliveries and other essential details. Thank you very much for your cooperation.

Yours sincerely,
[Signature]

Specimen 6
Reply

Dear Madams or Sirs,

Thank you very much for your inquiry dated July 9. We are pleased to attach the following information for your reference:

Items	Model		Remarks
	KJF-1000A	KJF-1000B	
Rated voltage	110-127V/60HZ 220-240V/50-60HZ	110-127V/60HZ 220-240V/50-60HZ	
Power Consumption	150W	150W	
Weight	32KG	32KG	
Dimensions	480×290×1700	480×290×1700	
Airflow	8003/h	8003/h	
Noise level	49 dB	49 dB	
Dust Purifying Rate	99.99%	99.99%	$30m^3$ space testing for 30min
Formaldehyde Purifying Rate	99.8%	99.8%	$30m^3$ space testing for 2 hours
Benzene Purifying Rate	98%	98%	$30m^3$ space testing for 1 hour

All the products will be packed in cartons and the delivery will be 15-20 days. The lowest quotation for air cleaner Model KJF-1000A and KJF-1000B is US $ 18,000 CIF Liverpool. The payment mode is L/C or T/T.

Air cleaner KJF-1000A and KJF-1000B, with stylish design and superior performance, will definitely satisfy your expectation. We are looking forward to your first order.

Yours sincerely,
[Signature]

Specimen 7
Credit Inquiry

Dear Sir,

<u>Credit inquiry on the Shengzhou Jinli Knitted Tie Co., Ltd.</u>

The subject company has recently written to us with an intent to establish business relations with us. It has referred us to your bank for detailed information about its credit standing and business capacity.

We will appreciate very much if you could make an effort to send us the relevant information. Any information given by you will be treated strictly in confidence and highly valued.

Yours respectively,
[Signature]

Specimen 8
Reply

Dear Sir,

<u>Credit information on the Shengzhou Jinli Knitted Tie Co., Ltd.</u>

The subject company you inquired by your letter of June 1, 2014 is a leader in knitted ties. With more than 10 years' knitting experience, it has enjoyed a high admiration both at home and abroad.

It has been maintaining an account with us from its establishing and has never failed to fulfill its obligation. Its balanced sheets of recent years enclosed will show you that its business has been operated satisfactorily.

Please note that the above information is provided without any responsibility on our part and should be treated strictly confidential.

Yours truly,
[Signature]

5. Writing Templates

General Inquiry

Dear _____,

We learn from _____ that you can supply _____. We would appreciate so much if you could kindly send us as soon as possible _____.

Please state clearly in your reply _____. Prices should be quoted _____.

We hope this will be a good start for a long and profitable business relation.

Yours faithfully,
[Signature]

Reply

Dear _____,

    In reply to your letter of _____, we are now enclosing you _____, together with _____. We are sending you _____ under separate cover as well. As you will see in the above list, our products are good in quality and reasonable in price. We believe you will favor us with your valued orders.

    We will offer a proper discount according to the quantity ordered. We usually require _____ for terms of payment.

    Your further inquiries of any kind are always welcome. We are looking forward to your early reply and doing business with you.

Yours faithfully,
[Signature]

Specific Inquiry

Dear _____,

    Thank you for your letter of _____. We have studied your _____ and are interested in your _____ Model _____. Please quote us your lowest price, _____ and tell us your minimum order quantity.

    Furthermore, please tell us the packing, weight, deliveries and other essential details.

    Thank you very much for your cooperation.

Yours sincerely,
[Signature]

Credit Inquiry

Dear _____,

Credit Inquiry on _____

    The _____ company has recently written to us with an intent to establish business relations with us. It has referred us to _____ for detailed information about its _____.

    We will appreciate very much if you could make an effort to send us the relevant information.

    Any information given by you will be treated strictly in confidence and highly valued.

Yours respectively,
[Signature]

Reply

> Dear _____,
>
> <u>Credit Information on</u> _____
>
>   The _____ company you inquired by your letter _____ is a leader in _____. With more than _____ years' _____ experience, it has enjoyed a high admiration both at home and abroad.
>
>   It has been maintaining an account with us from its establishing and has never failed to fulfill its obligation. Its _____ of recent years enclosed will show you that its business has been operated satisfactorily.
>
>   Please note that the above information is provided without any responsibility on our part and should be treated strictly confidential.
>
> Yours truly,
> [Signature]

6. Key Words and Expressions

(1) inquiry/enquiry   询价，询盘

(2) discount   折扣

(3) CIF: Cost, Insurance and Freight   成本加保险费运费价

(4) under separate cover   在另一包裹或另函内

(5) credit standing   信用情况

(6) thank you for your inquiry (letter) dated...   感谢你方××月××日的来信咨询

(7) enclosing   随信附寄

(8) illustrated catalogue   有插图的产品目录

(9) Letter of Credit payable by sight draft   信用证即期汇票支付

(10) appreciative   感激的

7. Useful Sentence Patterns

(1) Please state clearly in your reply your earliest delivery date, terms of payment, the minimum order quantity and discounts.   请在回复中写明贵方最早发货日期、付款方式、最小订单量以及折扣。

(2) As you will see in the above list, our products are good in quality and reasonable in price. 正如贵方在报价单里看到的那样，我们的产品物美价廉。

(3) We will offer a proper discount according to the quantity ordered.   我方将根据订购数量提供适当的优惠。

(4) We are looking forward to your early reply and doing business with you.   我们期待您的早日回复，并与您建立业务关系。

(5) We shall be appreciative if you will send us your latest catalogue and price list.　若贵方能惠寄最新的产品目录和价目单，我们将不胜感激。

(6) We believe you will place an order before further rises in costs after you examine the samples.　我们相信贵方看过样品之后会在成本上涨前下单。

(7) Please quote us your lowest price, CIF Liverpool and tell us your minimum order quantity. 请报最低的利物浦成本加保险费运费价，并告诉我们贵方的最小订单量。

(8) Furthermore, please tell us the packing, weight, deliveries and other essential details. 此外，请告诉我们包装、重量、运输和其他的重要细节。

(9) It has referred us to your bank for detailed information about its credit standing and business capacity.　该公司推荐贵方银行出具其信誉和经营能力的详细信息。

(10) Any information given by you will be treated strictly in confidence and highly valued. 对于贵方提供的所有资料，我们将高度重视并严格保密。

8. Exercises

Exercise 4-1

Direction: Rearrange the following information into a general inquiry.

(1) We look forward to receiving your quotation CIF Liverpool inclusive of our commission of 5% at an early date.

(2) We are ready to conclude substantial business with you if your quotation is attractive.

(3) We have read your advertisement in newspaper.

(4) It is our goal to establish direct business relations with you in order to promote trade between our two countries.

(5) We look forward to your early reply.

(6) Please state the earliest shipment and quantity available as well.

(7) Our company is one of the largest health food importers in Liverpool.

Exercise 4-2

Direction: Put the following sentences into English.

(1) 若贵公司能尽快惠寄产品目录、样品手册或样品，我方将不胜感激。

(2) 我方希望这是一个长期互利的业务关系的良好开端。

(3) 从价目表中你方可以看到我们在近几个月价格上涨的情况下已经报了最低价。

(4) 以上信息请注意严格保密，我方对这些信息不负任何责任。

(5) 该公司近几年的资产负债表显示他们的业务开展得令人满意。

Exercise 4-3

Direction: Write a reply according to the following information.

Write a reply to Guangzhou Liding Leather Industry Co., Ltd. They are in the market for all bags (ladies fashion bag, wallet, clutch). They requested an illustrated catalogue and samples.

This is the first time that you contact this company.

9. Supplementary Reading

How to Write an Inquiry Letter

Write an inquiry letter to ask for more information concerning a product, service or other information about a product or service. These letters are often written in response to an advertisement that we have seen in the paper, a magazine, a commercial on television when we are interested in purchasing a product, but would like more information before making a decision. Inquiries are also written to ask for business contact information to develop new business. For further types of business letters use this guide to different types of business letters to refine your skills for specific business purposes such as making inquiries, adjusting claims, writing cover letters and more.

Remember to place your or your company's address at the top of the letter (or use your company's letterhead) followed by the address of the company you are writing to. The date can either be placed double spaced down or to the right.

Important Language to Remember as following:

· The Start:

Dear Sir or Madam

· To Whom It May Concern - (very formal as you do not know the person to whom you are writing)

· Giving Reference:

With reference to your advertisement (ad) in...

Regarding your advertisement (ad) in...

· Requesting a Catalog, Brochure, etc.: (After the reference, add a comma and continue), would (could) you please send me...

· Requesting Further Information: I would also like to know...

Could you tell me whether...

· Signature:

Yours faithfully - (very formal as you do not know the person to whom you are writing)

Chapter 5
Offers and Promotions
报价与促销

1. Learning Objectives

By the end of this chapter, you will be able to do the following:

· Have a general view about offers and promotion.

· Know how to write an offer.

· Know how to write a promotion.

· Learn the proper words and expressions and sentence patterns in writing offers and promotion.

2. Case Study

> CREATIVE EYE AMERICAN APPAREL, INC. is a one-stop vertically integrated company—from fabric to finish, all processed under one roof. It is an apparel design and manufacturing company located in the United States and excels at producing private labels and custom-made apparels that are technical, fashionable and of exceptionally superior quality. Presently, CEAA has received an inquiry from the following Chinese company, asking for a catalogue, a quotation list and a sample book:
>
> Company Name: Qingdao Arrow Industry And Trade Co., Ltd.
>
> Operational Address: Bldg. C, 452 Jingfa Road, Yiwu, Zhejiang, China (Mainland)

Suppose you are a foreign trade clerk working in CEAA. Please write an offer to Qingdao Arrow Industry and Trade Co., Ltd., quoting the price of the goods for sale as well as stating all necessary terms of sales for the company's consideration and acceptance.

3. Introduction

Offers are promises to supply goods at a stated price and within a stated period of time. The offerer not only quotes the price of the goods for sale, but also states all necessary terms of sales for customers' consideration and acceptance. To justify the price and arouse the customers' interest, the seller, as the offerer, will make a price concession on conditions, or talk about the cost, rising market and the orders from other sources. While the buyer, being the offerer, will refer to the declining market or offers from other suppliers to ask for price reduction. The person to whom such letters are written to is called referee.

Offers are usually divided into firm offer and non-firm offer. Firm offers can not be withdrawn within its validity. It is the referee's opinion to accept or reject or counter-offer during the validity period. If the offer is accepted, it is a contractual obligation. Contrary to a firm offer, a non-firm offer has no binding force upon the offerer. It has no term of validity. A non-firm offer often uses such wording "this offer is subject to our final confirmation", or "the prices are subject to change without notice". Thus non-firm offer entails the offerees more freedom that they could make decisions according to the market situation. But the offerees might consider the non-firm offer to be ordinary business dealings and pay little attention. In this respect, firm offers could do better by encouraging the offerees to make decisions and close business.

To make it a satisfactory offer, the offerer should include the following:

· An expression of thanks for the inquiry, if any.

· Detailed information of the goods, like names of commodities, specifications, quality, quantity, packing, delivery, etc.

· A clear statement of prices, terms of payment, commissions, or discounts, if any.

· The period for which the offer is valid (if it is a firm offer).

· Favorable comments on the goods.

· An expression of hopes to conclude business.

There is another type of letters which are called sales or promotion. The sellers advertise their products in these letters in order to persuade the buyers into accepting the priced goods. A good promotion tries to represent the offer from the view point of the buyer with a purpose to arouse interest and promote the sales of the goods.

4. Specimen Letters

Specimen 1
Firm Offer

Dear Sir,

In reply to your letter of February 20, we are giving you an offer, subject to your reply here by 5 p.m. our time, Friday, March 13, as follows:
Commodity: Mountain Bike
Specifications: 26 Inch 24 Speed Mountain Bike
Packing: Carton Box 85% SKD
Quantity: 3,000 sets
Price: US $102
Shipment: Within 30 days after receiving deposit
Payment: by confirmed, irrevocable L/C payable by draft at sight to be opened 30 days before the date of shipment

We have given you our most favorable price and look forward to your early reply.

Yours faithfully,
[Signature]

Specimen 2
Firm Offer

Dear Sir,

We take pleasure in making you an offer as follows, subject to your reply reaching here by July 7 as follows:

Article: Menow Lipstick

Quality: Menow 62-P12014 Waterproof Longlasting Lipstick

Quantity: 10,000 Pieces

Price: US $ 7.5

Packing: 6 pcs/color box,12 dozs/inner box,12 inner boxes/ctn

Shipment: 40-50 days

Terms: Draft at 60 d/s under Irrevocable Letter of Credit

What's more, the prices quoted are for orders of invoice value below $ 3000. For larger orders we offer an extra 5 percent discount.

We highly appreciate your early reply.

Yours faithfully,
[Signature]

Specimen 3
Non-firm Offer

Dear Sir,

Thank you for your letter of June 7, inquiring for Fashion zipper lady purse. Based on your requirement, we are quoting as follows:

Product name	Fashion zipper lady purse
Gender	Female
Model no.	DLL-QB-0707
Type	Zip wallet
Material	PU
Color	Red
Size	19×10.5×2.5cm
Moq	500pcs
Price	US $ 2-5/piece FOB Guangzhou/Shenzhen

Payment term	by L/C at sight to be opened through a bank to be approved by us
Packing	Polybag or paper gift box
Shipment	By sea, by air, by express DHL UPS Fedex

The above quotation is made without engagement and is subject to our final confirmation.Looking forward to your early reply.

Yours faithfully,
[Signature]

Specimen 4
Promotion

Dear Sir,

We are glad to send you our catalogue for our custom stripe silk tie. The high quality of our products is universally acknowledged and we are confident that a trial order would convince you that the goods we are offering are the best choice.

To popularize the products, all the catalogue prices are subject to a special discount of 15% during this month only.

We are offering you the goods of the highest quality on the most generous terms and would welcome your earliest orders.

Yours sincerely,
[Signature]

Specimen 5
Promotion

Dear Sir,

A new style computer desk has been introduced recently by our company and the market response is very positive. Thus we sincerely introduce it to you.

The new style is both elegant and practical, with smooth and delicate surface and bright colored drawing on the desk. The structure of this computer desk is made of thicker steel pipes and it is of high quality that it can be used well within 10 years.

What's more, our price is very reasonable. Every computer desk is 150 RMB and we can offer 5000 sets every month. If you place order over 1000 sets, we will give you a 20% discount. We can guarantee you our good delivery speed.

New style, high quality, reasonable price and speedy delivery are our advantages compared with other company's similar products. Please contact us if you have any interest. And we wish we can build a long-term relationship.

Yours sincerely,
[Signature]

Specimen 6
To Promote Goods Available from Stock

Dear Sir,

Thank you for your order of January 20. We have enclosed a catalogue and price list, which we trust will reach you soon.

What we feel awfully sorry is that the traditional executive desks FOHS-A18112 are in short supply, and we cannot satisfy all the customers' demands. We sincerely recommend the traditional executive desks FOHS-A18113, with the size 1800*900*760mm, which is the only difference between FOHS-A18112. We now have plenty of this type of desk in stock and can offer 20% discount for bulk purchase.

We would be very much appreciated to receive your order soon.

Yours sincerely,
[Signature]

Specimen 7
To Promote to a Former Client

Dear Sir,

Looking through our records, we note with regret that we have not received any orders from you since last September. We wonder whether you have been dissatisfied either with our goods or with the way in which we have handled your orders. Would you please fill out the enclosed reply card if you have encountered some problems with us? We will give your comments immediate attention.

We think you may be interested to know that we have merged with Monica (Guangzhou) Textile Technology Co., Ltd. We are engaged in the research and development of fabric for men's wear. In order to be more professional, we have a powerful and professional Foreign Trade Team to serve clients.

You will see from the catalogue enclosed that our prices are much lower than those of other importers. In addition, we are offering very generous terms of payment. We look forward to the pleasure of your renewed orders.

Yours sincerely,
[Signature]

5. Writing Templates

Firm Offer

Dear _____,

In reply to your letter of _____, we are giving you an offer, subject to your reply here by _____, as follows:

Commodity: _____
Specifications: _____
Packing: _____
Quantity: _____
Price: _____
Shipment: _____
Payment: _____
We have given you our most favorable price and look forward to your early reply.

Yours faithfully,
[Signature]

Non-firm Offer

Dear _____,

Thank you for your letter of _____, inquiring for _____. Based on your requirement, we are quoting as follows:

Product name	
Gender	
Model no.	
Type	
Material	
Color	
Size	
Moq	
Price	
Payment term	
Packing	
Shipment	

The above quotation is made without engagement and is subject to our final confirmation. Looking forward to your early reply.

Yours faithfully,
[Signature]

Promotion

Dear _____,

We are glad to send you _____ for our _____. The high quality of our products is universally acknowledged and we are confident that a trial order would convince you that the goods we are offering are the best choice.

> To popularize the products, all the catalogue prices are subject to a special discount of
> _____ during _____ only.
> We are offering you the goods of the highest quality on the most generous terms
> andwould welcome your earliest orders.
>
> Yours sincerely,
> [Signature]

6. Key Words and Expressions

(1) offer 报盘，报价

(2) offerer 发盘人，发价人

(3) offeree 受盘人，被发价人

(4) firm offer 实盘

(5) non-firm offer 虚盘

(6) quote 报盘，报价

(7) 26 Inch 24 Speed Mountain Bike 26寸24速山地自行车

(8) FOB free on board 离岸价

(9) express: DHL UPS Fedex 快递公司：DHL、UPS和联邦快递公司

(10) custom stripe silk tie 定制条纹真丝领带

(11) in short supply 供不应求

(12) 6 pcs/color box,12 dozs/inner box,12 inner boxes/ctn 6件/彩盒，12打/内盒，12内盒/箱

(13) SKD（Semi Knock Down） 半散装件（在国际贸易中，特别是在国际汽车贸易中，整车出口国的汽车公司把成品予以拆散，而以半成品或零部件的方式出口，再由进口厂商在所在国以自行装配方式完成整车成品并进行销售）

7. Useful Sentence Patterns

(1) We are giving you an offer, subject to your reply here by... 我们给贵方的报价，以贵方在……前的回复为准。

(2) Within 30 days after receiving deposit. 收到定金后30天内。

(3) By confirmed, irrevocable L/C payable by draft at sight to be opened 30 days before the date of shipment. 以保兑的、不可撤销的信用证，凭装运日期前30天开立的即期汇票支付。

(4) Draft at 60 d/s under Irrevocable Letter of Credit. 在不可撤销信用证条件下凭即期汇票支付。

(5) By L/C at sight to be opened through a bank to be approved by us. 凭在我方批准的银行开立的即期信用证支付。

(6) The above quotation is made without engagement and is subject to our final confirmation. 以上报价无约束力，请以我方的最后确认为准。

(7) The high quality of our products is universally acknowledged and we are confident that a

trial order would convince you that the goods we are offering are the best choice. 我们产品的高质量是公认的，我们相信试订单会让贵方相信我们提供的商品是最好的选择。

(8) We can guarantee you our good delivery speed. 我们可以向贵方保证我们良好的交货速度。

(9) New style, high quality, reasonable price and speedy delivery are our advantages compared with other company's similar products. 款式新，质量高，价格合理、交货快捷是我们相比其他公司同类产品的优势。

(10) You will see from the catalogue enclosed that our prices are much lower than those of other importers. 从所附的产品目录中您可以看到，我们的价格比其他公司低很多。

8. Exercises

Exercise 5-1

Direction: Rearrange the following information into a non-firm offer.

(1) The above prices are understood to be on CIF Ningbo basis net. A discount of 15% may be allowed if the quantity for each specification is more than 1500 sets.

(2) Based on your requirement, we are quoting as follows:

26" Men's style   US $ 40 per set

26" Women's style   US $ 40 per set

(3) Payment term: Draft at 60 d/s under Irrevocable Letter of Credit

(4) We look forward to your early reply.

(5) The above quotation is made without engagement and is subject to our final confirmation.

(6) Thank you for your e-mail of October 1, inquiring for Sunshine bicycles.

Exercise 5-2

Direction: Put the following sentences into English.

(1) 所报价格针对发票价值低于3000美元的订单。

(2) 对于大订单，我们提供额外的5%的折扣。

(3) 为了推广这些产品，所有的产品目录价格在这个月都有15%的特殊折扣。

(4) 我们为您提供最高质量的商品和最优惠的价格条款，欢迎您尽早下订单。

(5) 此外，我们提供非常优惠的付款方式。

Exercise 5-3

Direction: Write a letter according to the following information.

Please write a firm offer for 200 pairs of Breeze No. 2 Shoes with the price of US $ 35 a pair CIF Liverpool. The shipment is September to October. The payment mode is confirmed, irrevocable L/C payable by draft at sight to be opened 30 days before the date of shipment.

9. Supplementary Reading

Pricing and Promotion Strategy

There is a delicate balance between pricing and promotion, as marketers aim to move units and make a profit, without sacrificing brand equity. The goal of pricing strategy is to set a value to the good that will cover costs of production and marketing, and produce a profit. By integrating promotional efforts, marketers make customers more aware of the brand and compel them to take immediate buying action. Coupons, discounts and rewards are all strategies used to temporarily drive down the price, and spur the customer to act within a fixed time. When properly implemented, price and promotion strategy can cause an instant, seasonal or predictable spike in sales.

Pricing Strategy

Price is determined by supply, demand, and competition—and within these parameters marketers can choose three types of pricing strategies: skimming, penetration or competitive. The competitive price of a good is set by the market, and marketers can set their price on par with competitors (competitive strategy), higher than competitors (skimming strategy), or lower than competitors (penetrating strategy). The strategy behind setting the price takes into account the cost of production plus the mark-up, as well as the desired perceived value of the branding. Marketers might choose to skim the market to position their brand as a luxury good. Or they might penetrate the market, marketing the product as a discount brand, to grab more market share. Either way the price, high or low, determines how they will use promotional strategy.

Limited Offers

Coupons and rebates are both examples of limited offers. These promotions reduce the price for one time only, pushing the customer to take buying action. If the marketer has skimmed the market, his main preoccupation is to discount the product without diminishing the perceived value of the premium brand. However, if the marketer is penetrating the market, he has to be careful not to set a promotional price so low that it will cut into profits. The time frame when marketers will see a return on investment is not so easily calculated, since the customer chooses when to cash in the coupon or rebate.

Seasonal Sales

Promotional periods are set by retailers, and the cost of the promotion is usually shared between the retailer and the brand. By designing a sale program that coincides with a specific holiday or seasonal time of year, retailers and marketers can predict a spike in consumer spending and recoup losses in sales and inventory. Choosing the discounted price in conjunction with the length of time is key, because marketers do not want the customer to get so accustomed to the lower price that they are less willing to pay full price for the product when the promotional period has expired.

Bulk Purchase

A bulk-buying promotion strategy lowers prices for buying more than one of a specific item. This ensures that marketers will sell more units, and take advantage of lower production costs because of economies of scale. Customers who buy competitive to low-priced goods in bulk reap the benefits of this strategy. A bulk-buying promotion doesn't work as well with a price-skimming strategy because the higher-priced items are not normally manufactured in quantities large enough to be considered a bulk purchase.

Membership Programs

Customer enrollment in a valued membership club—where she receives exclusive promotional discounts—is something that is used at all price points and can actually fortify perception of the brand. Because membership equates to exclusivity, it doesn't diminish brand equity in a luxury product, and it can spur multiple sales in lower-priced goods. Furthermore, by controlling the sales periods for valued customers, marketers can predict when a specific segment of their customers will be more likely to buy. Thus, businesses profit from two income streams: a discounted but more predictable income stream, and full-price but less-predictable stream.

Chapter 6
Counter Offers
还盘

1. Learning Objectives

By the end of this chapter, you will be able to do the following:

· Get to know the key words and expressions for writing counter-offers.

· Know the useful sentence patterns in writing counter-offers.

· Know how to write counter-offers.

2. Case Study

> Ningbo Chengqi Vehicle Co., Ltd. is specializing in the production of bicycle parts, with the clip-on brake, brake, cantilever brake, transmission, brake handle, V brake, saddle, etc. It has a certain scale of production, strong technical force, advanced factory equipment, science and technology management and a high-quality staff team.
>
> Recently, Ningbo Chengqi Vehicle Co., Ltd. has received an offer from USA EXPORTS GLOBAL LIMITED PARTNERSHIP (Operational Address: PO Box 6073, South Hackensack, New Jersey, United States):
>
> City Bike
> FOB Price: US $45 - 50 / Unit
> Min. Order Quantity:100 Unit/Units
> Supply Ability: 10000 Unit/Units per Month
> Port: Shanghai, China
> Payment Terms: T/T
> Ningbo Chengqi Vehicle Co., Ltd. could not agree on the price and payment term.

Suppose you are a foreign trade clerk working in it. Please write counter-offer to USA EXPORTS GLOBAL LIMITED PARTNERSHIP, showing your company's disagreement and seeking for compromise.

3. Introduction

Upon receiving a firm offer or non-firm offer, the offeree may not agree with any or some of the transactional terms, he would send a counter-offer, in which he would try to negotiate about some contents, such as the price, packing, terms of payment, time of shipment, and mostly the focus is on the price.

In the counter-offer, the offeree may show his disagreement to the certain terms and state his own ideas. Then the original offerer now becomes the offeree with the full right of acceptance or refusal. In the latter case, he may make another counter-offer of his own, which is called counter-counter offer. This process could go on for many rounds till business is concluded or called off.

A counter-offer usually covers the following contents:

- expression of thanks for the recipient for his offer
- expression of regret and statement of reasons for inability to accept the offer
- statement of desired business conditions and persuading the recipient to accept them
- expecting for a favorable reply

In international business negotiations, the seller, on one hand, wants to sell things at a high price on safe terms of payment; the buyer, on the other hand, wants to buy things at a low price with an earlier delivery date. So the offerer's quotation is often much higher than what the offeree has expected, and it is natural and common that the offeree will make a counter-offer.

4. Specimen Letters

Specimen 1
Counter-offer — Amendment to an Offer

> Dear Sir,
>
> Re: <u>2014 Fashion Women's Bag</u>
>
> Thank you for your offer of January 11 for the subject article.
> In reply, we are sorry to say that we can't accept it. Your prices are rather on the high side and not in line with the world market. Other suppliers are offering us much lower price.
> We have seen your samples and are satisfied with the high quality, but feel hard to accept the big gap between your price and that of other suppliers.
> In order to finalize the transaction, we suggest that you reduce the prices by 15%.
> We look forward to your acceptance and early reply.
>
> Yours faithfully,
> [Signature]

Specimen 2
Counter-offer — Amendment to an Offer

> Dear Sir,
>
> Re: <u>HY-9006 water tap</u>
>
> Thank you for your letter of September 20, offering us US $ 20/piece CIF Ningbo for the subject article.

We feel regretted to tell you that your price is too high and will leave us nothing. Actually, we have received quotations 20% lower than yours. But we don't deny our interest in your product. Thus if you reduce your prices by, say, 10%, we will conclude the business immediately.

Looking forward to your early acceptance of this special discount. We hope our cooperation will be fruitful and successful.

Yours faithfully,
[Signature]

Specimen 3
Counter-offer — Amendment on Payment Terms

Dear Sir,

Re: <u>Yue Xiu Curtain</u>

Thank you for your letter of September 20, offering us US $ 0.6/meter CIF Shanghai for the subject article. But we want you to consider an alternation of the payment terms.

The past mode confirmed, irrevocable letter of credit at sight has indeed cost us too much. From the opening of the credit till we receive the payment, the tie-up of our funds lasts about four months. This problem is more serious presently due to the tight money condition.

Considering our good cooperation over these years, we suggest you accept either "Cash against Documents on arrival of goods" or "Drawing on us at 60 day's sight".

We look forward to your favorable reply as soon as possible.

Yours faithfully,
[Signature]

Specimen 4
Counter-counter Offer — Declining Counter-offer

Dear Sir,

We have received your counter-offer of September 25, and regret to find that you think the price offered by us for HY-9006 water tap is on the high side.

You mention that you have received quotations 20% lower than ours. But we want you to notice that the quality of the other suppliers does not measure up to that of our products.

We believe our price is fixed at a reasonable level. Actually, we have received lots of orders from other buyers who are satisfied with our price. Thus we feel very sorry that we can't accept your counter-offer for the time being.

We value our relations and look forward to your favorable reply.

Yours faithfully,
[Signature]

Specimen 5
Counter-counter Offer — Agreeing Partly to Lower the Price

Dear Sir,

Re: <u>Fashion Cycling Clothing</u>

In reference to your counter-offer of October 1, we feel that the price we quoted to you for the subject article is very generous due to the rising cost of raw materials in the past three months.

However, considering the fact that we have cooperated so well for these years, we would like to grant your request by reducing the price by 5%, that is US $ 28 FOB Hong Kong, China. Taking the quality into consideration, we believe the prices are very competitive in this market.

Please note that this is the best we can offer and we can not entertain any counter-offer.

We hope you take our suggestion into serious consideration and give us your reply as soon as possible.

Yours sincerely,
[Signature]

5. Writing Templates

Counter-offer — Amendment to an Offer

Dear Sir,

Re:_____

Thank you for your offer of _____ for the subject article.

In reply, we are sorry to say that we can't accept it. Your prices are rather on the high side and not in line with the world market. Other suppliers are offering us much lower price.

We have seen your samples and are satisfied with the high quality, but feel hard to accept the big gap between your price and that of other suppliers.

In order to finalize the transaction, we suggest that you reduce the prices by _____.

We look forward to your acceptance and early reply.

Yours faithfully,
[Signature]

Counter-offer — Amendment on Payment Terms

Dear Sir,

Re:_____

Thank you for your letter of _____ , offering us _____ for the subject article. But we want you to consider an alternation of the payment terms.

The past mode confirmed, irrevocable Letter of Credit at sight has indeed cost us too much. From the opening of the credit till we receive the payment, the tie-up of our funds lasts about four months. This problem is more serious presently due to the tight money condition.

Considering our good cooperation over these years, we suggest you accept either "Cash against Documents on arrival of goods" or "Drawing on us at _____ day's sight".

We look forward to your favorable reply as soon as possible.

Yours faithfully,
[Signature]

Counter-counter Offer — Declining Counter-offer

Dear Sir,

We have received your counter-offer of _____, and regret to find that you think the price offered by us for _____ is on the high side.

You mention that you have received quotations _____ lower than ours. But we want you to notice that the quality of the other suppliers does not measure up to that of our products.

We believe our price is fixed at a reasonable level. Actually, we have received lots of orders from other buyers who are satisfied with our price. Thus we feel very sorry that we can't accept your counter-offer for the time being.

We value our relations and look forward to your favorable reply.

Yours faithfully,
[Signature]

Counter-counter Offer — Agreeing Partly to Lower the Price

Dear Sir,

Re:_____

In reference to your counter-offer of _____, we feel that the price we quoted to you for the subject article is very generous due to the rising cost of raw materials in the past.

However, considering the fact that we have cooperated so well for these years, we would like to grant your request by reducing the price by _____, that is _____. Taking the quality into consideration, we believe the prices are very competitive in this market.

Please note that this is the best we can offer and we can not entertain any counter-offer.

We hope you take our suggestion into serious consideration and give us your reply as soon as possible.

Yours sincerely,
[Signature]

6. Key Words and Expressions

(1) counter-offer　还价，还盘

(2) counter counter-offer　反还盘

(3) subject article　标题（所指的）商品

(4) on the high side　价格有点偏高

(5) raw material　原材料

(6) amendment　修改

(7) finalize　完成

(8) fruitful　有成效的

(9) alternation　改变，改动

(10) Cash against Documents on arrival of goods　货到后凭单付款

(11) Drawing on us at 60 day's sight　开出见票60天付款的汇票向我们收款

(12) Fashion Cycling Clothing　时尚自行车骑行服

(13) grant　同意，准许

(14) entertain　接受

7. Useful Sentence Patterns

(1) Your prices are not in line with the world market. 贵方的价格与市场价格水平不一致。

(2) We have seen your samples and are satisfied with the high quality, but feel hard to accept the big gap between your price and that of other suppliers. 我们已经看过贵方的样品，并且对其高质量十分满意。但我们无法接受贵方与其他供应商在价格上的巨大差距。

(3) We feel regretted to tell you that your price is too high and will leave us nothing.很遗憾我们认为贵方的价格过高，这样的价格将使我们无利可图。

(4) But we don't deny our interest in your product. 但是我们不否认我们对贵方的商品很感兴趣。

(5) If you reduce your prices by, say, 10%, we will conclude the business immediately. 如果贵方能降价10%，我们将立即成交。

(6) From the opening of the credit till we receive the payment, the tie-up of our funds lasts about four months. 从开立信用证到我们收到付款，我们的资金被占用达四个月之久。

(7) This problem is more serious presently due to the tight money condition. 由于银根紧缩，这个问题目前变得更为严重。

(8) We feel very sorry that we can't accept your counter-offer for the time being. 很抱歉我们目前不能接受贵方的还盘。

(9) We feel that the price we quoted to you for the subject article is very generous due to the rising cost of raw materials in the past three months. 由于过去三个月中原材料成本的上涨，我们认为我们对标题商品的报价非常优惠。

(10) Taking the quality into consideration, we believe the prices are very competitive in this market. 考虑到质量，我们相信这个价格在市场上很有竞争力。

(11) Please note that this is the best we can offer and we can not entertain any counter-offer.

请注意这是我们所能提供的最低价格，我们不能接受任何还盘。

8. Exercises

Exercise 6-1

Direction: Rearrange the following information into a counter-offer.

(1) If you can find out the reason and cut down the price, we would be pleased to place a big order till the end of this year.

(2) However, we find that we can get a price of US $ 5.00 per dozen with another supplier.

(3) That order would be one of our largest orders ever since.

(4) Looking forward to your early reply.

(5) This is sixty cents per dozen lower than your price.

(6) We are pleased to receive your offer of July 15, and satisfied with your product.

Exercise 6-2

Direction: Put the following sentences into English.

(1) 为达成交易，我们建议贵方降价15%。

(2) 但是我们想请贵方注意，其他供应商的产品质量比不上我们的产品质量。

(3) 我们相信我们的报价处于合理的价格水平。

(4) 考虑到我们已经合作了这么多年，我们想通过降价5%满足贵方的要求。

(5) 我们希望贵方认真考虑我们的建议，并尽快给我们回复。

Exercise 6-3

Direction: Write a letter according to the following information.

Please write a counter-offer asking for earlier delivery. The original delivery time "the end of October" needs to be shifted to "on or before September 15".

9. Supplementary Reading

The Ultimate Truth in Persuasion

As you know your intent directs the flow of energy in your interactions with others. So doesn't it just make sense to have in mind a really clear and strong intent before you engage in your powerful persuasion mission.

If you were to think about the person(s) you want to persuade what comes to mind in regards to the benefits they will gain from your persuasion?

Of course your' persuasive pitch' will be received much more receptively if your intent is strongly biased to their benefits.

So stepping into their shoes what benefits can you perceive from their angle and looking at the situation as if you were watching a movie what other ideas come to mind?

Having some idea of what the other person(s) want and keeping that positive intention nice and strong in mind when interacting with the person(s) will automatically create a "good vibe" between you, thus creating that well known fundamental persuasion skill—Rapport!

Now in your interaction with the other party you would increase your persuasion parlance greatly by asking well focused questions. Basically you want to ask questions that get the other person to open up so that you can discover one of the very powerful motivators-to-action in humans known as "values."

This is another aspect of the very fascinating way in which the human mind works because you find yourself becoming increasingly curious about people's values as your persuasion power increases, doesn't it?

Now an important point to remember in this curious adventure is when you have got them talking: You Shut Up! AND Listen!

Isn't that cool, you just sit there and listen as they give you loads of high quality information that you can then use to powerfully persuade and guide them!

By paying attention you will notice that people use certain words which have a lot of emotional value for them personally. You could call these words their personal trance words.

Let me give you an example to clarify what were talking about. Let's say you are helping someone make a change in their life. Now presuming the person has asked you to help them you can make the change process happen even more smoothly by asking them certain questions.

So during conversation with this person you could ask him/her, "Why exactly do you want to make this change?" And, "What would having made this change, give you?" And also you could ask, "Why is that important to you?"

As you ask these questions you will notice that they have to access deeper parts of their minds. So by paying attention and listening carefully you will discover some of their personal trance words.

Some possible examples of their personal trance words might be: inner peace, better energy, assertiveness. Keep in mind the important fact that these words could have a deep and powerful feeling associated with them in their internal experience.

Now what do you suppose would happen if you were to then describe and incorporate those wonderful personal trance words into your persuasive change "pitch"?

That's right, they would be much more likely to go along with your persuasive intervention because you are using words which stimulate powerful feelings inside them for the changes that they really want!

So just what is "the ultimate truth in persuasion"? Well the fact is in the art of persuasion, or indeed anything, there are many ways of doing things, many perspectives, techniques, methods and tools. The point being, by using it and paying attention to feedback, will it get you the results you want?

Chapter 7
Orders and Replies
订货与回复

1. Learning Objectives

By the end of this chapter, you will be able to do the following:

· Understand the essential components of an order letter.

· Know how to make order letters.

· Know how to make acknowledgements to order letters.

· Use the proper words and expressions and sentence patterns in writing orders and replies.

2. Case Study

> Victorian Trade Co. is a Canadian importing company. After the negotiation with Shelton (Jiaxing) Import & Export Co., it decides to place an order for 1,200 cartons of Essential Balm on the terms and conditions as follows:
> Article: Jade Rabbit Brand Essential Balm
> Quantity: 1,200 cartons
> Price: USD 30 per carton FOB Shanghai
> Payment: payable by irrevocable confirmed sight L/C
> Shipment: not later than November 30
> Packing: 100 packets in a box and 60 boxes in a carton

Suppose you were the manager in Victorian. Please write an official order letter to Shelton.

3. Introduction

All your efforts will pay off when you receive orders from your customers. An order is a formal request addressed from a buyer to a seller, indicating types, quantities and agreed prices for specific goods. It is true that an order letter creates one half of a contract. Therefore, for the buyer, the order letter should be written as accurately and clearly as possible, because any error or misunderstanding may cause unexpected trouble; for the seller, the order letter should be treated with extra care and discretion. Remember that when the official order is accepted, both parties will be legally bound.

An order may be given by letter, fax, e-mail, or a preprinted order form. You need to contain the following points when writing an order:

(1) a full description of the commodity, including article number, size, color, or any other relevant information

(2) quantity

(3) date and method of shipment

(4) price per item

(5) packing

(6) payment term

…

After the receipt of an order, if the goods required are available, you should lose no time to state your acknowledgement. For small routine orders a printed acknowledgement may be enough, but a detailed confirming letter is better and helps create goodwill. An acceptance or a confirmation is in fact an unreserved assent of the buyer's terms. When you receive the relative order and confirm its terms and conditions, you may begin to execute the order to the buyer's satisfaction. However, there are times when you cannot accept buyers' orders because the goods required are not available or prices and specifications have been changed. In such circumstances, letters declining orders must be written with the utmost care and with an eye to goodwill and future business. It is advisable to recommend suitable substitutes, make counter-offers and persuade buyers to accept them.

4. Specimen Letters

Placing an Order
Specimen 1

Dear Sir,

Your samples of Bed Sheets and Pillow Cases received favorable reaction from our customers, and we are pleased to place our Order No.345 with you as follows.

Qty	Item	Catalogue No.	Price net
2300	Bed Sheets, 106cm, blue	75	US$ 5.00 each
2500	Bed Sheets, 82 120cm, pink	US$ 6.00 each	
500	Pillow Cases, blue	150	US$ 1.50 each
5000	Pillow Cases, pink	162	US$ 1.70 each
			FOB Shanghai

The goods are urgently required, so prompt delivery will be most appreciated.

Yours faithfully,
[Signature]

Specimen 2

Dear Sir,

We are pleased to order 2000 sets of Toshiba Color TV 29 inches under the following terms and conditions:

2000 sets of Toshiba Color TV 29 inches, at US$585 CIF Dalian, packed in wooden cases, each containing 4 sets, shipment from Yokohama to Dalian within a week after receipt of the relative L/C.

We trust that you will give special care to the packing of the goods, lest the goods should be damaged during transit.

We are now arranging the establishment of the L/C, which will be opened in your favor upon receipt of your Sales Confirmation.

Yours faithfully,
[Signature]

Specimen 3

Dear Sir,

We are in receipt of your letter of Sept. 5th and glad to inform you that your samples are satisfactory. Enclosed please find our Order Form No.235 for three of the items.

As these items are in urgent need by our customers, we hope you will do everything possible to guarantee punctual shipment.

Yours faithfully,
[Signature]

Encl.

ORDER FORM

COMPANY: SIMPSON IMPORT & EXPORT CO.
DELIVERED TO: 124 Dalhousie Street, Toronto B3H 51A, Canada
DATE: Sep. 12th, 2014

Qty(M/T)	Item	Catalogue No.	Unit Price(FOB Yantai)
600	A Grade Canned Mushroom	A-528	US$1800 per M/T
800	B Grade Canned Mushroom	B-117	US$1600 per M/T
600	C Grade Canned Mushroom	C-927	US$1450 per M/T

Packing: In cartons of 200 cans each
Shipment: Prompt Shipment from Yantai to Toronto
Payment: By irrevocable L/C payable by sight draft

Specimen 4
Acknowledgement of Order

> Dear Sir,
>
> We acknowledge with thanks your order No. BD/135 of Jan. 20th for our Canned Beef. We accept the order and are enclosing our Sales Confirmation No. 354 in duplicate of which please sign and return one copy to us for our file.
>
> The terms of payment you suggested, a draft at sight under L/C are quite acceptable to us. Provided your L/C in our favor reaches us in time, we will proceed with the shipment of the captioned products well before March. Special attention will be paid to its packing, which we feel confident. We believe that our products will prove satisfactory to your clients in every respect.
>
> We hope that our handling of this order will lead to further business between us and to a happy and lasting association.
>
> Yours faithfully,
> [Signature]

Specimen 5
Declining an Order

> Dear Sir,
>
> Thank you very much for your order No. 98 for 180 units Y18 portable videos received on May. 20th.
>
> After careful consideration on your request, however, we have come to the conclusion that it would be better for us to decline your order in this case. We regret that, our manufacturers cannot undertake to fulfill your order owing to the uncertain availability of raw materials. We will, however, contact once supply improves.
>
> We do appreciate your coming to us and regret our inability to be more helpful this time. In the meantime, please feel free to send us your specific inquiries for other types of products. You can be assured of our best attention at all time.
>
> Yours faithfully,
> [Signature]

5. Writing Templates

Placing an Order

> Dear Sir,
>
> Your samples of _____ received favorable reaction from our customers, and we are pleased to place our Order No. _____ with you as follows.
>
> Qty　　Item　　Catalogue No.　　Price net
>
> _____　　_____　　_____　　　_____

The goods are urgently required, so prompt delivery will be most appreciated.

Yours faithfully,
[Signature]

Dear Sir,

　　We are in receipt of your letter of _____ and glad to inform you that your samples are satisfactory. Enclosed please find our Order Form No. _____ for _____.
　　As these items are in urgent need by our customers, we hope you will do everything possible to guarantee punctual shipment.

Yours faithfully,
[Signature]

Encl.

ORDER FORM

COMPANY: _____
DELIVERED TO: _____
DATE: _____

Qty(M/T)	Item	Catalogue No.	Unit Price(FOB Yantai)

Packing: _____
Shipment: _____
Payment: _____

Acknowledgement of Order

Dear Sir,

　　We acknowledge with thanks your order No. _____ of _____ for our _____. We accept the order and are enclosing our Sales Confirmation No. _____ in duplicate of which please sign and return one copy to us for our file.
　　The terms of payment you suggested, _____ are quite acceptable to us. Provided _____, we will proceed with the shipment of the captioned products well before _____. Special attention will be paid to its packing, which we feel confident. We believe that our products will prove satisfactory to your clients in every respect.
　　We hope that our handling of this order will lead to further business between us and to a happy and lasting association.

Yours faithfully,
[Signature]

Declining an Order

Dear Sir,

Thank you very much for your order No. _____ for _____ received on _____.

After careful consideration on your request, however, we have come to the conclusion that it would be better for us to decline your order in this case. We regret that, our manufacturers cannot undertake to fulfill your order owing to _____. We will, however, contact once supply improves.

We do appreciate your coming to us and regret our inability to be more helpful this time. In the meantime, please feel free to send us your specific inquiries for other types of products. You can be assured of our best attention at all time.

Yours faithfully,
[Signature]

6. Key Words and Expressions

(1) order/order form　订单

(2) acknowledgement　确认书

(3) official order　正式订单

(4) legally bound　（受）法律约束

(5) unreserved assent　无保留的同意

(6) execute the order　执行订单

(7) decline the order　拒绝订单

(8) in one's favor　以……为受益人

(9) in duplicate　一式两份

(10) for our file　供我方备档

(11) fulfill the order　履行订单

7. Useful Sentence Patterns

(1) We are pleased to place the following orders with you if you can guarantee shipment from Shanghai to Singapore by October 9. 若贵方能保证在10月9日之前将货物由上海运至新加坡，则我方乐于向贵方订购下列货物。

(2) We have now seen the samples and are prepared to order ... pieces as a trial. Please note that the goods should be exactly the same as the sample. 我们已收到样品，现准备试订购……件产品。请保证订购产品和样品完全一致。

(3) Thank you for your Order No ... We accept it and will dispatch the goods before ... 感谢贵方的××号订单。我们现确认该订单，并将于……号之前发货。

(4) Thank you very much for your order of ... for ... We are pleased to confirm our

acceptance as shown in the enclosed Sales Confirmation. 非常感谢贵方……号购买……的订单。我们很高兴地确认该订单，详见附件中的销售确认书。

(5) We have pleasure in informing you that we have booked your order No. … We are sending you our Sales Confirmation No. … in duplicate, one copy of which please countersign and return for our file. 我们很高兴地通知贵方，贵方的××号订单现已订舱。现寄去××号销售确认书一式两份。请会签并退还一份以便存档。

(6) To our regret, we are unable to accept your order at the price requested, since our profit margin does not allow us any concession by way of discount of prices. 我们很抱歉地通知您，我们无法以您期望的价格接受您的订单，因为我们的利润空间很小，无法再做价格上的调整了。

(7) As our factories are fully committed for … we regret our inability to entertain any fresh orders. 由于我们的工厂已经满单，因此我们抱歉地通知贵方，对该产品我们无法接受新订单。

(8) Something unexpected has compelled us to ask you to cancel part of our order and to deliver … instead of … 突如其来的变故使得我们不得不请求贵方取消我们的部分订单，并发送……以替代原来的……

(9) We find both quality and prices of your products satisfactory and enclose our trial order for prompt supply. 我方对贵方产品的质量和价格均感满意，现寄去试订单，请供应现货。

(10) We are pleased to find that your material appear to be fine quality. As a trial, we are delighted to send you a small order for 2500 dozen Rubber Shoes. 我方很高兴发现贵方原料品质优良，现寄去2500打胶鞋小额订单，作为试购。

(11) Thank you for your quotation for bicycle, but we regret that we have to place our order elsewhere as your prices are too high for this market. 谢谢贵方自行车报价，但遗憾的是，贵方价格对此市场来说过高，我们不得不向别处订购。

(12) We are very pleased to receive your order and confirm that all the items required are in stock. 很高兴接到贵方订单，并确认所需的全部货物均以现货供应。

(13) Your order is receiving our immediate attention and we will keep you informed of the progress. 我方正在迅速处理贵方订单，并将随时告知贵方进展情况。

(14) As our factories are fully committed for the fourth quarter, we regret our inability to entertain any fresh order. 由于我方工厂第四季度的货订单已满，很抱歉我们无法接受新的订单。

(15) Unfortunately, your order goods Model No. A21 are now out of stock, but we recommend No. A26 as a substitute which is very close to your choice in quality though slightly higher in price. 很抱歉，贵方所订购的A21型产品目前已无存货，故推荐A26型产品，此产品与贵方指定的产品在质量上极其相近，只是价格稍贵。

(16) We regret that we have to cancel our order because of the inferior quality of your products. 很抱歉，由于贵方产品质量低劣，我方不得不取消合同。

8. Exercises

Exercise 7-1

Direction: Put the following sentences into English.

(1) 附寄订单一份，请按你方最低价执行。这是我们第一次试购你方货物，我们将仔细检查货物的价值。

(2) 附上300辆自行车的试购订单一份，如货物质量能使我方满意,今后我们将大量定购。

(3) 你公司8月10号来函收悉，随函附有关第100号订单定购500台缝纫机(sewing machine)的销售确认书一式两份，编号为90SP–5861。

(4) 由于工资和原料价格大幅上涨，很抱歉无法按我方半年前所报价格接受订单。

(5) 很遗憾，由于贵方所需要的货物的订货已经预订到年底，我们不能接受任何年内交运的新订单。

Exercise 7-2

Direction: Write a letter based on the following information.

You are the manager of Meixin Imp. & Exp. Co. Ltd. in Hangzhou. One day, you check your mailbox and find the following letter.

Dear Sir,

Thank you for your previous letters and having sent us samples of canned mushroom. We find both quality and prices satisfactory and pleased to place an order for the following goods on the understanding that they will be supplied from stock at the prices stated:

Quality	Article No.	Prices	Shipment
12M/Ts	0801	USD1800per M/T	FOB Nigbo
8M/Ts	0802	USD1800per M/T	FOB Nigbo

If this first order is successfully executed, we shall place further and larger orders with you in the near future.

Our usual terms of payment are by D/P at sight and we hope that they will be acceptable to you.

Please send us your confirmation of sales in duplicate and see to it that the goods are strictly in accordance with the samples.

Yours sincerely,
David Spear
Manager
Messrs. Hawker Wood Trading Co., Ltd.

Please write a letter to accept this order.

Exercise 7-3

Supplementary task.

Click http://www.proceq.com/en/servicesfeedback/place-an-order.html?pqr=7. Please read the information on the page of Proceq. Make sure that you understand all the details in placing an order with Proceq.

9. Supplementary Readings

How to Place an Order

So you've done your research, compared products and pricing, and are finally ready to buy the brushes you need. Adding items to your shopping cart and checking out becomes much easier when you've created an account with your business or personal name, address, shipping and payment preferences. You are still able to order without taking that step though. Your information is transferred to our internal database, and order information is retained indefinitely. This is reassuring for many as sometimes many years go by before you need to purchase that "brush that lasts and lasts".

You need to be sure you are ordering the exact item you intend. Double check the part numbers and descriptions to ensure you are getting what you want. If at any time you are unsure, don't hesitate to call us and we will be more than happy to guide you through the process. We are just as available to take your order over the phone if you feel.

Some of our items are set up as "grouped"—a collection of similar brushes, like twisted in wire brushes, or a brush that simply has a variety of colors. This type of item you will see listed with a "starting at price". You need to click through to the listing of all brushes in that grouping to select whatever size, color, or type you need.

There are many new features brush.com site allowing you to compare products, forward the item to an email contact or save to your wish list. Another new addition to brush.com is that we encourage your reviews. You can also add a tag to items that you might feel is best recognized by a different name. This helps other people just like you find what they want much faster. We recognize this may be a popular feature, as most brushes have a variety of names and uses.

When you are ready, enter your desired quantity of one or more in the appropriate box, and then click "add to cart". You will be able to change your quantities when viewing the basket. From the basket, you can continue to shop, choose to save your cart for a future visit, or checkout.

Every customer may check out through PayPal express, or as a member. As a member, you can add more than one shipping address to the account to select from. Please remember to fill out all necessary information including your phone number and full name.

All orders ship via UPS. If you wish to ship using your shipper number, please enter it on checkout. If you are a tax exempt business from NY or CA, please provide your tax ID number in a notes field, and tax will be refunded. Because we cannot guarantee all items will be in stock at time of order, we cannot offer expedited shipping online. If you need the item fast, please call us.

To change your shipping and billing address once you are in the checkout process, you must go to "My Account" to edit. Thank you again for choosing Braun for your brush needs!

Chapter 8
Payment
支付

1. Learning Objectives

By the end of this chapter, you will be able to do the following:
· Understand the commonly-used terms of payment.
· Know how to write letters to negotiate on specific payment terms.
· Know how to write letters to urge the establishment, amendment or extension of L/C.
· Use the proper words and expressions and sentence patterns in writing.

2. Case Study

Mr. Brown is the manager of the import department, West DT Inc. in Hamburg. The branch handles large volumes of international trade finance business. At the beginning of February, Mr. Brown received the following letter from one client.

Dear Sir,

We received your letter of October 7, 2014 and learn that you proposed the payment by D/A.

We regret that we are unable to consider your request for payment on D/A basis. As a rule, we ask for payment by L/C. However, in view of our long-term business relations, we will, as an exceptional case, accept payment for your order by D/P at sight. We trust this will greatly facilitate your efforts in sales.

We hope the above payment terms will be acceptable to you and expect to receive your order on good time.

We look forward to your early reply.

Yours faithfully,
[Signature]

Suppose you were Mr. Brown. Please make a reply to accept the payment by D/P.

3. Introduction

Payment refers to the transfer of money from one party to another, in exchange for the provision of certain goods or services, or to fulfill a legal obligation. It is an indispensable step in the course of international trade. Both the importer and the exporter should make careful decision on the payment terms, trying to persuade the other side accept the terms which are advantageous to his own side.

Payment terms in international trade are much more complicated than that in domestic trade. Generally speaking, there are three basic terms of payment: remittance, collection and L/C.

Remittance

Remittance happens when an importer asks his bank to send a sum of money to an exporter abroad by one of the transfer methods at his option. The exporter then can be paid at the designated bank, which is either the remitting bank's overseas branch or its correspondent. There are three transfer methods, namely, by Mail Transfer (M/T), by Telegraphic Transfer (T/T) and by Demand Draft (D/D). In international trade, remittance is the simplest way to transfer funds.

Collection

Collection is an arrangement whereby the goods are shipped and a relevant draft is drawn by the exporter on the importer, and / or shipping documents are forwarded to the exporter's bank with clear instructions for collection through one of its correspondent bank located in the domicile of the importer. Basically, there are two kinds of collection: Documents against Payment (D/P) and Documents against Acceptance (D/A). D/P requires immediate payment by the importer to get hold of the documents, while D/A calls for delivery of documents against acceptance of the draft drawn by the exporter. The importer is then given a certain period to make payment.

L/C

Letter of Credit is a written undertaking by a bank given to the exporter at the request, and in accordance with the instructions of the importer to effect payment up to a stated sum of money, within a prescribed time limit and against stipulated documents. L/C is the most important and commonly-used payment term in international trade. As an usual practice, the L/C is to be established and to reach the seller at least one month prior to the date of shipment so as to leave enough time for the seller to make preparations for shipment.

Inquiries about terms of payment and replies are routine work. Most traders know the methods of payment available for settling international trade transactions. However, one should keep in mind that the receipt of payment is often dependent on the commercial, economic and political risks evident in a country and should dictate the payment term chosen for the trade. It is also necessary to know the merits and shortages of each payment term.

4. Specimen Letters

Asking for More Favorable Terms
Specimen 1

Dear Sir,

We are pleased that the business between us have proved to be very smooth and successful. Our past purchase of Green Tea from you has been paid as a rule by confirmed, irrevocable Letter of Credit.

On this basis, it has indeed cost us a great deal. From the moment we open the credit till the time our buyers pay us, our funds are tied up for about four months. Under the present circumstances, this question is particularly taxing due to the tight money condition and the unprecedented high bank interest. If you would kindly grant easier payment terms, we are sure that such an accommodation would be conductive to encouraging more business. We then propose payment for this time by D/A 30 days.

It will be highly appreciated if you can kindly give priority to the consideration of the above request and give us an early favorable reply.

Yours faithfully,
[Signature]

Specimen 2

Dear Sir,

We have examined the specifications and price list for your range of colored candles, and now wish to place an order with you. We enclose our Order No.569 for 2000 dozens of candles.

As we are in urgent need of candles for the coming holiday season, we would be grateful if you would make up the order and ship it as soon as possible.

We would now like to propose T/T for this order. When the goods are ready for shipment and the freight space booked, could you fax us and we will then remit the full amount by telegraphic transfer.

We are asking for this concession so that we can give our customers a specific delivery date and also save the expense of opening a letter of credit. As we believe that this arrangement should make little difference to you and help with our sales, we trust that you will agree to our request.

We look forward to receiving confirmation of our order and your agreement to the arrangement for payment.

Yours faithfully,
[Signature]

Replies
Specimen 3

Dear Sir,

Thank you for your letter of 4th April, which arrived this morning.

We are pleased that you have been able to ship our order in good time but we are surprised that you still demand D/P. After long years of satisfactory trading we feel that we are entitled to easier terms. Most of our suppliers are drawing on us at D/A 60 days after sight and we should be grateful if you could grant us the same terms.

We are looking forward to your favorable reply.

Yours faithfully,
[Signature]

Specimen 4

Dear Sir,

We have received your letter of December 20th and noted with interest your intention of pushing the sale of our automobiles in your country.

Although we are much appreciative of your efforts to help sell our automobiles, we regretbeing unable to consider your request for payment by D/A 60 days after sight. Our usual practice is to ask for sight L/C.

However, in order to facilitate developing the sale of automobiles in your market, we are prepared to accept payment by D/P at sight as a special accommodation.

We hope that the above payment terms will be acceptable to you and look forward to the pleasure of hearing from you soon.

Yours faithfully,
[Signature]

Urging Establishment of L/C
Specimen 5

Dear Sir,

With reference to the 4000 dozen Shirts under our Sales Confirmation No.AD275, we wish to draw your attention to the fact that the date of delivery is approaching. But up to the present, we have not received the covering L/C. Please do your utmost to expedite its establishment so that we may execute the order within the prescribed time.

In order to avoid subsequent amendments, please see to it that the L/C stipulations are in exact accordance with the terms of the contract.

We look forward to receiving your favorable response at an early date.

Yours faithfully,
[Signature]

L/C Amendment
Specimen 6

> Dear Sir,
>
> We have today received L/C No. 2398 covering Order No. 6125.
> After careful examination, we have found some discrepancies. Please make the following amendments without delay.
> 1. Increase the amount of your L/C by $ 5000.
> 2. Partial shipment and transshipment are allowed and delete the clause "by direct steamer".
> 3. Amend the quantity to read: 15,000 M/T (5% more or less at seller's option).
> Please see to it that your amendments reach us by October 30th; otherwise shipment will be further delayed.
>
> Yours faithfully,
> [Signature]

L/C Extension
Specimen 7

> Dear Sir,
>
> We confirm our fax of yesterday, reading as follows:
> L/C NSW6180 TIN PLATE ARRIVED ONLY TODAY JULY SHIPMENT IMPOSSIBLE EXTEND SHIPMENT VALIDITY 31/8 15/9 RESPECTIVELY
> We trust that you have received the above fax and are doing what is necessary.
> As stipulated in S/C 89STX-5491, shipment could be made in July provided your L/C reached us not later than 15th. However, we received your L/C only yesterday and it is absolutely impossible for us to ship the goods in July.
> In the circumstances, we regret to have to ask you to extend the above L/C to August 31st and September 15th for shipment and negotiation respectively, with the amendment to reach us by the 15th of July; otherwise shipment will be further postponed.
> We look forward to receiving the relevant amendment at an early date and thank you in advance.
>
> Yours faithfully,
> [Signature]

5. Writing Templates

Asking for more Favorable Terms

> Dear Sir,
>
> We are pleased that the business between us have proved to be very smooth and successful. Our past purchase of _____ from you has been paid as a rule by _____.

On this basis, it has indeed cost us a great deal. From the moment _____ till the time _____, our funds are tied up for about _____. Under the present circumstances, this question is particularly taxing due to the tight money condition and the unprecedented high bank interest.

If you would kindly grant easier payment terms, we are sure that such an accommodation would be conductive to encouraging more business. We then propose payment for this time by _____.

It will be highly appreciated if you can kindly give priority to the consideration of the above request and give us an early favorable reply.

Yours faithfully,
[Signature]

Replies

Dear Sir,

Thank you for your letter of _____, which arrived _____.

We are pleased that you have been able to ship our order in good time but we are surprised that you still demand _____. After long years of satisfactory trading we feel that we are entitled to easier terms. Most of our suppliers are drawing on us _____ and we should be grateful if you could grant us the same terms.

We are looking forward to your favorable reply.

Yours faithfully,
[Signature]

Urging Establishment of L/C

Dear Sir,

With reference to _____ under our Sales Confirmation No._____, we wish to draw your attention to the fact that the date of delivery is approaching. But up to the present, we have not received the covering L/C. Please do your utmost to expedite its establishment so that we may execute the order within the prescribed time.

In order to avoid subsequent amendments, please see to it that the L/C stipulations are in exact accordance with the terms of the contract.

We look forward to receiving your favorable response at an early date.

Yours faithfully,
[Signature]

L/C Amendment

Dear Sir,

We have today received L/C No._____ covering Order No._____.

After careful examination, we have found some discrepancies. Please make the following amendments without delay.

    1._____.

    2._____.

    3._____.

Please see to it that your amendments reach us by_____; otherwise shipment will be further delayed.

Yours faithfully,

[Signature]

L/C Extension

Dear Sir,

    We confirm our fax of yesterday, reading as follows:

_____

We trust that you have received the above fax and are doing what is necessary.

    As stipulated in S/C _____, shipment could be made in _____ provided your L/C reached us not later than _____. However, we received your L/C only yesterday and it is absolutely impossible for us to ship the goods in _____.

    In the circumstances, we regret to have to ask you to extend the above L/C to _____ and _____ for shipment and negotiation respectively, with the amendment to reach us by the _____; otherwise shipment will be further postponed.

    We look forward to receiving the relevant amendment at an early date and thank you in advance.

Yours faithfully,

[Signature]

6. Key Words and Expressions

(1) remittance 汇付

(2) M/T: mail transfer 信汇

(3) T/T: telegraphic transfer 电汇

(4) D/D: demand draft 票汇

(5) collection 托收

(6) D/P: documents against payment 付款交单

(7) D/A: documents against acceptance 承兑交单

(8) L/C: letter of credit 信用证

(9) on...basis 以……为基础（方式，条件）

(10) tie up 占用资金，挤兑资金

(11) L/C amendment 信用证修改

(12) L/C extension 信用证展期

7. Useful Sentence Patterns

(1) ...will only be accepted if the amount is below/above...　只有金额低于/超过······时我们才接受······的支付方式。

(2) Our rules only allow us to accept ... We must adhere to our customary practice.　我们一向只接受······的支付方式。我们必须遵照惯例。

(3) We suggest/suppose/propose that ... be adopted as the terms of payment.　我们建议/提议/计划采用······的支付方式。

(4) Please increase/reduce the amount from ... to ...　请增加/减少总金额······至······

(5) We are faxing you today asking for a ... extension of the L/C.　今天我们传真至贵方，要求对信用证进行为期······的展期。

(6) Our past purchase of Giant Bicycles from you has been paid as a rule by confirmed, irrevocable Letter of Credit.　我方以往一直采用保兑的、不可撤销的信用证支付从贵处购买捷安特自行车。

(7) This question is particularly taxing due to the tight money condition and the unprecedented high bank interest.　由于资金紧张和银行的高额利息，此种付款方式负担过重。

(8) We are asking for this concession so that we can give our customers a specific delivery date and also save the expense of opening a Letter of Credit.　我方请求你方行此方便，旨在使我方客户能确定到货日期，并能省去开立信用证的很多费用。

(9) Our usual mode of payment is by confirmed, irrevocable Letter of Credit, available by draft at sight for the full amount of the invoice value to be established in our favor through a bank acceptable to us.　我们的付款方式，一般是以保兑的，不可撤销的，以我公司为收益人的，按发票金额见票即付的信用证支付，该信用证应通过我们认可的银行开出。

(10) In view of the long business relations between us, we will, as an exception, accept payment terms by D/P at 30 days sight for your present trial order and hope you will accept our terms.　鉴于你我间的长期友好关系，对你方这批试购的货物，我们愿意例外地接受30天付款交单的方式付款，希望你们能接受。

(11) In order to pave the way for your pushing the sale of our products in your market, we will accept the payment by D/P at sight as a special accommodation.　为了你方在你市场推销我方产品铺平道路，我方将接受即期付款交单方式付款，以示特别照顾。

(12) The 800 bicycles under Contract 268 have been ready for shipment for quite some time, but we have not yet received your covering L/C to date. Please open the L/C as soon as possible so that we may effect shipment.　第268号合约项下的800辆自行车备妥待运已久，但至今我们尚未收到你们的有关信用证。请速开来，以便装运。

(13) We thank you for your L/C No.789, but on checking its clauses we find with regret that your L/C calls for shipment in October, 2014, whereas our contract stipulate for November shipment. Therefore, it is imperative for your to extend the shipment date

to November 30, and negotiation date to December 15, 2014 respectively. Please act promptly and let us have your cable reply the soonest possible.   收到你方789号信用证，谢谢。经核对条款，我们遗憾地发现你方信用证要求2014年10月装运，但我方合约规定11月份装运。因此，务请把装运期和议付期分别展至2014年11月30日和12月15日。请即办理展证事宜，并尽早电复。

8. Exercises

Exercise 8-1

Direction: Put the following sentences into English.

(1) 我们相信该付款方式对你方不会增添太多麻烦，但却能促进我方销售，希望你方能同意我方的请求。

(2) 很抱歉，我们不能同意"货到目的地付款交单"方式付款。

(3) 我方建议这次用付款交单或承兑交单方式来付款。

(4) 我们不认为你们会有任何困难开立以我方为受益人的保兑的不可撤销信用证来支付你方目前的这张订单，这样，我们可预期在一个确定的日期收到货款。

(5) 我们抱歉不得不谢绝你方要求D/P条款。对这些传统货物，我们一般的贸易支付方法是用信用证付款。

(6) 因为这是一张很大的订单，机器要按你方规格制造，我们只能在即期信用证的基础上接受你方订单。

(7) 非常抱歉,我们不能同意在装运货物前付款。

(8) 对这次交易,我们例外同意用信用证方式付款,但对以后的交易,我们要求更有利的付款条件,也就是付款交单。

(9) 如果能优先考虑上述要求，尽早给予令人满意的答复，我方将不胜感激。

(10) 我们要求以保兑的不可撤销的信用证为付款方式。

Exercise 8-2

Direction: Write a letter based on the following information.

You are the manager of Samdo Co. Ltd in London. Your company is in market for 200 Haier refrigerators. After communicate with Haier Group, you decide to negotiate with them on payment issues. Please write a letter to suggest payment by D/A 30 days.

Exercise 8-3

Supplementary task.

Click www.answers.com. Try to ask any questions about payment terms and take a good look at the answers.

9. Supplementary Readings

The Letter of Credit

In international trade it is almost impossible to match payment with physical delivery of the goods which constitutes conflicting problems to trade, since the exporter prefers to get paid before releasing the goods and the importer prefers to gain control over the goods before paying the money. The Letter of Credit is an effective means to solve these problems. It objective is to facilitate international payment by means of the creditworthiness of the bank. This method of payment offers security to both the seller and the buyer. The former has the security to get paid provided he presents impeccable documents while the latter has security to get: the goods required through the documents he stipulates in the credit. This bilateral security is the unique and characteristic feature of the Letter of Credit.

Letter of Credit is often shortened as L/C, and is sometimes referred to as "banker's commercial letter of credit", "banker's credit", "commercial credit" or simply "credit". Modern credits were introduced in the second half of the 19th century and had substantial development after the First World War. The credit is a letter issued by a bank at the request of the importer in which the bank promises to pay upon presentation of the relevant documents. It is actually a conditional bank undertaking of payment.

The operation of the Letter of Credit starts with the importer. He instructs his bank to issue an L/C in favor of the seller for the amount of the purchase. Here the importer is called the applicant, or opener, principal etc. ; the bank that issues the credit is called the opening bank, the issuing bank or the establishing bank, and the exporter in whose favor the credit is opened is called the beneficiary. The opening bank sends the credit to its correspondent bank in the exporter's country, who will, after examining the credit, advise the exporter of its receipt. Here the correspondent bank is called the advising bank. The exporter or beneficiary will make a careful examination of all the contents of the credit and will request the opener to make amendments to any discrepancies in the credit so as to ensure safe and timely payment. Sometimes the exporter may require a confirmed Letter of Credit either because the credit amount is too large, or because he does not fully trust the opening bank. The bank that adds its confirmation to the credit is called the confirming bank which is undertaken either by the advising bank or another prime bank. When everything with the credit is in order, the exporter will prepare the relevant documents based on the credit and dispatch the goods to the importer. Then he will present the draft and the accompanying documents to the advising bank that pays or accepts or negotiates the bill of exchange. The advising bank then also becomes the paying bank which acts as the agent of the opening bank. and gets reimbursed by the opening bank after paying the beneficiary. If a bank either nominated by the opening bank or at its own choice, buys the exporter's draft submitted to it under a credit, it is called a negotiating bank. The draft and the documents will then be sent to the opening bank for reimbursement.

Letters of Credit are varied in form, length, language, and stipulations. Generally speaking, however, they include the following contents: (1) The number of the credit and the place and time of its establishment. (2) The type of the credit. (3) The contract on which it is based. (4) The major parties relevant to the credit, such as the applicant, opening bank, beneficiary, advising bank. etc. (5) The amount or value of the credit. (6) The place and date on which the credit expires. (7) The description of the goods including name of commodity, quantity, specifications, packing, unit price, price terms, etc. (8) Transportation clause including the port of shipment, the port of destination, the time of shipment, whether allowing partial shipments or transshipment. (9) Stipulations relating to the draft. (10) Stipulations concerning the shipping documents required. (11) Certain special clauses if any, e. g. restrictions on the carrying vessel and the route. (12) Instructions to the negotiating bank. (13) The seal or signature of the opening bank. (14) Whether the credit follows the uniform customs and practice for documentary credits.

The letter of Credit provides security to both the exporter and the importer. However, it only assures payment to the beneficiary provided the terms and conditions of the credit are fulfilled. It does not guarantee that the goods purchased will be those invoiced or shipped. It is stipulated in Article 4 of the uniform customs and practice for documentary credit that "in credit operations all parties concerned deal in documents, and not in goods, service and/or other performance to which the documents may relate". That is to say the banks are only concerned with the documents representing the goods instead of the underlying contracts. They have no legal obligation whether the goods comply with the contract. They will be considered as having fulfilled their responsibility so long as all the documents comply with the stipulations of the credit. The quality and quantity of merchandise shipped, although specified in the documents, ultimately depend on the seller who has manufactured, packed, and arranged shipment for the goods. If the importer finds any problems with the goods, e. g. inferior quality or insufficient quantity, he has to contact or even take legal action against the exporter instead of the bank so long as the documents are "proper" on their face.

Chapter 9
Packing
包装

1. Learning Objectives

By the end of this chapter, you will be able to do the following:

· Get familiar with three package types and different marks.

· Know how to make packing instructions.

· Know how to write letters on packing issues.

· Use the proper words and expressions and sentence patterns in writing.

2. Case Study

> Lily is the general manager of James Importing Inc. in Canada. The company is trading with Shercon (Hangzhou) Rubber Co., Ltd. One morning, Lily makes the following shipment instructions to Shercon:
>
> Dear Sir,
>
> We are glad to learn from your letter of April 25th that you have confirmed our order for 1000 bags of Model Hup5-4 Ultrabake Hollow Masking Rubber Plugs. We believe in the quality of your products.
>
> As the products are susceptible to heat and moisture, they must be packed in seaworthy cases. They should also be protected from water dampness in transit by a coating of grease that will keep out dampness.
>
> We trust that the above instructions are clear to you and that shipment will give the users entire satisfaction.
>
> Yours faithfully,
> [Signature]

Suppose you are the manager in Shercon. Make a reply to the above email, trying to reassure Lily.

3. Introduction

Packing in foreign trade is of particular and crucial importance due to the long distance in which the unpredictable risks that may occur. It is reasonable to assume that packing is to goods as what clothing to man. Except from bulk cargo and nude cargo, most goods need to be packed in a proper way. The real art of packing is to get the contents into a nice, compact shape that will stay that way during the roughest journey.

Needless to say, every buyer expects that his goods will reach him in perfect condition. Nothing is more exasperating to a buyer than to find his goods damaged or part missing on arrival. It has been estimated that as much as 70% of all cargo loss could be prevented by proper packaging. Therefore, the seller must pack the goods according to the buyer's instructions. Apart from this reason, attention should be drawn to the fact that requirements for packing vary according to the differences in the nature and features of the commodities.

Generally speaking, there are three packing types in international trade in terms of their functions: outer packing, inner packing, and neutral packing.

Outer Packing

Outer packing is also known as transport packing. The main purposes of outer packing include: (1) to protect goods from damaging or stealing; (2) to facilitate loading, unloading and transporting; (3) to create convenience for storage and check. Bags, barrels, drums, boxes, cases, cartons, crates and carboys are some of the most often used types of outer packing in international trade.

Outer packing needs to be marked. The marks may be a combination of simple shapes, letters, numbers and words. Conventionally, outer marks mainly include shipping marks, directive marks and warning marks.

Inner Packing

Inner packing or sales packing, on the other hand, aids marketing, consumer advertising, display, presentation, protection, handling and self-service retailing. Skin packing, blister packing and shrink wrapping are the commonly-used packing in international trade. Each has its own functions.

Neutral Packing

Neutral packing refers to the packing that makes no mention at all of the name and the country of the exporter on the commodity and on the outer and inner packages. The purpose of neutral packing is to break the tariff and non-tariff barriers in some importing countries and regions and to satisfy the special need of transaction. It is used as one means of exporters to expand trade and strengthen competitiveness.

An importer shall make the exporter understand his requirements for packing so as to avoid the subsequent disputes. A good way is to send a letter of packing instructions in which the importer lists all the detailed packing information. The exporter will then make a reply to ensure that the packing conditions will satisfy the importer.

4. Specimen Letters

Giving Packing Instructions
Specimen 1

Dear Sir,

We thank you for your letter dated May 20th, enclosing the sales confirmation in duplicate but wish to state that the packing clause in the contract is not clear enough. Now we are making our packing instructions:

1. Seaworthy export packing, suitable for long distance ocean transportation.
2. The furniture under the contract should be packed in wooden case. One set to a case, and each case is lined with foam plastics in order to protect the goods against press.
3. On the outer packing please mark our initials: MT in a triangle, under which the port of destination and our order number should be stenciled.
4. Directive marks like KEEP DRY AWAY FROM PRESSURE, etc. should also be indicated.

We have made a footnote on the contract to that effect and are returning herein one copy of the contract, duly countersigned by us. We hope you will find it in order and pay special attention to the packing.

We look forward to receiving your shipping advice and thank you in advance.

Yours faithfully,
[Signature]

Specimen 2

Dear Sir,

In reply to your fax of May 25th, 2014, we regret having forgotten to mention the inner packing requirements of Taste Brand Brown Sugar we ordered at the Canton Spring Fair this year.

Now we have discussed the matter with our customers. They request as follows: As brown sugar is moisture absorbent especially in hot rainy seasons, it should be packed in kraft paper bags containing 30 small paper bags of 1 kg net each, two kraft paper bags to a carton lined with water-proof paper.

We hope the above requirements will be acceptable to you and look forward to your early confirmation.

Yours faithfully,
[Signature]

Specimen 3

Dear Sir,

We are now writing to you in regard to the packing of the cargo of chinaware, which we feel necessary to clarify for our future dealings.

As chinaware is fragile, we would like hard foamed plastic padding for each and wooden cases outside. In addition, please remember to stencil warning markings such as "FRAGILE", "HANDLE WITH CARE"on the wooden cases. We hope you pay special attention to the packing.

Please let us know whether these requirements could be met.

Yours faithfully,
[Signature]

Negotiation on Packing
Specimen 4

Dear Sir,

We are pleased to inform you that for your future orders we shall pack our garments in carton instead of in wooden cases, as packing in cartons has the following advantages:

1. It will prevent skillful pilferage, for the traces of pilferage will more in evidence.
2. It is fairly fit for ocean transportation.
3. Our cartons are well protected against moisture by plastic lining.
4. Cartons are comparatively light and compact, so they are more convenient to handle.

Our comments above come from a comparative study of the characteristics of the two modes of packing, i.e. carton packing and wooden case packing, as well as the results of shipments already made.

We hope you will accept our carton packing and assure you of our sincere cooperation.

With best regards.

Yours faithfully,
[Signature]

Specimen 5

Dear Sir,

We thank you for your order of October 15th, 2014 and have pleasure in informing you that we can accept all the terms but the packing.

We would like to recommend you our latest package, which is economical and strong. The packing mentioned in your order was of the old method we adopted several years ago. From then on we have improved it with the result that our recent goods have all turned out to the complete satisfaction of our clients.

Our Men's Shirts are now packed in a poly bag and then in a cardboard box, 5 dozen to a carton, with a gross weight about 10 kgs.

We are looking forward to your prompt reply and wondering if our proposal meets your requirement.

Yours faithfully,
[Signature]

Specimen 6

Dear Sir,

    We have received your letter of Feb 23rd with pleasure. Totally speaking, your suggestion about packing is pretty good. But we believe wooden case is not necessary because it is too heavy.

    We maintain that waterproof carton is a better choice because cartons are comparatively light and compact. So you can use cartons instead. Each carton contains 10 bags.

    We hope you will accept our opinion and appreciate your cooperation.

Yours faithfully,
[Signature]

Accepting the Packing Details
Specimen 7

Dear Sir,

    In conformity with the packing instructions made in your letter of October 17th, we find your proposal quite reasonable and acceptable. We are glad to inform you that your goods are packed in wooden cases and with stated shipping marks. Since we have been packing pillowcases for so many years, any damage due to the packing has never occurred on the way of transportation. In addition, we would hope the result of packing in wooden cases turns out to your satisfaction.

    We assure you of our effort to pack according to your instructions. We can meet your special requirements for packing. We sincerely hope that you will rest assured on the packing.

Yours faithfully,
[Signature]

5. Writing Templates

Giving Packing Instructions

Dear Sir,

    We thank you for your letter dated _____, enclosing the sales confirmation in duplicate but wish to state that the packing clause in the contract is not clear enough. Now we are making our packing instructions:

        1. _____.
        2. _____.
        3. _____.
        4. _____.

    We have made a footnote on the contract to that effect and are returning herein one copy of the contract, duly countersigned by us. We hope you will find it in order and pay special attention to the packing.

We look forward to receiving your shipping advice and thank you in advance.

Yours faithfully,
[Signature]

Negotiation on Packing

Dear Sir,

We are pleased to inform you that for your future orders we shall pack our _____ in _____ instead of in _____, as packing in _____ has the following advantages:
1. _____.
2. _____.
3. _____.
4. _____.
Our comments above come from a comparative study of the characteristics of the two modes of packing, i.e. _____ and _____, as well as the results of shipments already made.
We hope you will accept our _____ packing and assure you of our sincere cooperation.
With best regards.

Yours faithfully,
[Signature]

Accepting the Packing Details

Dear Sir,

In conformity with the packing instructions made in your letter of _____, we find your proposal quite reasonable and acceptable. We are glad to inform you that your goods are packed in _____ and with stated shipping marks. Since we have been packing _____ for so many years, any damage due to the packing has never occurred on the way of transportation. In addition, we would hope the result of packing in _____ turns out to your satisfaction.
We assure you of our effort to pack according to your instructions. We can meet your special requirements for packing. We sincerely hope that you will rest assured on the packing.

Yours faithfully,
[Signature]

6. Key Words and Expressions

(1) packing   包装

(2) outer packing   外包装

(3) inner packing   内包装

(4) packing instructions   包装要求

(5) container   集装箱

(6) carton　纸板箱，纸箱

(7) wooden case　木箱

(8) seaworthy（尤指船舶）适航的

(9) kraft paper bag　牛皮纸袋

(10) fragile　易碎的

(11) pilferage　盗窃,偷窃

(12) plastic lining　塑料衬里

7. Useful Sentence Patterns

(1) ... pieces to a box, ... boxes to a case, totally ... cases only.　每……件装一盒子，每……盒子装一箱，共……只箱子。

(2) We need a better design for this batch of ..., because attractive designs will be good for sales promotion.　对于这批……，我们需要更好的设计。因为具有吸引力的设计将更好地促进销售。

(3) In reply to your email of ... inquiring about the packing of our ... we wish to answer as follows.　对贵方××月××日来函提出的……的包装要求，现回复如下。

(4) The goods under Order No ... shall be packed in seaworthy...　订单号……项下的货物需要用适合航运的……包装。

(5) Any damage resulted from rough handling must be compensated by ...　任何由于粗暴装卸导致的损失将由……进行赔偿。

(6) Thank you very much for informing us that the goods are packed in cartons as usual practice.　感谢通知我们该订单项下商品按惯例用纸板箱包装。

(7) We hope our packing will serve your purpose and look forward to your early reply.　我们希望我们的包装将满足你们的要求，同时希望尽早回复。

(8) Our cartons are well protected against moisture by plastic lining.　纸板箱垫有一层塑料能防潮。

(9) The goods are to be packed in strong seaworthy wooden cases.　货物须用适用于海运的坚固的木箱包装。

(10) Each to be wrapped with paper, then to a plastic bags, every dozen to a new strong wooden case, suitable for long sea voyage and well protected against dampness, moisture, shock, rust and rough handling.　每只用纸包，并套上塑料袋，每一打装一坚固的新木箱，适合长途海运，防湿、防潮、防震、防锈，耐粗暴装运。

(11) Please take necessary precautions that the packing can protect the goods from dampness or rain, since cement is liable to be spoiled by damp or water in transit.　由于水泥在途中非常易于受潮或遭雨淋而变质，因此务必采取必要的防护措施使得包装能够防潮和免遭雨水侵蚀。

(12) The insurance company requires that this class of merchandise should be packed in extra strong boxes.   保险公司要求这类商品用特别坚固的箱子包装。

(13) We can meet your requirements to have the goods packed in wooden cases but you have to bear the extra packing charge.   我们能满足你方将货物装木箱的要求，但是你方必须承担额外的包装费用。

8. Exercises

Exercise 9-1

Direction: Put the following sentences into English.

(1) 我方棉布须用木箱包装，内衬牛皮纸和防潮纸。

(2) 鸡蛋要用内衬防震纸板的纸箱包装。

(3) 每件衬衫装一个塑料袋，6袋装一盒。

(4) 货物应采用一种能保证安全完好到达目的地和便于在转运中搬运的方式进行包装。

(5) 出口货物的包装必须足够牢固，以经受途中最野蛮的搬运。

(6) 服装装在衬有塑料袋的纸箱里比装在木箱里更不易受到潮损。

(7) 在外包装上，请刷上一菱形，内刷我公司首字母SCC。

(8) 每个包装上应标上"易碎"字样。

(9) 我方罐头食品纸箱包装不仅可适合海运，而且很结实，能防止货物受损。

(10) 折叠椅两把装入一个纸板箱。

Exercise 9-2

Direction: Write a letter based on the following information.

You have finished negotiation with your partner on the main terms and conditions and would discuss the packing instructions. The following information is given about the goods and packing. Please try to write a letter to clarify the packing instructions.

Name of the commodity: Dolphin Beach Towel D149 (picture is shown below)

Specifications: A cotton towel featuring Bottlenose Dolphins. 30 "wide×60" high

Price: $15.99

Packing: The towel was packed in a zip-lock style reusable clear plastic package, with a cardboard insert covering the front and back of the package. The towel was neatly folded inside, and the color of the towel was clearly visible.

Shipping marks: gross weight, net weight and tare weight will be included in a diamond and "Made in China" is to be stenciled as well.

Notes:

Mark the outside of each shipping carton with S/C Number (s).

Mark the total number of cartons shipped on the outside of cartons (example: 1 of 6, 2 of 6, etc.).

9. Supplementary Readings

Packing

Packing is of great importance in foreign trade. The ultimate purpose of packing is to keep the transported goods in prefect condition with nothing missing on arrival. Good packing must be able to stand the roughest transportation. Packing can be divided into transport packing (usually known as outer packing) and sales packing (usually known as inner packing). Transport packing is done mainly to keep the goods safe and sound during transportation. It must not only be soiled enough to prevent the packed goods from any damage, but also pilferage-proof, easy to store, convenient to load and unload. Sales packing is done mainly to push sales. It is now universally recognized as a decisive aid in selling household consumer goods. It can be realized in various forms and with different materials as long as it is nice to look at, easy to handle and helpful to the sales. Still, there is another category of packing, called "neutral packing". This kind of packing carries no mark of the name of the origin country of the packed goods and no sign of the original trademark, with the view to elude the tariff of the import country or satisfy the buyer's special requirements.

Packing must be strikingly marked. Conventionally, outer packing marks mainly include transport marks, directive marks and warning marks. Transport marks consist of:

(1) consignor's or consignee's code name.

(2) number of the contract or the L/C.

(3) the port of destination.

(4) numbers of the packed goods.

And sometimes weight and dimensions, all of which can greatly facilitate identification and transportation,

Directive marks are eye-catching figures and concise instructions concerning manners of proper handling, storing, loading and unloading of the packed goods,

e.g. (See Figure 9.1)

USE NO HOOKS

THIS SIDE UP

HANDLE WITH CARE

KEEP DRY

DO NOT DROP

Figure 9.1 Mark of "Keep Dry"

Warning marks are obvious symbols or words to warn people against the hidden danger of inflammable, explosives and poisonous products,

e.g. (See Figure 9.2)

DANGEROUS GOODS

KEEP AWAY FROM HEAT

Figure 9.2 Mark of "Dangerous Goods"

ACID—WITH CARE

INFLAMMABLE

EXPLOSIVE

Requirements for inner packing are increasingly high, with beautiful color, creative design and convenient handling as its chief concern. The primary motive for inner packing is to promote the sales of the particular goods.

Letters about packing issues should be concise and clear. In such letters, the seller can describe in detail to the buyer his customary packing of the goods concerned and also indicate clearly that he may accept any required packing at the expense of the buyer. The buyer can inform the seller of any formerly unexpected requirements or fears about the packing. Any changes regarding packing stipulated in the contract should be mutually discussed and determined before shipment.

Chapter 10
Shipment
装运

1. Learning Objectives

By the end of this chapter, you will be able to do the following:

· Learn essential components of major shipment terms.
· Understand the basic structure of a letter of shipment.
· Learn to use proper words, phrases and sentence patterns in writing effective shipment letters.
· Learn to reply to shipment letters.

2. Case Study

> Omni Garment and Textile Trading Company is eager for the shipment of its order for 800 dozens of men's shirts. According to the terms of Contract 201402COT790, the shipment is to be effected by February 15th, 2015, and the significance of punctual execution of this order has been explicitly stated, however, up to now no information concerning this lot is received. As the goods are in bad need and the selling season is drawing near. What can be done now?

Suppose you were a foreign trade clerk in charge of this case, please write a letter to urge the supplier for immediate shipment.

3. Introduction

Shipment is an important part of international trade as goods have to be transported from where they are manufactured to where consumers can buy and the transportation of the goods is to be made possible by different means of transport. Carriage of goods can take place by sea, rail, air, road, inland waterway, parcel post, container and multimodal transport. Among the diverse means of transportation available, ocean freight is the most widely applied means of transportation which enjoys the advantage of easy passage, large capacity and low cost. However, compared with road or air transport, ocean transport is not without problems, being slow, vulnerable to bad weather and less punctual.

When negotiating a transaction, the buyer and the seller should come to an agreement on major terms of shipment such as time of shipment, port of shipment and port of destination, partial shipment and transshipment and state them clearly in the sales contract. Without contract statement, contract performance cannot be ensured.

There are three parties involved in most delivery of goods: the consignor who sends the goods; the carrier who carries them and the consignee who receives them at the destination. Under the term of FOB, CFR and CIF, the seller must load the goods onto the particular vessel at the named port of shipment and ship them to the port of destination. In the meantime, the seller has to submit relevant shipping documents such as commercial invoices, certificate of origin, packing lists and bills of lading.

Shipment covers rather a wide range of work. Before the goods are to be dispatched, the following must be duly seen to:

(1) send the shipping instructions by the buyer.

(2) select a shipping line and a particular vessel.

(3) book shipping space or chartering and sign the contract of carriage.

(4) register the cargo on shipping note and send the shipping note to a shipping company.

(5) register details on customs, entry forms and send them to customs.

(6) arrange adequate packing, including shipping marks.

(7) receive the bill of lading from the shipping company.

(8) pay the freight bill.

(9) arrange the shipment.

(10) send the shipping documents and shipping advice.

4. Specimen Letters

Shipment Instruction

Shipping instruction is a kind of document offered by the buyer to the seller before the shipment for the requirement and instruction of the goods about its mode of packing, the stencil of the shipping marks and mode of transportation and so on.

Specimen 1

Dear Sir,

Re: Your Contract No E215 covering 1,000 Dozen Shirts

We hereby acknowledge the receipt of your letter dated April 20th in connection with the above subject.

In reply, we have the pleasure of informing you that the confirmed, irrevocable Letter of Credit No. BA 4698, amounting to £ 500 has been opened this morning through the District Bank, Ltd., Manchester. Upon receipt of the them, please arrange shipping company that S.S. "Victory" is due to sail from your city to our port on or about May 10 and, if possible, please try your best to ship by that steamer.

Should this trial order prove satisfactory to our customers, we can assure you that repeat orders in increased quantity will be placed.

Your close cooperation in this respect will be highly appreciated. Meanwhile, we await your shipping advice by cable.

Yours faithfully,
[Signature]

Urging Immediate Shipment
Specimen 2

Dear Sir,

We wish to draw your attention to our Order No. 6558 covering 5000 pieces of sweater, for which we issued in your favor about 25 days ago an irrevocable L/C with expiration date on April 20th.

Our retailers are badly in need of the goods. As the season is rapidly approaching, any delay in shipping our order will undoubtedly result in big trouble.

To enable our retailers to catch the brisk demand at the start of the season, we shall greatly appreciate if you effect shipment in time.

Yours faithfully,
[Signature]

Asking for Partial Shipment
Specimen 3

Dear Sir,

Subject: Your Order No. 596

Thank you for the above order for our furniture.

It is stipulated in our Sales Confirmation No. 2014021 that the 2,000 sets you ordered are to be shipped in two equal lots in March and April 2014. However, in your letter of February 20 you requested that 70% of the furniture be shipped in March and the balance in April.

Although we have the quantity in stock, it is too late for us to ship 70% of your order in March. It is hard to book shipping space at short notice, especially due to few direct sailings to your port of destination. Besides, no relevant L/C has been opened yet.

We are suggesting that 50% be shipped in March and the rest in April provided that the L/C can reach us on March 12 at the latest.

We are looking forward to receiving your prompt reply.

Yours faithfully,
[Signature]

Asking for Allowing Transshipment

In cases where direct sailing from one port to the other is not available, transshipment is a necessity. Aiming to avoid dispute that might arise in future, the seller should first obtain consent from the buyer that the goods ordered may be sent to the port of destination with transshipment. As such, the stipulation "transshipment is allowed" should be laid down in the L/C as well as in the contract.

Specimen 4

Dear Sir,

We are in receipt of the Letter of Credit No. S1677 you established through the Barclays Bank, London on May 2nd, covering our contract No. L2015.

On perusal, we find that the port of destination should be Belfast and no transshipment is allowed. Since there are only one or two direct steamers monthly from Dalian to Belfast, we usually have to make shipment via Hong Kong, China. In order to make sure that the goods will be duly delivered, which is to our mutual benefit, we request that you amend the said L/C to allow us transshipment.

In case the above amendment is not agreeable to you, you may change the port of destination Belfast to Liverpool because there are more direct steamers available from Dalian to Liverpool.

Your kind acknowledgement will be highly appreciated.

Yours faithfully,
[Signature]

Request for Extending L/C
Specimen 5

Dear Sir,

<u>L/C No. SM289</u>

We are sorry to advise you that the recent flood damaged part of the railway from our factory to the port of shipment, causing some delay in making delivery of the goods under your order No. 6799.

The authorities concerned say that they are doing rush repairs and the transportation is expected to return to normal in March.

As this is the case, we hereby request you to extend your L/C No. SM289 for one month, that is, the shipment date to March 20th and validity to August 10th.

Many thanks for your cooperation.

Yours faithfully,
[Signature]

Reply to the Request for Extending L/C
Specimen 6

Dear Sir,

<u>L/C No. SM289</u>

We regret to learn the present trouble you are involved in from your letter of February 15th. As the matter stands, we have to allow you a one-month extension of our L/C.

The delay of delivery will cause great inconvenience to us. Therefore, it is vital that the shipment be made within the extended time limit. We will not stand any further delay.

Yours faithfully,
[Signature]

Shipping Advice

The shipping advice is a notice to the importer on summary of the shipment. If a transaction is concluded on a CIF or CFR basis, the exporter should, before or after effecting shipment, notify their dispatch to the importer. In case of CFR transaction, a shipping advice is also a necessity for the importer to cover insurance of their goods based on the shipping advice. Besides, the importer may know when to receive the goods and arrange with a customs broker for the cargo clearance.

A shipping advice usually includes the following information:

(1) The name of the ship used to dispatch the goods.

(2) The name of the goods, the quantity and value.

(3) The date and number of Bill of Lading.

(4) The date and number of The Contract.

(5) The name of the shipping port/loading port.

(6) The estimated time of departure (ETD).

(7) The estimated time of arrival.

(8) The packing conditions.

(9) Whether the draft drawn under the relevant L/C has been negotiated.

(10) Together with relevant shipping documents.

(11) Other information as delay of shipment, transshipment or change of L/C.

(12) Thanks for patronage.

Specimen 7

> Dear Sir,
>
> <u>Contract NO. 215 for 3,000 Pieces of Cases and Bags</u>
>
> We are pleased to inform you that we have shipped the subject goods on board S.S "Star" which is due to leave here on or about November 20th and arrive at your port on or about November 26th. Enclosed please find the following shipping documents covering the consignment:
>
> 1. Commercial Invoice No. 2355 in duplicate.
> 2. Packing List No. 637 in triplicate.
> 3. One non-negotiable copy of B/L.
> 4. One copy of Insurance Policy.
> 5. One copy of Certificate of Quality.
> 6. Weight Memo in duplicate.
>
> We are very glad to have been able to deliver the goods as contracted and assure you that the goods will reach you in good time and prove to be entirely satisfactory to you.
>
> We assure you our full cooperation and look forward to more opportunities to serve you.
>
> Yours faithfully,
> [Signature]

5. Writing Templates

Shipment Instruction

> Dear Sir,
>
> We wish to draw your attention to our contract No. _____ covering _____ (goods), for which we opened the confirmed, irrevocable Letter of Credit No. _____ in your favor this morning through _____ (bank).
>
> Upon receipt of the above-mentioned L/C, please do make delivery of the goods on time as any delay in shipment would bring our goods out of the best sale season and result in harm to our future business.
>
> We are informed by the local shipping company that _____ (name of conveyance) is due to sail from your city on or about _____ (date) and, if possible, please try your best to ship by that steamer.
>
> Your close cooperation in this respect will be highly appreciated. We trust you will see to it that the order is shipped within the stipulated time and the consignment arrives in good order.
>
> Yours faithfully
> [Signature]

Urging Immediate Shipment

Dear Sir,

   With reference to our Order No. _____ of _____ (goods) with stipulated time of shipment in _____ (time of shipment), we wish to remind you that up to now we have not had any definite information from you about delivery, although the time of shipment has expired.

   As our buyers are in urgent need of the goods, the long delay has caused us considerable inconvenience and we may be compelled to seek an alternative source of supply. If you fail to effect delivery in _____ (time of delivery), we will have to lodge a claim against you for the loss and reserve the right to cancel the contract.

   Please make your best efforts to get the goods dispatched with the least possible delay. We look forward to receiving your shipping advice, by _____ (means of communication), within _____ (date).

Yours faithfully,
[Signature]

Asking for Partial Shipment

Dear Sir,

Re: <u>No. E215 Order</u>

   We have received your letter of _____ (date), concerning the captioned order. We are sorry for not having given you any news about the delay of shipment. Owing to an unexpected shortage of _____ as raw material in our market, it is impossible for us to ship _____ (goods) in one lot.

   We learn your clients need the goods badly, so we request you to allow us to make a partial shipment. We are suggesting that _____ (%) be shipped in _____ (date) and the remaining in _____ (date).

   We should be obliged if you would kindly understand the situation and you would comply with our request.

Yours faithfully,
[Signature]

Asking for Allowing Transshipment

Dear Sir,

Re: No. _____ <u>Order</u>

   With regard to shipment of No. _____ Order, we regret very much to inform you that despite painstaking efforts having been made by us, we are still unable to book space of a vessel sailing to your _____ (port of destination) direct. Therefore, it is very difficult, if not impossible, for us to ship _____ (goods) to your _____ (port of destination) direct.

   In view of the difficult situation faced by us, you are requested to amend the L/C to allow transshipment of the goods in _____ (name of place) where arrangements can easily be made for transshipment. Please be assured that we will ship the goods to _____ (name of place) right upon receipt to the L/C amendment. And your understanding of our position will be highly obliged.

  We are expecting your early reply.

Yours faithfully,
[Signature]

Export's Advice of the Delay of Shipment

Dear Sir,

  We are very sorry to inform you that the shipment during _____ (date) covering your Order No. _____ is impossible to be executed within the stipulated date on account of (cause of delay).

  The manufactures are suffering _____ . Although they are making every effort to deliver the goods as requested, they inform us that a _____ delay of shipment is unavoidable. We ask, therefore, that you approve this situation with a _____ % price discount and we deeply apologize for the possible inconvenience you may be put into.

  We assure you that we will take every precaution against such trouble arising in the future.

Yours faithfully,
[Signature]

Shipment Advice

Dear Sir,

  We are pleased to inform you that your order No. _____ covering _____ dated _____ under L/C No. _____ has been shipped by _____ (means of conveyance), which is scheduled to sail from _____ (loading port) on _____ (date), and is due to arrive at _____ (port of destination) on _____ (date).

  We are sending you under cover one set of duplicate shipping documents as follows, so that you may make all the necessary preparations to take the delivery of the goods when they duly arrive at your port.

  _____ Commercial Invoice
  _____ Packing List
  _____ Bill of Lading, Non-Negotiable Copy
  _____ Insurance Policy/Certificate
  _____ Inspection Certificate (Report)
  _____ GSP Form A
  _____ Certificate of Origin
  _____ Customs Invoice
  _____ Beneficiary's Certificate

  We hope this shipment will reach you in perfect condition and look forward to your further order.

Yours faithfully,
[Signature]
Ecl.a/s

6. Key Words and Expressions

(1) shipment　装运，运输

(2) shipping advice　装运通知

(3) shipping instructions　装运指示 (由出口商发出，证明运输及交付方法)

(4) consign　运送，托运

(5) consignor　发货人

(6) consignee　收货人

(7) enclose　附上

(8) shipping documents　运单据

(9) non-negotiable copy of B/L　不可转让的提单副本

(10) commercial invoice　商业发票

(11) in duplicate　一式两份

(12) packing list in triplicate　装箱单一式三份

(13) insurance policy　保险单

(14) ETD: Estimated Time of Departure　预计离开时间

(15) ETA: Estimated Time of Arrival　预计到达时间

(16) S.S = steamship　轮船

(17) partial shipment　分批装运

(18) transshipment　转船

(19) consignment　托运的货物, 寄售产品

(20) the stipulated time　规定的时间

(21) port of destination　目的港

7. Useful Sentence Patterns

(1) Up to the present moment, we have not yet received your irrevocable L/C. 到目前为止我们还没有收到你方开来的不可撤销的信用证。

(2) Upon receipt of the L/C, please arrange immediate shipment. 收到信用证后，请立即安排装运。

(3) As we are in urgent need of crude oil, please complete the shipment of 60, 000 tons under the captioned contract within this month. 我们急需石油，请你方将标题所指的合同项下的6万吨石油在这个月内装完。

(4) We shall give 30 days definite notice of cargo readiness and expect the ship to be at Antwerp on April 15th ready to take cargo on board. 我公司将于30天前发出货物备妥通知，并希望船只于4月15日在Antwerp准备装货。

(5) We regret to inform you that there is no shipping container sailing from Dalian to London prior to April 12th. 非常遗憾地通知您，4月12日前没有从大连开往伦敦的集装箱船，因此，无法按你方要求提出报价。

(6) Please book the shipping container for the goods and let us know the ocean freight as

soon as possible. 请为货物洽订海运集装箱，并尽快告知海运运费。

(7) We hereby give 40 days' notice that the goods under Contract No. 1488 will be available for shipment on July 20th. 兹通知，第1488号合同项下货物将于40天后，即7月20日备妥待运。

(8) Please arrange to send the consignment to Dubai to be shipped by S.S. "Victory". 请即刻安排将货物发往迪拜，装"胜利号"轮船。

(9) As our users are in urgent need of the consignment, please get the goods dispatched within the stipulated time. 由于我方客户急需此货物，请按规定的时间发运。

(10) This consignment of goods we've ordered is of a strong seasonal nature. If we miss the season, we won't be able to... 我们订的这一批货，季节性很强，错过了季节就没办法……

(11) So please by all means guarantee the date of shipment so that we would not miss the sales season. 所以，请千万保证船期，使我们能赶上销售旺季。

(12) We have contacted a number of shipping companies and agents, but none of them has ships available before 25th next month. 我们联系了几家船运公司和代理，但他们在下月25号之前都没有船。

(13) Shipment is to be made in five equal lots beginning from May, with transshipment at Hong Kong, China. 装运应从5月份开始，分五次平均装运，在中国香港转船。

(14) The goods ordered are all in stock and we assure you that the first steamer will make the shipment available in October. 贵公司订购的货物我方均有现货，可保证在10月份将货物装上第一条船。

(15) As there is no direct steamer, shipment has to be made by an indirect steamer with transshipment at Hong Kong, China. 因无直达船，货物只能由非直达船装运，在中国香港转船。

(16) As the goods are ready for shipment, please designate a steamer and let us know its name as early as possible. 因货物已备妥待运，请尽快选派船只并将船名告知我们。

(17) Your will be duly informed when shipment of your order is effected. 一旦发货，就会及时通知你们。

8. Exercises

Exercises 10-1

Direction: Put the following sentences into English.

(1) 我们已于今日，将下列书籍通过美国铁路快运至至你处，运费已付。

(2) 货物已于旧金山港卸货。

(3) 收到信用证后，请立即安排装运我方所订货物，勿误。

(4) 我们接到当地轮船公司通知，"胜利"号轮船定于本月10日左右开往上海。

(5) 这批货已装上"公主"号轮船，该轮已于3月20日从上海起航，预计于4月5日抵达纽约。

(6) 遗憾地告诉您，由于我们在原产地的供应商的延误，我们无法在本月底前将货物备妥。

(7) 货物在5月至7月间分三次平均发货。

(8) 请告知您要求我们以什么方式发运这两批货物。

(9) 由于从上海到你方港口没有直达船，货物必须至香港转船。

(10) 信用证已按要求修改，现在一切已就绪，望尽早将我方订货装船。

Exercises 10-2

Direction: Write a letter according to the fouowing hints.

假设你是某家具出口公司的业务员，你昨天已将客户所订的200套家具装运于"公主"号轮船，该轮船预计在5月25日抵达客户港口。现要求你写一篇装船通知，告知客户相关事宜，并表达长久合作的意愿。

Exercises 10-3

Direction: Write a letter according to the following hints.

(1) 兹通知对方第3979号订单项下的货物已发运。

(2) 咖啡机分别装入50个纸板箱，箱外的运输标志是UMT IND MANILA, 箱号为1—50.

(3) 货物装于"美人鱼"号轮，12月5日驶离上海，12月16日抵达马尼拉。

(4) 你方已向华侨银行(the Overseas Chinese Banking Corporation)提示了汇票，其金额为对方信用证金额，同时提示的还有全套货运单据：清洁已装船提单一式三份、保险凭证、原产地证书及你方的发票一式三份。

(5) 希望这些咖啡机会适合对方客户的需要，盼望你方再来订货。

9. Supplementary Readings

Shipment

The effectuation of shipment signifies the exporter's fulfillment of the obligation to make delivery of the goods. In international transactions, shipment is mostly made by ocean vessels-tramp or liner. The former is a freight-carrying vessel, which has no regular route or schedule of sailings while the latter has both regular route and schedule of sailings and arrivals on a stated date between specified ports. The article of shipment usually consists of: (1) time of effecting shipment; (2) loading port & port of destination; (3) notice of assigning vessel and notice of shipment; (4) partial shipments and transshipment. In addition, as the most important document in shipping, the bill of lading is also covered in this article.

Time of effecting shipment can be specified to a specific date or a term or by a specific event. As the exporter is prone to be in breach of the contract if a specific date for effecting shipment is contracted, it is advisable that shipment is to be effected when some specific event happens. To avoid subsequent disputes, some terms of expression without universal or uniform interpretation, such as "shipment as soon as possible", "immediate shipment", "shipment with the least possible delay", or "shipment in time" shall not be used in an international transaction contract.

Under a FOB or CIF or CFR contract, port of loading is usually proposed by the exporter and is worded in the international transaction contract when confirmed by the importer. As far as profit is concerned, the exporter often assigns a port, which is adjacent to the origin of the goods, as the port of loading. But if the goods are of great number or volume or there are several suppliers, who are not in the same region or are not adjacent to the same port, it is advisable, for the advantage of the exporter, that more than one port is contracted to be port of loading, and the final port of loading shall be selected and confirmed by the exporter in accordance with the goods' supplying. And of course, in the interest of the importer, a term for the importer to decide the final port of loading shall be stipulated in the contract.

Under a C&F or CIF contract, the port of destination shall be specified. It is often proposed by the importer and is worded in the contract when confirmed by the exporter. For the advantages of the exporter, it is not good to contract that "main ports in × × × shall be the port of destination", as there is no universal or uniform interpretation about the main port in a certain area. If a port, to which there is no direct sail, is contracted to be port of destination, "transshipment shall be allowed" is an essential article in the contract.

Under an FOB contract, the exporter shall, prior to the contracted date of shipment, notify the importer the goods under the contract are ready for shipment so that the latter can have ample time to assign a vessel to the loading port for embarking. Upon receipt of the notice, the importer shall inform the exporter of the anticipated arriving date for the vessel to the loading port.

Under FOB, C&F and CIF, the Seller shall notify the Buyer the contract number, name of commodity, quantity or weight, invoiced value, name of steamer and the date of shipment immediately after the effecting of shipment so that the Buyer can make preparation for receiving the goods at the port of destination. The notice of shipment under C&F is particularly important, as under this term the Buyer will effect insurance upon receipt of the notice.

Partial shipments and transshipment affect direct the interests of the Seller and the Buyer, so whether partial shipments and transshipment are allowed shall be specified in an international transaction contract.

"Partial shipments" is also called shipment on installments. It means that the goods under one contract are shipped in different terms or by different lots. In international transaction contracts, partial shipments is often stipulated as follows: Partial shipments is only stipulated in principle, the terms of shipments, lots and quantity or weight are not detailed. This kind of stipulation is advantageous for the Seller as he can effect shipment within the contracted term according to the supplying of commodities and conditions of shipment.

Transshipment means unloading and reloading from one means of conveyance to another means of conveyance, in different modes of transport, during the course of carriage from the place of shipment to the place of destination stipulated in the Letter of Credit. Even if the Letter of Credit prohibits transshipment, banks will accept a road, rail, or inland waterway transport document which indicates that transshipment will or may take place, provided that the entire carriage is covered by one and the same transport document and within the same mode of transport.

The most important document in shipping is the bill of lading signed by or on behalf of the transporter or the ship's master. Originally called a bill of loading, it is used to certify that the Seller's goods have been received for transportation and delivery as stipulated in bill of lading. A bill of lading is a contract of carriage between an exporter and a service provider (i.e. airline, steamship line, freight forwarder or shipping company, etc.) that identifies the parties to the transaction and their responsibility for payment of transportation and other accessorial fees, such as transfers and delivery. In international trade, the origin and the destination on the bill of lading are usually for the "main carriage" transportation between the port of departure and the port of importation.

Chapter 11
Shipping Documents
货运单证

1. Learning Objectives

By the end of this chapter, you will be able to do the following:

· Know the definition of shipping documents.

· Learn the classification of shipping documents.

· Get familiar with some very often seen shipping documents.

2. Case Study

Please get prepared the Commercial Invoice, Certificate of Origin (or Country of Origin), Packing List, Bill of Lading etc. based upon the following given information.

根据以下案例背景材料，完成国际物流和国际贸易过程中涉及的制作商业发票、原产地证书、装箱单、提单等操作步骤。

外贸公司：	TENGSUN TRADING CO.,LTD. HUARONG MANSION RM2901 NO. 185 GUANJIAQIAO, BEIJING 210005, CHINA TEL: 0086-10-87156004 FAX: 0086-10-84711365
国外客户：	NEON GENERAL TRADING CO. P.O. BOX 79552, RIYADH 23566, KSA TEL: 00966-1-4769220 FAX: 00966-1-4689213
交易商品：	CANNED MUSHROOMS PIECES
CIF付款方式：	L/C AT SIGHT
通知行：	中国银行北京市分行
出口口岸：	上海
供应厂商：	杭州市华通食品厂

印刷厂商：	徐州市恒远印刷厂
货运代理公司：	上海凯通国际货运代理有限公司
承运船公司：	中国远洋集装箱运输有限公司
备注说明：	该外贸公司的业务形态是每名业务员负责业务的始末，直到收汇后转交财务部门办理核销退税事宜

3. Introduction

A great number of documents are needed in the global transport. The documents required for all commercial shipments, irrespective of value or mode of transportation, generally include a commercial invoice, a certificate of origin, a bill of lading, a steamship or an airlines company certificate, an insurance certificate (if goods are insured by the exporter) and a packing list. Depending on the nature of goods being shipped, or upon certain requests from the importer or in a Letter of Credit (L/C), or according to clauses in a contractual agreement, specific additional documents may also be required.

Each document should be prepared in (at least) one original and one copy. All documents (originals or copies) should bear the handwritten signature of the person issuing the document.

4. Specimens

Commercial Invoice

This document is required for exporting and includes all the terms of sale. The commercial invoice must conform exactly to Letters of Credit, including misspellings and foreign languages. Product descriptions, prices, weights, and other information must follow requirements specified by the target country.

Specimen 1

发　票
INVOICE

To: Messrs. SAM WOO EXPRESS CO. LTD. RM1101
DONG-A JEIL BLDG. 37-16, 4KA,
CHUNGANG-DONG, CHUNG-KU, PUSAN,
KOREA

No. 8963066G
Date: June. 4. 1998
FROM HSINKANG
To PUSAN KOREA

CONTRACT NO. 98BG1653　　SHIPPED BY VESSEL GLORY STAR V. 821E　　B/LADING NO. DYSCR005

Marks & Nos.	Descriptions & Quantity	Unit price	Amount
			BY L/C AT ······· SIGHT FOB HSINKANG
N/M	CUSHION　　5,000PCS	USD3. 25000	USD16,250.00
	PACKED IN 625CTNS G. WT. 14,125 kgs. NWT. 13,500 kgs.		USD16,250.00
	Total Quantity: 5,000.000 0　　PCS		
	ORIGIN: CHINA		

(签章)

Specimen 2

发 票
INVOICE

EIRENE BUSINESS SOLUTION PRIVATE LIMITED		INVOICE NO.:		PD1501-10
2A,SARAT BOSE ROAD,		DATE:		MAR 30,2015
KOLKATA-700020,		S/C NO.:		HPEM1501-10
WEST BENGAL,INDIA				

SHIPPING MARKS	DESCRIPTION	QTY	UNIT PRICE	AMOUNT USD
				C & F MUMBAI
N/M	LAMINATION MACHINE	3600 PCS	USD 23.77	USD 85560.00
	FREIGHT			USD 500.00
	TOTAL	**3600 PCS**		**USD 86060.00**

1200 CTNS   G.W.:   21840 KG   N.W.:   20370 KG

(Signature)

Certificate of Origin

This certificate must be issued by the manufacturer (or the exporter). In addition to the name of the vessel and the date of sailing, name(s), nationality(ies), and full street address(es) of the manufacturer of all items to be shipped, and components thereof, must be declared. Furthermore, the origin of each item or component must be stated clearly. Although these usually appear on the invoice, many countries require a separate certificate of origin.

Specimen 3

1. Exporter　TRADE LTD　CO.,LIMITED	Serial No.　CCPIT700 1501458669　Certificate No.　15C4403B5945/01757

ICC CERTIFICATE OF ORIGIN

CERTIFICATE OF ORIGIN
OF
THE PEOPLE'S REPUBLIC OF CHINA

2. Consignee	5. For certifying authority use only

3. Means of transport and route FROM NINGBO CHINA TO BREMERHAVEN, Germany by sea	CHINA COUNCIL FOR THE PROMOTION OF INTERNATIONAL TRADE IS CHINA CHAMBER OF INTERNATIONAL COMMERCE

4. Country / region of destination GERMANY	VERIFY URL:HTTP://WWW.CO-CCPIT.ORG/

6. Marks and numbers	7. Number and kind of packages; description of goods	8. H.S.Code	9. Quantity	10. Number and date of invoices
Produced for:EXPO BORSE GMBH INDUSTRIESTR.12 DE 49577 ANKUM Item:TOASTER 700W WIEB Item-no.t Packing 6 Order-No. Barcode Item Barcode VE	ONE THOUSAND FIVE HUNDRED AND FORTY (1540) CTNS OF TOASTER TOASTER AS PER S/C NO. 15-SC-195/APPLICANT ORDER NO. GE001584 TO BE SHIPPED FROM NINGBO NOT LATER THAN 31.05.2015.	8516722000	10472KGS	15WTC0526 MAY.26.2015

11. Declaration by the exporter The undersigned hereby declares that the above details and statements are correct, that all the goods were produced in China and that they comply with the Rules of Origin of the People's Republic of China. ,CHINA JUN.1.2015 Place and date, signature and stamp of authorized signatory	12. Certification It is hereby certified that the declaration by the exporter is correct. CHINA COUNCIL FOR THE PROMOTION OF INTERNATIONAL TRADE ,CHINA JUN.1.2015 Place and date, signature and stamp of certifying authority

Specimen 4

1. Products consigned from (Exporter's business name, address, country)	Reference No.
	ASEAN-CHINA FREE TRADE AREA PREFERENTIAL TARIFF CERTIFICATE OF ORIGIN (Combined Declaration and Certificate) **FORM E** Issued in THE PEOPLE'S REPUBLIC OF CHINA (Country) See Overleaf Notes

2. Products consigned to (Consignee's name, address, country)	

3. Means of transport and route (as far as known)	4. For Official Use
Departure date Jul. 2015 Vessel's name / Aircraft etc. Port of Discharge	☐ Preferential Treatment Given ☐ Preferential Treatment Not Given (Please state reason/s) ----- Signature of Authorised Signatory of the Importing Party

5. Item number	6. Marks and numbers on packages	7. Number and type of packages, description of products (including quantity where appropriate and HS number of the importing Party)	8. Origin criteria (see Overleaf Notes)	9. Gross weight or other quantity and value (FOB)	10. Number and date of invoices
1	N/M	SIXTEEN (16) BAGS OF BED SHEET H. S. CODE: 63023290	"WO"	864KGS 1460PCS USD: 365. 00	DTL15AP0701 JUL. 01, 2015
2		SIX (6) BAGS OF PILLOWCASE H. S. CODE: 63023290	"WO"	420KGS 7300PCS USD: 803. 00	
3		FIFTY-ONE (51) BAGS OF QUILT H. S. CODE: 94049040	"WO"	3066KGS 1460PCS USD: 1752. 00	
		TOTAL: SEVENTY THREE (73) CTNS ONLY *** *** *** *** *** *** MANUFACTURER: ADD: PARK TEL:			

11. Declaration by the exporter	12. Certification
The undersigned hereby declares that the above details and statement are correct; that all the products were produced in ----- and that they comply with specified for these products ... -TA for the products expor... ----- (Importing Country) ----- Place and date, signature of authorised signatory	It is hereby certified, on the basis of control carried out, that the declaration by the exporter is correct. ----- Place and date, signature and stamp of certifying authority

13. ☑ Issued Retroactively ☐ Movement Certificate	☐ Exhibition ☐ Third Party Invoicing

Packing List

A packing list is a document prepared by the shipper at the time the goods are dispatched, including names and addresses of consignor and consignee, description and value of the exported goods, net and total weight, number of packages and their contents, number of containers and contents, numbers of seals, and number of L/C (if applicable). Its prime purpose is to give an inventory of the shipped goods, and it is usually required by the customs for clearance purposes.

Specimen 5

装　箱　单
PACKING LIST/WEIGHT LIST

INV NO. 89630666

BEIJING June. 4. 1998

SHIPPING MARKS:	DESCRIPTION & QUANTITY	G.W.: (KGS)	N.W.: (KGS)	MEAS.
	CUSHION			
@8/5.000PCS/625CTNS		@22.6/14.125	@21.6/13.500	
N/M	5.000PCS　625CTNS	14.125KGS	13.500KGS	15.23M³

TOTAL QUANTITY: 5.000.0000PCS

TOTAL: SIX HUNDRED AND TWENTY FIVE CTNS ONLY.

(签章)

Specimen 6

装 箱 单

PACKING LIST

		INVOICE NO.:	PD1501-10
		DATE:	MAR 30.2015
		S/C NO.:	HPEM1501-10

TO:
EIRENE BUSINESS SOLUTION PRIVATE LIMITED
2A,SARAT BOSE ROAD,
KOLKATA-700020,
WEST BENGAL,INDIA

SHIPPING MARK	DESCRIPTIONS & PART NO.	PKGS CTN	QTY PCS	G.W. (KG)	N.W. (KG)	V (M3)
N/M	LAMINATION MACHINE	1200	3600	21840	20370	67.23
TOTAL		**1200 CTN**	**3600 PCS**	**21840 KG**	**20370 KG**	**67.23 (M3)**

电子机械有限公司
ELECTRIC & MACHINERY CO.,LTD

(Signature)

Bill of Lading (B/L)

A bill of lading is a document issued by the transportation carrier to the shipper acknowledging that they have received the shipment of goods and that they have been placed on board a particular vessel for a particular destination. Separate bills of lading are issued for the inland or domestic portion of the transportation and the ocean or air transportation, or a through bill of lading can be obtained covering all modes of transporting goods to their destination.

Bills of lading, inland or ocean, can be issued in either non-negotiable (straight) form or in negotiable form. If the bill of lading is specified as being non-negotiable, the transportation carrier must deliver it only to the consignee named in the bill of lading, thus the bill of lading acts both as a receipt of goods and as an agreement to transport these goods to a specific destination and consignee in return for payment of the transportation charges. If the bill of lading is specifically labeled as being negotiable, ownership to the goods and the right to re-route the shipment are with the person who has ownership of the bill of lading properly issued or negotiated to it. Such bills of lading are issued to shipper's order, rather than to a specific, named consignee. Where collection and payment is through banking channels, such as under a Letter of Credit or documentary collection, negotiable bills of lading are required (except for air shipments). The exporter must endorse the bill of lading and deliver it to the bank in order to receive payment.

Three Functions of the Bill of Lading

(1) A receipt of the goods given to the shipper by the shipping company.

(2) Evidence of the contract by the shipping company and the shipper.

(3) A document of title, entitling the person named on it to claim the goods when they arrive at the port of destination.

Contents of the Bill of Lading

The shipper, consignee, date and place of shipment, name of the vessel, port of shipment and destination, description of the goods, and the shipping marks.

Ocean Bill of Lading

Ocean Bill of Lading is an essential document in making a shipment. It is a contract between an exporter and an international carrier for transport of merchandise to a specified foreign market overseas.

Specimen 7

Shipper SHANGHAI ORIENT TRADING CO. LTD. SICHUAN EAST ROAD, SHANGHAI, CHINA	BILL OF LADING B/L No. COSCO 中国远洋运输公司 CHINA OCEAN SHIPPING COMPANY
Consignee TO THE ORDER OF INDUSTRIAL BANK OF KOREA (HEAD OFFICE SEOUL) SEOUL	Cable: Telex COSCO PEKING 22264CPCPK CN
Notify Party DAIWAN ART AND CRAFTS CO. LTD NO.4002 SEOCHO-DONG SEOCHO-GU,SEOUL, KOREA	COSCO CANTON 44080COSCA CN COSCO SHANGHAI 33057COSCO CN COSCO TSINGTAO 320370CSQD CN COSCO TIENTSIN 23221TOSCO CN COSCO DAIREN 86162DOSCO CN
*Pre-carriage by	*Place of Receipt by Pre-carrier	ORIGINAL
Ocean Vessel Voy. No. EASTWIND V.008E	Port of Loading SHANGHAI, CHINA	

Port of Discharge BUSAN PORT, KOREA	*Final Destination (if goods to be transshipped at port of discharge)	Freight payable at FREIGHT PREPAID	Number of original Bs/L THREE
Marks & Nos.	Number and Kind of Package; Destination of Goods N/M 284 CARTONS GLASSWARE AS PER SALES CONFIRMATION NO. RS303/007 DATED 5-5-2014 CIF-BUSAN PORT, KOREA	Gross Weight kgs 4668	Measurement m³ 27.64

TOTAL PACKAGES (IN WORDS) SAY TWO HUNDRED AND EIGHTY FOUR CARTONS ONLY

Freight and Charges	Shipped on board the vessel named above in apparent good order and condition (unless otherwise indicated) the goods or packages specified herein and to be discharged at the above mentioned port of discharge or as near thereto as the vessel may safely get and be always afloat. The weight, measure, marks, numbers, quality, contents and value being particulars furnished by the Shipper, are not checked by the Carrier on loading. The Shipper, Consignee and the Holder of this Bill of Lading hereby expressly accept and agree to all printed, written or stamped provisions, exceptions and conditions of this Bill of Lading, including those on the back hereof. In witness whereof, the Carrier or his Agents has signed Bills of Lading all of this tenor and date, one of which being accomplished, the others to stand void. Shippers are requested to note particularly the exceptions and conditions of this Bill of Lading with reference to the validity of the insurance upon their goods.
FREIGHT AS ARRANGED	Place and Date of Issue: SHANGHAI JUNE 25, 2014
	Signed for the Carrier [Signature]

Through Bill of Lading

Through Bill of Lading is a document that establishes the terms between a shipper and a transportation company covering both the domestic and international transport of export goods between specified points for a specified charge. For example, an air shipment can be covered with a through bill of lading; however, ocean shipments require both an inland bill of lading (for domestic transport) and an ocean bill of lading (for international transport).

Specimen 8

Shipper SHANGHAI ORIENT TRADING CO. LTD. SICHUAN EAST ROAD, SHANGHAI, CHINA	BILL OF LADING B/L No. COSCO 中国远洋运输公司 CHINA OCEAN SHIPPING COMPANY
Consignee TO THE ORDER OF INDUSTRIAL BANK OF KOREA (HEAD OFFICE SEOUL) SEOUL	Cable: Telex COSCO PEKING 22264CPCPK CN COSCO CANTON 44080COSCA CN
Notify Party DAIWAN ART AND CRAFTS CO. LTD NO.4002 SEOCHO-DONG SEOCHO-GU,SEOUL, KOREA	COSCO SHANGHAI 33057COSCO CN COSCO TSINGTAO 320370CSQD CN COSCO TIENTSIN 23221TOSCO CN COSCO DAIREN 86162DOSCO CN ORIGINAL

Pre-carriage by WAGON NO. 124334	Place of Receipt by Pre-carrier NINGBO	
Ocean Vessel Voy. No. EASTWIND V.008E	Port of Loading SHANGHAI, CHINA	

Port of Discharge BUSAN PORT, KOREA	Final Destination (if goods to be transshipped at port of discharge)	Freight payable at FREIGHT PREPAID	Number of original Bs/L THREE

Container No.	Marks & Nos.	Number and Kind of Package; Destination of Goods	Gross Weight kgs	Measurement m³
20'DWTU2200129 37740 CY/CY F.C.L 96046 PENANG No. 1-750	780 CARTONS	TEA SAUCER	15,850kgs	24.760m³

TOTAL PACKAGES (IN WORDS) SAY SEVEN HUNDRED AND EIGHTY CARTONS ONLY

Freight and Charges	Shipped on board the vessel named above in apparent good order and condition (unless otherwise indicated) the goods or packages specified herein and to be discharged at the above mentioned port of discharge or as near thereto as the vessel may safely get and be always afloat. The weight, measure, marks, numbers, quality, contents and value being particulars furnished by the Shipper, are not checked by the Carrier on loading. The Shipper, Consignee and the Holder of this Bill of Lading hereby expressly accept and agree to all printed, written or stamped provisions, exceptions and conditions of this Bill of Lading, including those on the back hereof. In witness whereof, the Carrier or his Agents has signed Bills of Lading all of this tenor and date, one of which being accomplished, the others to stand void. Shippers are requested to note particularly the exceptions and conditions of this Bill of Lading with reference to the validity of the insurance upon their goods.

F R E I G H T A S ARRANGED	Place and Date of Issue: SHANGHAI JUNE 25, 2014
	Signed for the Carrier [Signature]

Air Waybill

With the rapid development of international trade, transportation facilities have greatly improved to meet the demand. Besides transport by sea, road, or rail, nowadays in order to speed up delivery, carriage by air has become popular. Instead of a bill of lading, an air waybill is used if goods are sent by air. Air Waybill is a bill of lading which covers both domestic and international flights transporting goods to a specified destination. The air waybill is a contract enforceable by law. It has to be signed by the shipper or his agent and by the carrier or its authorized agent. Although the same individual or organization may act on behalf of both the carrier and the shipper, the air waybill must be signed twice one each in the respective carrier and shipper boxes. Both signatures may be of the same person. It establishes the terms between a shipper and an air transportation company for the transport of goods. Included in the document are the conditions, limitations of liability, shipping instructions, description of commodity, and applicable transportation charges. In addition, the air waybill is a non-negotiable document which serves as a receipt for the shipper, indicating that the carrier has accepted the goods listed and obligates itself to carry the consignment to the airport of destination according to specified conditions.

Specimen 9

Shipper's Name and Address		Shipper's Account Number	Not Negotiable	
CHINA NATIONAL FOOD STUFFS IMPORT & EXPORT CORPORATION, ZHEJIANG BRANCH, 145 JIANGUO ROAD, HANGZHOU, CHINA			Air Waybill Issued by	**AIR CHINA** 中国国际航空公司

Copies 1,2 and 3 of this Air Waybill are originals and have the same validity

Consignee's Name and Address		Shipper's Account Number	
TOKYO TRADING CO. LTD TEL: FAX:			BEIJING CHINA

It is agreed that the goods described herein are accepted for carriage in apparent good order and condition (excepted as noted) and SUBJECT TO THE CONDITIONS OF CONTRACT ON THE REVERSE HEREOF. ALL GOODS MAY BE CARRIED BY ANY OTHER MEANS INCLUDING ROAD OR ANY OTHER CARRIER UNLESS SPECIFIC CONTRARY INSTRUCTIONS ARE GIVEN HEREON BY THE SHIPPER. THE SHIPPER'S ATTENTION IS DRAWN TO THE NOTICE CONCERNING CARRIER'S LIMITATION OF LIABILITY. Shipper may increase such limitation of liability by declaring a higher value for carriage and paying a supplemental charge if required.

Issuing Carrier's Agent Name and City	
SINOAIR SHANGHAI COMPANY, HANGZHOU	

Agent's IATA Code	Account No.	Accounting information
		FREIGHT PREPAID

Airport of Departure (Addr of First Carrier) and Requested Routing
SHANGHAI

To	By First Carrier	Routing & Destination	To	By	To	By	Currency CNY	CHGS Code	WT/VAL		Other		Declared Value for Carriage	Declared Value for Customs
NRT									PPD X	COLL X	PPD X	COLL X	NVD	NCV

Airport of Destination	Flight/Date	For carrier Flight/Date	Amount of Insurance	INSURANCE-If carrier offers insurance and such insurance is requested in accordance with the conditions thereof. Indicate amount to be insured in figures in box marked "Amount of insurance".
TOKYO	FX0070/8 NOV.2005	, use only		

Handing Information

NOTIFY: SAME AS CONSIGNEE,

THIS SHIPMENT CONTAINS NO SOLID WOOD PACKING MATERIALS

(For USA only) These commodities licensed by ultimate destination _____, diversion contrary to US law is prohibited.

No. of Pieces RCP	Gross Weight	kg lb	Rate Class		Chargeable Weight	Rate	Charge	Total	Nature and Quantity of Goods (incl. Dimensions or Volume)
			Commodity Item No.						
210 CARTONS	3205	k C	0300		3020	20.81		63 342.20	LIVING ARKSHELL

Prepaid	Weight Charge		Collect				Other Charger AWC: 60.00
63 342.20					Valuation Charge		
					Tax		
	Total Other Charges Due Carrier				Shipper certifies that the particulars on the page hereof are correct and that insofar as any part of the consignment contains dangerous goods. Such part is properly described by name and is in proper condition for carriage by air according to the applicable Dangerous Goods Regulations.
60.00					
	Total Other Charges Due Agent				Signature of Shipper or his Agent

Total Prepaid	Total Collect					
63 402.20					8/NOV/2005 SINOAIR SHANGHAI COMPANY
Currency Conversion Rates	CC Charges in Dest Currency				**Executed on (date) at (place) Signature of Issuing Carrier or His Agent**
For Carrier's Use only At Destination	Charges at Destination				Total Collect Charges	999-8887 5566 AS AGENTS FOR THE CARRIER AIR CHINA

ORIGINAL 3 (FOR SHIPPER) A

Specimen 10

501 PVG 0123 7714		501-0123 7714

Shipper's Name and Address

ELECTRIC CO., LTD

▮▮▮▮▮▮, ZHEJIANG,
CHINA 87096330 315020

Air Waybill
Issued By

Copies 1, 2 and 3 of this Air Waybill are originals and have the same validity.

SMARTWARES SAFETY & LIGHTING LTD
ADDRESS: BYRON HOUSE 34 SHERWOOD
ROAD ASTON FIELDS INDUSTRIAL ESTATE
BROMSGROVE B60 3DR U.K. MARTIN BEER
T +44 1527 557 700 EXT 240
M +44 2585 610 207, F +44 1527 557 701
E MARTIN.BEER@SMARTWARES.EU
FCI / SHA

It is agreed that the goods described herein are accepted in apparent good order and condition (except as noted) for carriage SUBJECT TO THE CONDITIONS OF CONTRACT ON THE REVERSE HEREOF. ALL GOODS MAY BE CARRIED BY ANY OTHER MEANS INCLUDING ROAD OR ANY OTHER CARRIER UNLESS SPECIFIC CONTRARY INSTRUCTIONS ARE GIVEN HEREON BY THE SHIPPER, AND SHIPPER AGREES THAT THE SHIPMENT MAY BE CARRIED VIA INTERMEDIATE STOPPING PLACES WHICH THE CARRIER DEEMS APPROPRIATE. THE SHIPPER'S ATTENTION IS DRAWN TO THE NOTICE CONCERNING CARRIER'S LIMITATION OF LIABILITY. Shipper may increase such limitation of liability by declaring a higher value for carriage and paying a supplemental charge if required.

Accounting Information

FREIGHT PREPAID
FCI SHA

Agent's IATA Code	Account No.
1111111	

Airport of Departure (Addr. of First Carrier) and Requested Routing

SHANGHAI PUDONG

Reference Number	Optional Shipping Information

To	By First Carrier Routing and Destination	to	by	to	by	Currency	CHGS Code	WT/VAL PPD COLL	Other PPD COLL	Declared Value for Carriage	Declared Value for Customs
GYD	7L		LHR	7L		CNY		PP	PP	N.V.D.	N.C.V.

Airport of Destination	Requested Flight/Date	Amount of Insurance	
LONDON	7L034 / 31MAR	XXX	INSURANCE - If carrier offers insurance, and such insurance is requested in accordance with the conditions thereof, indicate amount to be insured in figures in box marked 'Amount of Insurance'

NOTIFY: SMARTWARES SAFETY & LIGHTING LTD
ADDRESS: BYRON HOUSE 34 SHERWOOD ROAD ASTON FIELDS INDUSTRIAL ESTATE
BROMSGROVE B60 3DR U.K.

No. of Pieces RCP	Gross Weight	kg lb	Rate Class / Commodity Item No.	Chargeable Weight	Rate / Charge	Total	Nature and Quantity of Goods (incl. Dimensions or Volume)
2	707.0	K	Q	707.0	50.22	505.54	LED LAMPS V: 2.808 CBM
MARKS:							
SMARTWARES SAFETY & LIGHTING							PO7631
CODE:							
QTY:							
BATCH: RXXWXX							
GW:							
CARTON: OF							
SMARTWARES SAFETY & LIGHTING,							
BROMSGROVE, UK							
2	707.0					505.54	

Prepaid	Weight Charge	Collect	Other Charges
35505.54			AWC: 50.00, MYC: 7070.00, MSC: 848.40
	Valuation Charge		
	Tax		
	Total Other Charges Due Agent		Shipper certifies that the particulars on the face hereof are correct and that insofar as any part of the consignment contains dangerous goods, such part is properly described by name and is in proper condition for carriage by air according to the applicable Dangerous Goods Regulations.
	Total Other Charges Due Carrier		
7968.40			
			FCI/SHA
Total Prepaid	Total Collect		Signature of Shipper or his Agent
43473.94			
Currency Conversion Rates	CC Charges in Dest. Currency	2015-03-30	SHANGHAI	MIN
	Charges at Destination	Total Collect Charges	Executed on (date)	at (place)	Signature of Issuing Carrier or its Agent

5. Writing Templates

Commercial Invoice

INVOICE

Invoice No.: _____   Date: _____

    Seller: _____

    Buyer: _____

L/C No.: _____   Contract No.: _____

Shipped by _____ from _____ to _____

Shipping Mark	Description of Goods				Total Amount
	ART.NO	QTY(PCS)	UNIT PRICE	AMOUNT (USD)	

_____(Company Name)

_____

                               [Signature]

Certificate of Origin

Exporter	Certificate No.
Consignee	CERTIFICATE OF ORIGIN OF THE PEOPLE'S REPUBLIC OF CHINA
Means of Transport and Route	For certifying Authority Use Only
Country/Region of Destination	

Marks and Numbers	Number and Kind of Packages; Description of Goods	H.S. Code	Quantity	Number and Date of Invoices

Declaration by the Exporter The undersigned hereby declares that the above details and statements are correct, that all the goods were produced in _____ and that they comply with _____ (Rules of Origin) _____(Company Name) [Signature] Place/Date/Name	Certification It is hereby certified that the declaration by the exporter is correct. (OFFICIAL STAMP) [Signature] Place/Date
Place and date, signature and stamp of authorized signatory	Place and date, signature and stamp of authorized signatory

Packing List

PACKING LIST						

Invoice No.: _____   Date: _____

Seller: _____

Buyer: _____

Shipped by _____ from _____ to _____

Shipping Mark	Name of Commodity & Specifications		Qty (PCS)	Gross Weight (KGS)	Net Weight (KGS)	Measurement (CM)
	CARTONS NO.	ARTS NO.				
TOTAL	_____CARTONS					

Ocean Bill of Lading

Shipper	BILL OF LADING B/L No. COSCO
Consignee TO THE ORDER OF _____ (Bank) (HEAD OFFICE) _____ (Place) Notify Party	中国远洋运输公司 CHINA OCEAN SHIPPING COMPANY Cable: Telex COSCO PEKING 22264CPCPK CN COSCO CANTON 44080COSCA CN

★Pre-carriage by	★Place of Receipt by Pre-carrier	COSCO SHANGHAI 33057COSCO CN
Ocean Vessel Voy. No.	Port of Loading	COSCO TSINGTAO 32037OCSQD CN COSCO TIENTSIN 23221TOSCO CN COSCO DAIREN 86162DOSCO CN ORIGINAL

Port of Discharge	★Final Destination (if goods to be transshipped at port of discharge)	Freight payable at FREIGHT PREPAID	Number of original Bs/L THREE
Marks & Nos.	Number and Kind of Package; Destination of Goods	Gross Weight kgs	Measurement m³

TOTAL PACKAGES (IN WORDS) SAY _____ ONLY

Freight and Charges	Shipped on board the vessel named above in apparent good order and condition (unless otherwise indicated) the goods or packages specified herein and to be discharged at the above mentioned port of discharge or as near thereto as the vessel may safely get and be always afloat. The weight, measure, marks, numbers, quality, contents and value being particulars furnished by the Shipper, are not checked by the Carrier on loading. The Shipper, Consignee and the Holder of this Bill of Lading hereby expressly accept and agree to all printed, written or stamped provisions, exceptions and conditions of this Bill of Lading, including those on the back hereof. In witness whereof, the Carrier or his Agents has signed Bills of Lading all of this tenor and date, one of which being accomplished, the others to stand void. Shippers are requested to note particularly the exceptions and conditions of this Bill of Lading with reference to the validity of the insurance upon their goods.
F R E I G H T A S ARRANGED	Place and Date of Issue:
	Signed for the Carrier [Signature]

Through Bill of Lading

Shipper	BILL OF LADING B/L No.
	COSCO

Consignee	中国远洋运输公司
TO THE ORDER OF _____ (Bank)	CHINA OCEAN SHIPPING COMPANY
(HEAD OFFICE) _____ (Place)	Cable: Telex
Notify Party	COSCO PEKING 22264CPCPK CN
	COSCO CANTON 44080COSCA CN

Pre-carriage by	Place of Receipt by Pre-carrier	COSCO SHANGHAI 33057COSCO CN
		COSCO TSINGTAO 32037OCSQD CN
		COSCO TIENTSIN 23221TOSCO CN
Ocean Vessel Voy. No.	Port of Loading	COSCO DAIREN 86162DOSCO CN
		ORIGINAL

Port of Discharge	Final Destination (if goods to be transshipped at port of discharge)	Freight payable at F R E I G H T PREPAID	Number of original Bs/L THREE

Container No.	Marks & Nos.	Number and Kind of Package; Destination of Goods	Gross Weight kgs	Measurement m³

TOTAL PACKAGES (IN WORDS) SAY SEVEN HUNDRED AND EIGHTY CARTONS ONLY

Freight and Charges	Shipped on board the vessel named above in apparent good order and condition (unless otherwise indicated) the goods or packages specified herein and to be discharged at the above mentioned port of discharge or as near thereto as the vessel may safely get and be always afloat. The weight, measure, marks, numbers, quality, contents and value being particulars furnished by the Shipper, are not checked by the Carrier on loading. The Shipper, Consignee and the Holder of this Bill of Lading hereby expressly accept and agree to all printed, written or stamped provisions, exceptions and conditions of this Bill of Lading, including those on the back hereof. In witness whereof, the Carrier or his Agents has signed Bills of Lading all of this tenor and date, one of which being accomplished, the others to stand void. Shippers are requested to note particularly the exceptions and conditions of this Bill of Lading with reference to the validity of the insurance upon their goods.
F R E I G H T A S ARRANGED	Place and Date of Issue:
	Signed for the Carrier [Signature]

6. Key Words and Expressions

(1) S.S. (steamship)　船运

(2) DOC (document)　文件、单据

(3) P/L (packing list)　装箱单，明细表

(4) INV (invoice)　发票

(5) S/M (shipping mark)　装船标记

(6) S/C (sales contract)　销售确认书

(7) packing instruction　包装说明

(8) packing list　装箱单

(9) B/L (bill of lading)　提单

(10) bill of lading original　正本提单

(11) bill of lading copy　副本提单

(12) Ocean Bill of Lading　海运单

(13) sea waybill　海运单

(14) air waybill　空运单

(15) through bill of lading　直达提单

(16) certificate of origin　原产地证书

7. Useful Sentence Patterns

(1) Enclosed please find one set of the shipping document covering this consignment, which comprises: the commercial invoice, bill of lading, packing list, certificate of origin and insurance certificate. 现附上这批货物的装运单据一套，包括商业发票、提单、装箱单、原产地证明和保险凭证。

(2) The originals of the shipping documents are being sent to you through the Bank of China. 装运单据正本通过中国银行寄送你方。

(3) The Commercial Invoice and Insurance Policy, together with clean on board ocean Bill of Lading have been set through the National Bank. 商业发票、保险单和清洁已装船海运提单已交国家银行转送。

(4) In compliance with the terms of the contract, a full set of duplicate documents were airmailed to you immediately after the goods were shipped. 按照合同条款，在货物装船后即将全套单据副本空邮给你方。

(5) The seller shall present to the negotiating bank, Clean On Board of Lading, Invoice, Quality Certificate issued by the China Commodity Inspection Bureau or the Manufacturers, Survey Report on Quantity/Weight issued by the China Commodity Inspection Bureau, and Transferable Insurance Policy and Insurance Certificate when this Contract is made on CIF basis. 卖方应向议付银行提供已装船清洁提单、发票，中国商品检验局或工厂出具的品质证明和中国商品检验局出具的数量/重量鉴定书。如果合同按CIF条件，应提供可转让的保险单或保险凭证。

8. Exercises

Exercises 11-1

Direction: Put the following sentences into English.

(1) 卖方须将下列单据提交付款行议付货款/托收货款。若为信汇付款，下列单据须邮寄买方。

(2) 全套可转让的清洁提单、已装船提单，空白抬头，空白背书，注明"运费付至"，并通知目的港中国对外贸易运输公司。

(3) 制造厂出具的品质/数量/质量证书和检验报告，各一式二份。

(4) 装船10天内，除上述装船电报副本外，卖方须另外准备上述各种单据副本三套，其中一套航寄给买方，另外两套寄给目的港中国对外贸易运输公司。

9. Supplementary Reading

The Commercial Invoice

The commercial invoice acts as a bill to the buyer. The invoice contains basic information concerning the transaction. The invoice should contain a description of the products, shipper and seller, delivery date, and payment terms. The description of the products must exactly match the description on the Letter of Credit or other method of payment.

The bill of lading acts as a contract between the owner (seller) of the products and the carrier. The carrier agrees that he has received the shipment and will transport it to a stated designated site. Bill of lading can be issued in either a non-negotiated (straight) or a negotiated (shipper's order) form. The straight bill of lading (non-negotiated) cannot be negotiated, whereas, the shipper's order bill of lading (negotiated) can be brought, sold, or traded while the product is in transport. The original proof of ownership is required to take possession of the products.

The export packing list is a detailed export packing list that itemizes individual packages. The list contains information ranging from the type of packages (drum, crate, carton, etc.), gross weights and measurements, and shipper's and buyer's references. The list is used to determine the total shipment weight and volume and the cargo being shipped.

The destination control statement appears on the commercial invoice, ocean or air waybill of lading to notify the carrier and all foreign parties that the item may be exported only to certain destinations.

Consular invoice is required by certain nations and used to identify goods. The invoice is purchased from the consulate of that country into which the goods are being shipped and must be prepared in the language of that country.

Documentation must be detailed and precise. Discrepancies (intentional or unintentional) could result in seizure of cargo and/or failure of payments. The exporter must deal with a variety of documents depending on the final destination of the exports. Because each country has different import regulations, you must be careful to provide proper documentation. Remember, the exporter is accountable for the accuracy of the documentation, regardless if the exporter uses a forwarder or customs broker.

Chapter 12
Insurance
保险

1. Learning Objectives

By the end of this chapter, you will be able to do the following:

· Learn the risks frequently insured.

· Understand the basic structure of a letter of insurance.

· Learn to use proper words, phrases and sentence patterns in writing effective letters of insurance.

· Learn to reply to letters of insurance.

2. Case Study

> 　　某外贸公司按CIF价格条款出口一批大蒜，装运前已向保险公司按发票总值110%投保平安险，9月初货物装妥顺利开航。但是，在运输途中，该载货船舶于9月15日在海上突遇暴风雨，致使一部分货物受到水渍损害，损失价值10000美元。一个月后，该船又突然遇到海盗袭扰，经中国护航编队保护，该船撤离了海盗袭扰水域，却又不幸触礁，致使该批货物又遭到部分损失，价值为20000美元。试问：保险公司对该批货物的损失是否赔偿?为什么?

3. Introduction

Insurance is an indispensable part of foreign trade. In international business, the transportation of goods from the seller to the buyer generally covers a long distance by air, by land or by sea and has to go through the procedures of loading, unloading and storing. During this process the goods are quite likely to encounter diverse kinds of perils and sometimes suffer loss of one kind or another. In order to defend the goods against possible losses in case of such perils, the buyer or seller before the transportation of goods usually applies to an insurance company for insurance covering the goods in transit.

In insurance business, the insured (or insurant) is one who pays the insurance company for the coverage of risks of the cargo. The insurer is the insurance company that agrees to make payment in case of loss or damage occurred to the insured.

An insurance policy is released when goods are insured, but it is a common practice to use a "certificate of insurance" which is used as evidence of insurance. A policy is a contract, a legal document, and principally it acts as evidence of the agreement between the insured and the insurer.

There are three kinds of risks which can be covered under an insurance policy. They are as follows:

(1) Basic risks, such as:

    Free from Particular Average (F.P.A.)

    With Particular Average (W.P.A.) or With Average (W.A.)

    All Risks (A.R.)

(2) General additional risks, such as:

    Theft Pilferage & Non-Delivery (T.P.N.D.)

    Fresh and /or Rain Water Damage (F.R.W.D.)

    Shortage Risk

    Risk of Intermixture and Contamination

    Leakage Risk

    Clash & Breakage Risks

    Risk of Odor

    Sweating & Heating Damage

    Hook Damage Risk

    Risk of Rusting

    Breakage of Packing Risk

(3) Special additional risks, such as:

    Strikes, Riots, Civil Commotions (S.R.C.C.)

    War Risk

    Import Duty Risk

    On Deck Risk

    Rejection Risk

    Failure to Delivery Risk

    Aflatox in Risk

    Survey in Customs Risk

    Survey at Jetty Risk

The additional risks cannot be covered independently and should go with F.P.A. or W.P.A. and are included in All Risks coverage.

There are a great many insurance companies worldwide. Lloyd's is a famous organization incorporated in London in 1871. The People's Insurance Company of China (PICC), established in 1949, is the sole state-owned insurance organization in China. It underwrites almost all kinds of insurance and has agents in all ports and regions throughout the world. Since its birth, it has become a traditional practice of many foreign trade corporations to have their imports insured with the PICC. Insurance on China's exports may also be covered here if the foreign buyers view it advisable to do so. But on no account should the buyers be forced to accept CIF terms if they intend to do business on CFR or FOB basis with insurance at their destination.

4. Specimen Letters

Specimen 1
Enquiry of Insurance

Dear Sir,

We have received your fax of 10th May, quoting us for 500 sets of pottery.

The quotation you faxed is on CIF terms. We feel regretful, however, that we prefer to have your quotation and offer on CFR terms.

For your information, we have taken out an open policy with the Lloyd Insurance Company, London. When a shipment is made, all we have to do is advise them of the particulars. Furthermore, we cooperate with each other well. We usually receive from them quite a handsome premium rebate at regular intervals.

Meanwhile, we show great interest in knowing the scope of cover handled by your usual insurance company for our reference. Your reply in this respect will be much appreciated.

Yours faithfully,
[Signature]

Specimen 2
Reply

Dear Sir,

Thank you for your fax of May 12th. Attached is our CFR quotation for pottery. We are sure you will find our price reasonable.

With respect to insurance on our side, we usually cover insurance with the People's Insurance Company of China (PICC) for 110% of the invoice value against All Risks and War Risk as per the Ocean Marine Cargo Clauses of the PICC of January 1, 1981. If additional coverage is required, the extra premium will be for buyer's account.

The People's Insurance Company of China is a state-owned company with agents throughout the world. It enjoys a high reputation in handling claims promptly and effectively. As far as we know, the rates they quote are among the most competitive in the line.

We hope the above information will be of great help to you and look forward to receiving orders from you.

Sincerely yours,
[Signature]

Specimen 3
Explaining Insurance Practice

Dear Sir,

We have received your letter of June 20 in regard to insurance terms. Now we would like to inform you of the following:

Normally we cover insurance WPA and War Risk in the absence of the definite instructions from our customers. If you desire to cover All Risks, we can provide such coverage at a slightly higher premium. As to the insured value, our usual practice is to insure at invoice value plus 10%. Any additional premium for insurance coverage over 110% of the invoice amount, If so required, shall be for buyer's account.

Risks other than All Risks and War Risk can also be covered here, and the extra premium will be borne by the buyer.

We hope the above information will serve your purpose.

Yours faithfully,
[Signature]

Specimen 4
Asking the Seller to Arrange Insurance on Buyer's Behalf

Dear Sir,

We wish to refer you to our Order No. B356 for 2,500 pieces of Spotlights, from which you will certainly note that this order is placed on CFR basis.

As we now desire to have the consignment insured at your end, we shall be pleased if you will arrange to insure the goods on our behalf against All Risks at invoice value plus 10%, i.e. USD 5,000.

We shall of course refund you the premium upon receipt of your debit note or, if you like, you may draw on us at sight for the amount required.

We sincerely hope that our request will meet with your approval and await your reply with keen interest.

Yours faithfully,
[Signature]

Specimen 5
Reply

Dear Sir,

Re: Your Order No. B356 for 2,500 pieces of Spotlights

This is to acknowledge receipt of your letter dated June 20th requesting us to effect insurance on the captioned consignment for your account.

We are pleased to inform you that we have covered the above shipment with the People's Insurance Company of China against All Risks for USD 5,000. The policy is being prepared accordingly and will be forwarded to you by the end of the week together with our debit note for the premium.

For your information, we are making arrangements to ship the 2,500 pieces of spotlights by S.S. "Princess", sailing on or about August 20.

Yours faithfully,
[Signature]

Specimen 6
Asking the Buyer to Cover Insurance

Dear Sir,

Re: Your Order No.645 for 30 cases of assorted canned foods

We are pleased to inform you that the Order No.645 for 30 cases of assorted canned foods has been ready now. Since the business is concluded on FOB basis, the insurance should be arranged by you.

For your information, the goods will be shipped not later than September, 2014 by S.S. "Princess" and they will reach you at the later part of October. So you can cover insurance for the goods.

Should you need any other information, please feel free to let us know.

Yours faithfully
[Signature]

Specimen 7
Effecting Insurance for the Buyer

Dear Sir,

Re: Your Order No. 1992 for 1000 Cases of Toys

This is to acknowledge the receipt of your letter dated January 20 requesting us to effect insurance on the captioned shipment for your account.

We are pleased to inform you that we have covered the above shipment with the People's Insurance Company of China against All Risks for 2,500. The policy is being prepared accordingly and will be forwarded to you by the end of the week together with our debit note for the premium.

For your information, we are making arrangement to ship the 1000 cases of toys by S.S. "Victory" sailing on or about February 11.

Yours faithfully,
[Signature]

Specimen 8
Insurance Policy

PICC 中国人民财产保险股份有限公司
PICC PROPERTY AND CASUALTY COMPANY LIMITED

总公司设于北京 Head Office Beijing	一九四九年创立 Established in 1949	保险单号(POLICY NO.) PYIE201533020000012865

货物运输保险 保险单 CARGO TRANSPORTATION INSURANCE POLICY

发票号(INVOICE NO.) PD1501-11	提单号(B/L NO.)	NGBCB15003561
合同号(CONTRACT NO.) HPEM1501-11	信用证号(L/C NO.)	

被保险人(THE INSURED): ██████████ CO.,LTD

中国人民财产保险股份有限公司(以下简称本公司)根据被保险人要求，以被保险人向本公司缴付约定的保险费为对价，按照本保险单列明条款承保下述货物运输保险，特订立本保险单。
THIS POLICY OF INSURANCE WITNESSES THAT PICC PROPERTY AND CASUALTY COMPANY LIMITED (HEREINAFTER CALLED "THE COMPANY") AT THE REQUEST OF THE INSURED AND IN CONSIDERATION OF THE AGREED PREMIUM PAID TO THE COMPANY BY THE INSURED, UNDERTAKES TO INSURE THE UNDERMENTIONED GOODS IN TRANSPORTATION SUBJECT TO THE CONDITIONS OF THIS POLICY AS PER THE CLAUSES PRINTED OVERLEAF.

标记(MARKS & NOS.)	包装及数量(PACKAGE & QUANTITY)	保险货物项目(GOODS)	保险金额(AMOUNT INSURED)
N/M	1200CTNS	LAMINATION MACHINE	USD21780.00

总保险金额(TOTAL AMOUNT INSURED): US DOLLARS TWENTY ONE THOUSAND SEVEN HUNDRED AND EIGHTY ONLY

保险费(PREMIUM): AS ARRANGED   起保日期(DATE OF COMMENCEMENT): AS PER B/L

装载运输工具(PER CONVEYANCE): HAMMONIA ISTRIA V.1509

自(FROM): NINGBO, CHINA   经(VIA):   至(TO): MUMBAI

承保险别(CONDITIONS):

COVERING ALL RISKS AS PER OCEAN MARINE CARGO CLAUSES (2009) OF THE PICC PROPERTY AND CASUALTY COMPANY LIMITED.
B/L NO.: NGBCB15003561

所保货物如发生保险单项下可能引起索赔的损失，应立即通知本公司或下述代理人查勘，如有索赔，应向本公司提交正本保险单(本保险单共有____份正本)及有关文件，如____份正本已用于索赔，其余正本自动失效。
IN THE EVENT OF LOSS OR DAMAGE WHICH MAY RESULT IN A CLAIM UNDER THIS POLICY IMMEDIATE NOTICE MUST BE GIVEN TO THE COMPANY OR AGENT AS MENTIONED. CLAIMS, IF ANY, ONE OF THE ORIGINAL POLICIES WHICH HAS BEEN ISSUED IN ONE ORIGINAL(S) TOGETHER WITH THE RELEVANT DOCUMENTS SHALL BE SURRENDERED TO THE COMPANY IF ONE OF THE ORIGINAL POLICIES HAS BEEN ACCOMPLISHED, THE OTHERS TO BE VOID.

GLADSTONE AGENCIES LIMITED
BOMBAY OFFICE
419 HIMALAYA HOUSE 79 PALTON ROAD
BOMBAY 400001 INDIA
TEL: 0091-22-22675974, 22675975
FAX: 0091-22-22675976 MOBILE: 0091-9820025611
EMAIL: MUMBAI@GLADSTONEAGENCIES.COM

保险服务请联系:
CONTACT INFORMATION OF INSURANCE SERVICE:

中国人民财产保险股份有限公司宁波市分公司
PICC PROPERTY AND CASUALTY COMPANY LIMITED NINGBO BRANCH
871190111
传真(FAX):
EMAIL:
地址(ADD): 宁波市█████下应街道诚信路967号
████████ IN ROAD,
XIAXING STR
DISTRICT, N
UNDERWRITER:

赔款偿付地点(CLAIM PAYABLE AT): MUMBAI
签单日期(ISSUING DATE): Mar.31, 2015

5. Writing Templates

Explaining Insurance Practice

> Dear Sir,
>
> We refer to _____ under Sales Contract No. _____ and are pleased to inform you of our usual practice.
>
> Regarding insurance on our side, we usually cover insurance with _____ (insurance company) for _____ % of the invoice value against _____ as per _____ (insurance clause). If a higher percentage or broader coverage is required, the extra premium will be for buyer's account.
>
> We hope the above information will serve your purpose and look forward to receiving your _____ .
>
> Yours faithfully
> [Signature]

Asking the Seller to Arrange Insurance

> Dear Sir,
>
> We thank you for your shipment advice of _____ (commodity descriptions).
>
> As we now desire to have the consignment insured for your account, we would be pleased if you would kindly arrange to insure the goods to be shipped by _____ on Coverage.
>
> Please send us the policy, together with a note for charges.
>
> Yours faithfully
> [Signature]

Reply

> Dear Sir,
>
> In reply to your letter of _____ requesting us to effect insurance on the captioned goods, we are pleased to inform you that we have covered the shipment with _____ against _____ for US $ _____. The Policy is being prepared accordingly and will be forwarded to you by _____ together with our debit note for the premium.
>
> For your information, we are making arrangements to ship the contracted goods by _____ which is due to sail for your port on or about _____.
>
> Yours faithfully,
> [Signature]

Asking the Buyer to Cover Insurance

Dear Sir,

    We refer to_____.
    We have booked shipping space for the consignment on S.S. _____ which sails for your port on or about_____.
    We would be grateful if you would please arrange insurance cover for the consignment at your end.
    Please fax your confirmation as soon as possible.

Yours faithfully,
[Signature]

Effecting Insurance for the Buyer

Dear Sir,

Re: Your Order No. _____ for _____

    This is to acknowledge the receipt of your letter dated _____ requesting us to effect insurance on the captioned shipment for your account.
    We are pleased to inform you that we have covered the above shipment with the People's Insurance Company of China against _____ for _____. The policy is being prepared accordingly and will be forwarded to you by _____ together with our debit note for the premium.
    For your information, we are making arrangement to ship _____ by S.S. _____ sailing on or about _____.

Yours faithfully,
[Signature]

---

6. Key Words and Expressions

(1) insure *v.* 保险，投保

    to insure WPA / to insure…against… 投保……险 e.g. We have insured the goods F.P.A. and against All Risks.

    to insure … for 按……金额投保 e.g. We shall insure the goods for 110% of invoice value. to insure… with… 向……投保 e.g. We have insured the shipment with the People's Insurance Company of China against All Risks for $7000.

    insurance: *n.* e.g. 保险 we can say: to arrange insurance / to effect insurance / to provide insurance

(2) policy 保险单

(3) All Risks 一切险，综合险

(4) War Risk 战争险

(5) Theft, Pilferage & Non-Delivery (T.P.N.D)Risks　偷窃、提货不着险

(6) Aflatox in Risk　黄曲霉素险

(7) Fresh and / or Rain Water Damage Risks　淡水雨淋险

(8) Shortage Risks　短量险

(9) Inter-mixture & Contamination Risks　混杂、沾污险

(10) Leakage Risk / Risk of Leakage　渗漏险

(11) Rust Risk　锈损险

(12) Breakage of Packing Risk　包装破裂险

(13) Risks other than All Risks and War Risk　除了一切险和战争险以外的其他险别

(14) premium　保险费

(15) debit note　借记通知单

(16) at your end / in your country　在你处

(17) normal practice / usual practice　惯例，一般的做法

(18) for your account / for sb.'s account　指（某笔钱）由某人来出，记到某人的账上

7. Useful Sentence Patterns

(1) We have covered insurance with the People's Insurance Company of China on the 200 metric tons of coal for 110% of the invoice value against all risks at the rate of 4%. 我们已向中国人民保险公司为200公吨煤按发票金额的110%投保一切险，保险费用为4%。

(2) Please see to it that you will arrange insurance on our behalf with the People's Insurance Company of China. 请务必代表我方向中国人民保险公司投保。

(3) Insurance is to be covered by the seller against F.P.A. and breakage risk for 130% of the invoice value. 保险由卖房按发票金额的130%投保平安险和破碎险。

(4) Regarding insurance, the coverage is for 110% of the invoice value up to the port of destination only. 关于保险，是按发票金额的110%投保至目的港。

(5) The extra premium should be borne by you. 额外保费将由你方承担。

(6) We generally insure W.P.A. on CIF sales. 按到岸价交易，我们一般保水渍险。

(7) The cover shall be limited to sixty days upon discharge of the insured goods from the seagoing vessel at the final port of discharge. 被保险货物在卸货港卸离海轮后，保险责任以60天为限。

(8) This risk is coverable at a premium of 6%. 这个险别是按6%的保险费率投保。

(9) We cannot comply with your request for insuring your order for 130% of its invoice value. 我们不能为你方订货办理发票金额130%的保险。

(10) Insurance on the goods shall be covered by us for 110% of the CIF value, and any extra premium for additional coverage, if required, shall be borne by the buyer. 我方将按照到岸价的发票金额110%办理该货的保险，如需增加额度，额外费用将由买方承担。

(11) The underwriter is responsible for the claim as far as it is within the scope of cover. 只要是在保险责任范围内，保险公司就应负责赔偿。

(12) If there are no definite directions from you, we'll take out insurance against F.P.A. and War Risk. 如你方没有明确指示，我们将投保平安险和战争险。

(13) The extent of insurance is stipulated in the basic policy form and in the various risk clauses. 保险的范围写在基本保险单和各种险别的条款里。

(14) It is important for you to read the "fine print" in any insurance policy so that you know what kind of coverage you are buying. 阅读保险单上的"细则"对你是十分重要的，这样就能知道你要买的保险包括那些项目。

(15) The rates quoted by us are very moderate. Of course, the premium varies with the range of insurance. 我们所收取的费率是合理的，当然，保险费用要根据投保范围的大小而有所不同。

(16) According to co-insurance clauses, the insured person must pay usually 20 percent of the total expense covered. 根据共同保险条款，保险人通常必须付全部费用的20%。

(17) You should study not only the benefits but also the terms and limitations of an insurance agreement that appears best suited to your needs. 你不仅要研究各种保险所标明的给予保险人的赔偿费用，还要研究它的条件与限制，然后选出最适合你需要的一种。

(18) W.P.A. coverage is too narrow for a shipment of this nature, please extend the coverage to include T.P.N.D. 针对这种性质的货物只保水渍险是不够的，请加保偷窃、提货不着险。

(19) In the insurance business, the term "average" simply means "loss" in most cases. 在保险业中"average"一词是"海损"的意思。

(20) Should any damage be incurred you may approach the insurance agent at your end and submit an insurance claim supported by a survey report. 如果货物发生损坏，你方可凭检验报告与你处保险代理联系并提出保险索赔。

(21) Since the loss is caused by clashing which is included in the insurance, the insurance company should admit liability. 由于损失是因碰撞造成的，而这属于货物投保范围内，因此，保险公司应该承担责任。

(22) Insurance is to be covered by the seller for a sum equal to the amount of the invoice. 卖方按发票金额进行保险。

(23) We insure the goods for RMB ￥5000 against All Risks with PICC. 我们向中国人民保险公司办理投保一切险，保险金额为人民币5000元。

(24) As usual, the goods have been insured on WPA terms. 按常规做法，货物已保水渍险。

(25) Please insure at invoice value plus 10%. 请按发票金额的110%投保。

(26) We have insured your Order No. 879 for the invoice cost plus 20% up to the port of destination. 我方的879号订单项下货物我们已按发票金额的120%投保至目的港。

(27) Please reply whether we are to insure the above shipment. 请告知我方是否要对上述货物投保。

(28) We shall provide such insurance (coverage) at your cost. 我们将投保这种险别，费用由你方负担。

(29) We thank you for your instructions to arrange the shipment of… We take it that you

wish us to insure this cargo against the usual risks, for the value of the goods plus freight. Unless we hear from you to the contrary we shall arrange this. 你们有关×××货物装运指示获悉，谢谢。我们推定，你们要我们按货价加运费投保通常险别。除非另有指示，我们要按此办理了。

(30) Cover Note (Insurance Certificate) follows as soon as we receive it from the underwriter. 一接到保险人的保险凭证，我们就立即寄给你方。

(31) Breakage is a special risk, for which an extra premium will have to be charged. 破碎险是一种特殊险别，要额外收费。

(32) We shall of course refund the premium to you upon receipt of your debit note. 收到你借方结账单后，我即将保险费汇付给你们。

(33) If you desire us to insure against a special risk, an extra premium will have to be charged. 如果你方想投保特殊险别，将向你们收取额外保费。

(34) W.P.A. plus Risk of Breakage suit your consignment. 贵方货物适合投保水渍险及破碎险。

(35) They will undertake to compensate you for the losses according to the risks insured. 他们将根据所投保的险别，对损失负责赔偿。

(36) How long is the period from the commencement to termination of the insurance? 保险责任的起讫期限是多长？

(37) The loss in question was beyond the coverage granted by us. 损失不包括在我方承保的范围里。

8. Exercises

Exercises 12-1

Direction: Translate the following sentences into English.

(1) 另外，合同中规定保险由卖方按高出发票金额10%向中国人民保险公司投保一切险和战争险。

(2) 本保险在货物到达内地目的地后60天内有效。

(3) 保险单一式三份，投保一切险和战争险包括破碎损失。

(4) 我们公司可以承保海洋运输的一切险别。

(5) 由于我们的订单按CIF条件达成，保险由你方办理，所以若你方为我方保险公司接洽此事，我方十分感激。

(6) 如果您愿意，我们可以受理更广的保险范围，但额外保险费用由你方承担。

(7) 现确认收到你方8月8日来函，要求我方对所购货物按发票金额的110%投保。

(8) 如客户没有明确要求，我们一般投水渍险和战争险。

(9) 关于保险，请按发票金额130%投保到目的港为止。

(10) 承保上述货物一切险，包括战争险的现行费率是0.6%。

Exercises 12-2

Direction: Write a letter according to hints.

假如你是某进口公司的业务员，你从英国进口一批手机，货物将在10月份从伦敦港运往你方港口。现要求你方向本地的保险公司联系，要求保险公司以最优惠条款为你所定货物开具预约保险单。随函附上货物详细情况表。

Exercises 12-3
Direction: Write a reply to the following letter in English.

> Dear Sir,
>
> We hereby refer to our Order No. HA96 for 2,000 pairs of Women's shoes.
> As the order is based on CFR basis, the insurance for the goods should be arranged at your end. We shall be obliged if you will cover insurance on our behalf again All Risks including War Risks for 110% of the invoice value.
> We will refund you the relevant premium once we receive your debit note. We hope that you can pay your immediate attention to the above matter.
>
> Yours sincerely,
> [Signature]

9. Supplementary Readings

Insuring Your Shipment

When shipping to a foreign market, cargo insurance is strongly recommended. It is essential if the terms of sale require the exporter to arrange for insurance, for example a CIF. contract (cost, insurance and freight). In any event, the cost of cargo insurance is nominal in most cases, amounting to less than 1% of the value of the shipment and the freight bill.

With the proper insurance policy, exporters can recover losses if their shipments are accidentally lost, stolen, damaged or delayed, although the extent of recovery will depend on the type of insurance purchased. Without insurance, an exporter could have no recourse. Unfortunately, insurance does not cover the possible loss of a customer, who may shift to another source of supply because the goods ordered do not arrive in a usable condition or are late in arriving.

When buying insurance, the exporter should consider several things, such as the amount of coverage (all risks or limited), time of year, route and destination port (the North Atlantic during the winter months can be treacherous; some ports can have higher than usual rates of pilferage), the loss and damage record of competing carriers, and cargo stowage and packing.

Insurance should be viewed as part of the total rate and service package that the carrier (or forwarder) offers, so don't treat insurance in isolation. Even though a carrier may have an impeccable record, there is always an element of risk and exporters should protect themselves against this risk.

Moreover, insurance coverage is part of a carrier's marketing strategy. It is more than likely that cost, coverage and the number of loss and damage claims will vary from carrier to carrier, so ask several and compare ask the carrier, whether it is a rail, motor, marine or intermodal carrier, what it charges for insurance, what the insurance covers, the deductible (if any) and how claims are handled.

This suggests that the first step in insurance selection is to ask the carrier about its loss and damage record. Ask other exporters or, if you are a member of an organization such as the Canadian Industrial Transportation Association, ask if it has any record on a particular carrier.

Before exporting, make clear that the terms of sale specify who is responsible for arranging insurance. For example, an exporter selling "CIF." will be responsible for arranging and paying for freight insurance. In many transactions, it is common for Canadian exporters, even those selling "FOB" or "FAS", to control or arrange for marine insurance.

Which kind of insurance the exporter should buy depends on the mode of transport selected, as certain levels are established according to legal requirements. Railway carriers are completely responsible for loss and damage to cargo. Motor carriers are responsible for $2.00 per pound, but will provide full coverage for a fee of 1% of the value of the load. Ocean carriage is limited to $500 per package, which is frequently below the value of the shipment. Consequently, the exporter must arrange for coverage separately. Exporters should be aware that there are certain exceptions which override the carrier's liability, such as "Acts of God" or a defect in the goods.

Obviously, for highway/ocean shipments or intermodal shipments moving partly by a marine carrier, full coverage may require the purchase of separate insurance from each carrier. For shipments that involve ocean carriage, it is recommended that exporters include an "all risks" clause.

Insurance can be arranged directly with a carrier, an insurer, an insurance broker or agent or through a freight forwarder or customs broker. Whether you purchase from a carrier or a third party, make sure that the insurance purchased covers the entire journey, that is from the time it leaves your plant or warehouse until it is in the importer's warehouse. In some instances, a carrier will provide coverage only while it is handling the shipment.

It should be noted that this discussion is meant for shipments of general freight and for lost or damaged cargo. Insurance for products such as dangerous goods and hazardous wastes are covered by separate insurance regimes. Responsibility for issues such as cleanup costs in the event of an accident involving your goods is not covered.

Chapter 13
Complaints and Settlements
投诉与处理

1. Learning Objectives

By the end of this chapter, you will be able to do the following:

· Get to know the key words and expressions for dealing with complaints and settlement.
· Know the useful sentence patterns in writing complaint letters.
· Know how to write general complaint letters.
· Know how to reply the complaints.

2. Case Study

某中国大型国有公司向一国外客户进口1000MT 特种化工原料，价格为USD1,450,000.00，由于国际石油行情看涨，化工原料也因此走俏，中方公司和卖方联系过程中，对方要求中方公司方立即开立信用证，因为中方公司是一大型国企，在支付款项上没有任何问题，对方提出不用签合同，只要开出L/C即可。但中方公司坚持要签订一个正式的书面合同，于是对方就通过传真传来一个已签字盖章的非常简单的一般性合同，主要条款涵盖了GOODS DESCRIPTION, TOTAL WEIGHT, CIF SHANGHAI PRICE, TOTAL CONTRACT PRICE, PACKING: STANDARD PACKING STUFFED IN 20'/40' CONTAINERS, PAYMENT: BY AN IRREVOCABLE L/C 90 DAYS FROM B/L DATE IN FAVOR OF SELLER 等。某天，中方公司发现卖方在工厂的包装没有按照以往的惯例进行包装，而是把通常用的编织袋包装改为牛皮纸袋包装，在与对方沟通中，对方强调牛皮纸袋也一样牢固，且用集装箱运输，不会有什么问题。由于市场需求急迫，中方公司也就没有再坚持。最终，在中方公司收到货物之后，发现经过一路颠簸的长途运输，造成许多包装袋破损，造成了不小的损失。于是，中方公司向对方提出了索赔要求。

In the above case, the Chinese importer complains that the supplies packing is against the general practice, which causes some damages to the importer. See how the importer shall write a complaint and how the supplier shall have to reply.

3. Introduction

In business transactions, when conducted traditionally or in the context of electronic commerce, everything should be hopefully done so carefully, with details of offers and orders checked, packing supervised, handling of goods carried out expertly, that no mistake is made and nothing is damaged. Unfortunately, something unexpected always happens in spite of the well-planned and careful work in the performance of a sales contract, which results in the occurrence of complaints.

Customers sometimes receive the goods of inferior quality or wrong ones; or they may find the goods damaged, missing or short; or the received goods unmatched with the order; unsatisfactory packing conditions of the goods. Under all such conditions, customers may make complaints or file a claim against the supplier. The complaints may cover but not limited as under:

· complaints of the goods in inferior quality;
· complaints of wrong goods delivered;
· complaints of shipment damaged;
· complaints of short supply, or missing;
· complaints of goods delayed;
· complaints of goods unsatisfactorily packed.

Sellers in business, at some point, have to deal with an upset customer. A business owner's ability to effectively deal with customer complaints in fact may provide a great opportunity to turn the dissatisfied customers into active promoters of your business. As a matter of fact, it costs much less to keep an existing customer than to win a new customer, so retaining existing customers is more profitable for your business.

If a company has effective customer complaints systems in place, many of those customers with questions or problems can be retained. Satisfied complainants can be nearly as, or even more loyal than, customers who did not have a problem, while poor service drives customers away.

Customers are looking for their problem to be easy to report, acknowledged and dealt with quickly, sensitively, and fairly. Generally, customers value highly the following complainants dealing services:

· having a problem fixed first time, and on time;
· having confidence that you know what you are doing;
· not being blamed for the problem;
· showing concern for their situation;
· being kept informed of progress;
· being advised what they can do to help avoid the problem recurring.

When the problem is reported, you should:
· Thank the customer for bringing the problem to your attention.
· Treat the customer with empathy, courtesy, patience, honesty and fairness.

· Speak to the customer in person, and do not rely solely on written complaints, or records of conversations.

· Show the customer that you clearly understand their problem by listening and taking notes.

· Ask questions to clarify the situation.

· Do not jump to conclusions, apportion blame, or become defensive.

· Summarize back to the customer your understanding of the problem.

· Respond to the problem quickly, tell the customer how it will be handled and tell them when they can expect a response.

When starting to solve the problems, you should:

· Tell the customer you are taking responsibility for dealing with the problem.

· Familiarize yourself with any background information. This could include checking internal records, speaking to staff and checking how this compares with the customer's version of events.

· Be solution-focused by involving the customer in this process.

· Make sure the customer is happy with the proposed solution before going ahead.

· Ensure that the solution meets any legal obligations. If the customer is asking for more than their legal right and you feel they are making an unrealistic demand, explain what the law says.

· Where there are no legal obligations, offer a solution that in the circumstances best meets the needs of your business. For example, if the law says a customer is entitled to a repair, you may be willing to offer a replacement if that is what the customer wants. The cost of satisfying the customer is likely to be less than the cost of losing them.

· Make sure you do what you promised to do, and don't delay—quick action will keep customers happy, but stalling and delays will lose customers. If there is going to be a delay, tell the customer.

· Tell the customer what your business will do to prevent the problem from happening again.

The following points might be the good advices for you to deal with customer complaints effectively, which can improve customer retention and help your company gain a reputation for providing good service, so keep in mind:

· Acknowledge their anger and apologize

Whilst you are listening to them, make a note of the main points of their grievance. Once they are finished, thank them for their comments, acknowledge their anger and apologize.

· Reassure the customer

Use the notes you made whilst listening to demonstrate that you have a secure grasp on the problem by giving them a précis of what they have just told you. Assure them that is exactly what you're going to do and explain the realistic options you have available to you. If the customer wants something that simply is not possible, apologize, give reasons why this is not an available option and then tell them what you can do for them.

· Take actions

Once you have explained what you are going to do to resolve the customer's problem, do it. Follow it through and ensure that what you promised is delivered.

· Aggressively promote the fact that you want feedback

You want to know when you get it wrong. And, make it easy for customers to contact you and get immediate access to empowered and empathetic agents. If customers can't find a convenient way to give feedback, they may just defect to another company without saying a word.

· Empathize with the customer

The first thing you need to think about when dealing with complaints is how you would feel if you were the one making the complaint. Empathy and understanding are paramount to giving good customer service whether it is in sales, customer service or customer complaints departments.

Allow the customer to vent their feelings and then remind them that you are here to help them and will do everything in your power to resolve the issue. This gives them the feeling that you see them as more than just a number on a system and can act to calm the customer down especially if it is a difficult or challenging situation.

· A complaint is an opportunity for the business to learn and grow

As a business, every complaint should be treated as serious and the customer with a small "expression of dissatisfaction" should be given the same courtesy as someone whose complaint is huge. Be thankful that your customer is voicing their problem, but realize that they may still use your competition the next time they need your product or service.

· Act on the new knowledge you have

One of the most important factors in complaint handling is to demonstrate that the company has acknowledged the complaint for the future. After the complaint has been dealt with and is coming to a close, advise them that you hope that this recent situation hasn't adversely affected their long term relationship with you as a company. Reiterate that you hope the compensation you are offering may go some way to restoring their faith in the company / product or service.

The key to a successful complaint or claim consists in your sincerity and tone, as well as the words you choose in writing the letter. Here are the rules for writing complaints.

· Address the reader politely. Make sure that your letter is polite and business-like.

· Regret the need to complain.

· Mention the date of the order, the date of delivery and the goods complained about.

· Explain the problem clearly by providing specific details. You should make it clear what your grievances are and what has failed to be done. Refer to the inconvenience caused.

· Make a specific request. Suggest how the matter should be put right.

Letters in reply to complaints or claims should always be courteous. The following are the rules for replying to complaints.

· Take the complaint or claim seriously.

· Explain what has happened and why it happened.

  a. Include a goodwill-building sentence saying that you welcome the customer's comments as a way of making improvement.

  b. State briefly the reason for mishap.

  c. Be quick to admit error if the product or the company's service was at fault.

· Avoid negatives that recall the problem. Do not repeatedly recall or apologize for the disappointing aspects with a backward look.

· Ask for any necessary cooperation from the customer.

· Do not shirk responsibility. If you are wrong, you should admit your mistake and apologize sincerely. You can state that you will try every effort to prevent the error from happening again, but you should never say that such errors would never happen again. If the trouble is caused by other people, you may promise to contact them and resolve the problems.

· End with a friendly, positive comment.

4. Specimen Letters

Specimen 1
Complaint about inconformity with Contract

Dear Sir,

Subject: <u>Supply of ABS 750</u>

We regret to advise that the first lot of ABS 750 dispatched on April 15th, 2015, against our purchase Contract No. 20140201 has been carefully examined and found the packing done by your factory is against the specification in the Contract, which causes serious damages during shipment. The Inspection Certificate will be airmailed to you as soon as it comes to hand.

Please look into the matter at once and take urgent measures to ensure that nothing like this will happen in the following lots.

The storage of this shipment causes us considerable difficulty and hamper us in our efforts to dispose of it. We consider ourselves entitled to an allowance for the loss we have to suffer. Hence, we reserve our right to lodge a claim against you.

Yours faithfully,
Li Zhiming

Specimen 2
Reply

Dear Mr. Ali,

We are very sorry to learn from your letter dated June 12th, 2014 that the packing of ABS 750 supplied against the standard stipulated, which causes some damages.

From what you describe it seems possible that a big mistake has been made in the the use of packing materials by our factory and we are arranging our representative in Shanghai to call on you within the next week to have a joint examination of the poorly packed ABS 750.

If the case is confirmed not up to the standard stipulated in your order, you can rely on us to make proper treatment or compensation, and we shall do everything we can to ensure that such mistake will never happen again.

Yours faithfully,
Edward
General Manager

Specimen 3
Complaint about Inferior Quality

Dear Sir,

We should like to invite your attention to the defective goods shipped by the M/S "Moonlight" on 20th September, 2014.

Upon opening the packages, we found that the quality was much inferior to the sample on which we approved the order No.071. Moreover the length of some pieces is short by approximately 6 meters.

After examining the enclosed cutting samples we sent as evidence from the Lloyd's Survey Report, we are sure you will agree to the inferiority of the goods.

We are now in a very awkward situation, because our customers, who have been very strict about the quality, are becoming impatient to take delivery of the goods.

We hope that you will immediately take this matter into your careful consideration and favor us with a prompt solution by return call.

Yours faithfully,
John Smith
Business Manager

Specimen 4
Reply

Dear Mr. John Smith,

Your Order No.071

  With reference to your letter dated 20th October, 2014, we feel grateful for your straightforwardness in pointing out that quality was inferior to the sample.

  Our manufacturers were really regretted to learn that some of the products had caused you so much inconvenience. Would you please give us a list of the products which need to replace? Please be assured that all the substitutes will be shipped by S.S. "Victoria" which is due to leave Ningbo for London around the beginning of next month.

  We apologize for the trouble caused you by the error and wish to assure you that care will be taken in the execution of your further orders.

Yours sincerely,
Li Jian
Manager

Specimen 5
Complain about Late Delivery

Dear Sir,

Our S/C No. 072

  We regret to inform you that the goods under S/C No. 072 haven't been received yet up to the moment of writing. As you have been informed in one of our previous letters, the customers are in urgent need of the goods and have in fact pressed us for assurance of early delivery.

  We should be glad to hear from you the causes of the late delivery. If you are not able to ship the goods immediately, we shall have to cancel our contract and find replacement elsewhere.

  Looking forward to your early and favorable reply.

Yours sincerely,
[Signature]

Specimen 6
Reply

Sept. 2, 2014

Dear Sir,

<u>Your S/C No. 072</u>

With reference to your letter dated September 2nd, 2014 concerning the delay of shipment, we are quite sorry for the delay in delivering the goods. This is a result of problems at our supplier's factory due to an unexpected serious breakdown in their machinery. These problems are completely beyond our control. We have arranged the shipment on September 12, 2014 by S.S. "Victoria", which is about to arrive your port before the end of this month. Please find enclosed herewith our shipping advice.

We expect you do not cancel the contract in consideration of our long-term cooperation and trust this unavoidable occasion will not influence you unfavorably in the matter of future orders.

Yours sincerely,
[Signature]
Encl.

Specimen 7
Complaint about Short Weight

Sept. 25, 2014

Dear Sir,

<u>Our Order No.073</u>

Please refer to our Order No. 073 in connection with the anthracite coal which was shipped per S.S. "Dahua" and discharged at NIIGATA, Japan.

On its arrival at the destination, the shipment was found of short weight.

We now lodge claims with you as follows:

Claim number	Claim for	Amount
50	short weight	USD 153,500.00

Please find enclosed herewith a copy of Inspection Certificate No. 0723 with our statement of claims, which amounts to USD153,500.00.

We are looking forward to a satisfactory conclusion of the matter.

Yours sincerely,
[Signature]
Encl.

Specimen 8
Reply

Oct. 15, 2014

Dear Sir,

<u>Your Order No. 073</u>

With reference to your letter of Sept 25, 2014, a claim has been lodged for a short delivery. We feel deeply regretful over the unfortunate case.

While we are regretful for this unfortunate situation, we must point out that the anthracite coal underwent physical weighing by independent surveyors and superintendent of shipping company at our end. The Guangzhou Commodity Inspection Bureau had also carefully inspected the goods before they were shipped as evidence by their certificate now in your possession. We don't think we should be responsible for the shortage. It must be due to pilferage or some other reasons while the goods were in transit under such circumstances.

We therefore suggest you make a claim immediately against the Insurance Company. If you will send us the documents which can show exactly the shortage of the shipment having reached you, we will take up the matter for you with a view to recovering the shortage in weight from the Insurance Company.

We are looking forward to your soon reply.

Yours sincerely,
[Signature]

Specimen 9
Complaint of Unsatisfactorily Packed Goods

May 15, 2014

Dear Sir,

We have to regretfully inform you that the Cotton Goods under our Order No.074 and shipped per S.S."Mayflower" arrived in such an unsatisfactory condition that we cannot but lodge a complaint against you. Upon careful examination, it is found that nearly 10% of the packages broken, which is obviously attributed to the improper packing. As such, our only recourse and solution was to have them repacked before delivering to our customers, which inevitably resulted in extra expenses amounting to £5650. We expect compensation from you for this, and should like to take this opportunity to suggest that special care be taken in your future deliveries as prospective customers are apt to misjudge the quality of your goods by the faulty packing.

Yours faithfully,
[Signature]

Specimen 10
Reply

Dear Sir,

　　With reference to your letter dated May 15, 2014 and are very sorry to note your complaint regarding the Cotton Goods delivered to you by S.S."Mayflower". We can assure you, however, that the goods in question were in perfect order when they left here, hence the damage complained of must have occurred in transit. In such circumstances, we are apparently not liable for the damage and would advise you to claim on the shipping company who should be held responsible.

　　In any case, we deeply regret to learn from you about this unfortunate incident and should it be necessary we shall be pleased to take the matter up on your behalf with the shipping company concerned.

Yours faithfully,
[Signature]

Specimen 11
Reply

Dear Sir,

　　I am very sorry you did not accept the eight 6-hp gasoline engines you wanted, and I guess both of us should share the equal blame.

　　Your order (photocopy enclosed) lists the 7.5-hp gasoline engine along with its stock number, yet the price indicated is for the 6-hp gasoline engines. Since you've regularly ordered the 7.5, we assumed that this one was what you really wanted, and we went ahead and shipped it. We should have checked with you, and I'm sorry we didn't.

　　We will, of course, ship the eight 6-hp motors immediately. Do you think you might sell the 7.5s? If so, you may wish to keep them a while, and if they don't move, you can return them to us. In any event we'll pay all shipping charges.

　　I'm delighted you're having such a good season with the gasoline engines. We'll be ready for your next order and will definitely avoid the similar mistakes.

Yours Sincerely,
[Signature]

5. Writing Templates

Complaint

Dear Sir,

　　We should like to invite/draw/call your attention to ＿＿＿＿ (goods) shipped by the ＿＿＿＿＿ (ship name) on ＿＿＿＿ (date). We regret to inform you that ＿＿＿＿ of the cases of your consignment arrived in badly damaged condition.

In support of our claim, we are sending you a Survey Report issued by _____. We are now in a very awkward situation, because our customers, who have been very pressing on the delivery, are becoming impatient to take delivery of the goods. We have to ask for compensation of _____ to cover the loss incurred as a result of the damaged goods concerned

We hope that you will immediately take this matter into your careful consideration and favor us with a prompt solution by return call.

Yours faithfully,
[Signature]

Reply (Claim Accepted)

Dear Sir,

Sub:_____

With reference to your letter dated _____ informing us of the mistake in our shipment to you on _____, we feel grateful for your straightforwardness in pointing out _____ and send you hereby our sincere apologies.

We have done careful investigation of the matter and found your claim perfectly justified. We shall remit to you an amount of _____ in compensation for the loss arising therefrom. Please be assured that such a mistake will not take place again in the future.

We apologize for the trouble caused you by the mistake and wish to assure you that care will be taken in the execution of your further orders.

Yours sincerely,
[Signature]

Reply (Claim Rejected)

Dear Sir,

With reference to your letter dated _____, in which you remind us of _____ package(s) having been damaged came as a great shock to us.

I am very sorry that we are unable to accept your claim because the package(s), when being loaded, left nothing to be desired. The damage was due to the rough handling by the shipping company. You should lodge a claim against them for the recovery of the loss.

At any rate, we deeply regret to learn from you about the unfortunate situation and should it be necessary we shall be pleased to take this matter up on your behalf with the shipping company involved.

Yours sincerely,
[Signature]

6. Key Words and Expressions

(1) discharge　卸货

(2) lodge　提出

(3) claim　索赔

(4) transit　运输

(5) at any rate　无论如何

(6) take the matter up　处理此事

(7) on one's behalf　代表……

(8) in compensation for the loss arising from...　补偿因……造成的损失

(9) lodge a claim on ... for recovery of the loss　向……提出要求赔偿损失的索赔

7. Useful Sentence Patterns

Complaints about Quality

(1) When unpacking the case, we found the color unsatisfactory. 开箱后，我们发现颜色不符合要求。

(2) On careful examination we found that the goods delivered do not agree with the original samples. 经过认真检查，我们发现所交付的货物与原样品不相符。

(3) Upon examining the goods, we discovered to our surprise that they were altogether inferior in quality to the samples on which basis we placed the order. 经过对货物的检查，惊讶地发现货物的质量与我们下订单时所依据的样品质量不相符。

(4) The quality of this consignment is far from being satisfactory. 该货物的质量与要求相差甚远。

(5) We regret to inform you that your last shipment is not up to your usual standard. 我们遗憾地通知你方，上一批货不符合你方通常的质量标准。

(6) On examination, we have found that the quality of the products is too inferior to meet the requirement at our local market. 经检查，我们发现产品的质量太差，不能满足当地的市场要求。

(7) Although the quality of these goods is not up to our usual lines, we are prepared to accept them if you will reduce the price, say, by... 虽然这些货物的质量不符合我们的常规标准要求，但是如果你们能够降低价格，比如说……我们愿意接受这批货物。

(8) We have to ask a compensation to cover the loss incurred as a result of the inferior quality of the goods concerned. 我们不得不要求对这批货物质量差而造成的损失给予补偿。

Complaints about Shortage

(1) In checking the contents against your enclosed invoice, it was found that several items were missing. 对照你方所附的发票进行了检查，发现好几项货物缺失。

(2) On checking the goods received, we find that several items on your invoice have not been included; we enclose a list of the missing articles for your inspection. 在检查了所

收到的货物之后，发现你方发票中所列的货物有几项缺失；附上一份缺失货物清单供你方核查。

(3) While thanking you for the promptness with which you executed the order, we have to point out that 5 cases are missing. 谢谢你方快速供货，但我们必须指出缺失了5箱货物。

(4) After inspection of the shipment, we found that it was 8 boxes short. 经过检查，发现短供了8箱货物。

(5) We very much regret to point out that a shortage in weight of 500 pounds was noticed when the food arrived. 非常遗憾地指出，食品到货后，发现短缺500磅重的货物。

(6) Please take up the matter immediately and send us the goods to meet the shortage as soon as possible. 请抓紧处理此事，并尽快补发短供的货物。

Complaints about Delay

(1) We have to inform you that the mobile phone units we ordered from you last month have not arrived here, nor we heard anything from you concerning the consignment. 我们必须通知你方，上个月从你方订购的手机仍未到货，也没有收到你方有关该批货物的任何信息。

(2) This delay will surely cause us a loss of business, so we must have these goods by the end of September. 该延期肯定会造成我方生意上的损失，因此9月底前，我们必须要拿到这些货物。

(3) The goods we ordered from you on July 4 have not been received. 我方7月4日从你方所订购的货物仍未收到。

(4) We have lost considerable business on account of your delay in shipment. 因为你方的延期交货，我方已经损失了大量的生意。

(5) The demand for these goods is seasonal, we, therefore, urge you to do everything possible to hasten the dispatch. 这批货属于季节性的货物，因此，我方敦促你方尽一切努力尽快发货。

(6) As our clients are pressing us for prompt shipment, we must accordingly insist on your sending them by air. 由于我们的客户催促我方迅速交货，因此我方必须坚持要你方空运。

(7) If you cannot deliver the goods within ten days, we'll reluctantly turn this matter to our attorney. 如果你方在10天之内仍不能交货，我方只好将此事交由我方的律师处理。

(8) Unless your consignment reaches us no later than July 4, we will cancel our order. 我方必须在7月4日之前收到货物，否则我方将取消订单。

Complaints about Poor Packing

(1) We regret to inform you that the goods were badly damaged, because the packing inside the case was too loose (insufficient). 我们非常遗憾地通知你方，由于箱内货物装填太松散（不充分），致使货物严重受损。

(2) We regret that we have to complain about the way in which the consignment just received had been packed. 很遗憾，我方不得不对刚收到的货物的包装方式进行投诉。

(3) We have examined the goods duly received and found the packing was wet through. 我方已充分地检查了所收到的货物，发现包装全部湿透。

(4) A careful examination indicated that the broken bags were due to improper packing for which the suppliers are definitely responsible. 经过仔细检查，发现破损的箱子完全是因为包装不当所致，供货方理应对此承担责任。

(5) We hope you will pack the goods of our next order more carefully. 我们希望你方能够认真地包装我方的下一批货物。

Accepting Claims

(1) With mutual efforts, this case has been settled amicably and we shall remit to you an amount of USD1000 in compensation for the loss rising there from. 通过双方的努力，本案已得到友好解决，我方将向贵方汇去1000美元，以补偿由此造成的损失。

(2) Your proposal is reasonable, we can accept it. 你的建议是合理的，我方可以接受。

(3) We regret to find that the goods have been wrongly shipped by the mistake on the part of our shipping clerk. 我们遗憾地发现，由于我方运务员的失误而误发了货物。

Rejecting Claims

(1) The shortage you raised might have occurred in the course of transit, and that is a matter over which we can exercise no control. 你方提出的短货问题可能是在运输过程中造成的，这是我方所无法控制的。

(2) The damage was due to the rough handling by the shipping company, you should lodge a claim on them for recovery of the loss. 货损是由于船运公司的野蛮搬运造成的，你方应当向他们提出索赔，要求赔偿损失。

(3) We regret that we cannot entertain your claim. 很遗憾，我方无法接受你方的索赔。

(4) We can hardly be expected to accept your claim after a lapse of over one month. 时间已经过去一个多月，我方已无法接受你方提出的索赔。

8. Exercises

Exercise 13-1

Direction: Rearrange the following information into a complaint letter about inferior quality.

(1) We should like to draw your attention to the defective sewing machine.

(2) Please inform us when we can expect delivery of a replacement for the machine under order No.20 on August 2nd, 2013.

(3) The machine is now out of order again. Although it is still on a one-year warranty, we really don't want to have it repaired again and again. Instead, we want you to replace it

with a new one.

(4) But by the end of June 2014, the machine has broken down four times. The breakdown has led to the loss of more than 15 days' production time while we waited for your local agents' maintenance.

(5) Thanks for your cooperation.

(6) We bought this machine on the basis of your company's reputation for quality and service. We believe that both of us will neither expect nor permit the interruptions caused by repeated breakdowns.

Exercise 13-2

Direction: Put the following sentences into English.

(1) 我们在检验时发现近15%的包装破裂，显然是由于包装不良所致。

(2) 遗憾的是货物不能令人满意，质量太差无法达到市场的要求。

(3) 经中国商检局检验后发现，贵方出运的货物短重。对此，我方非常遗憾。

(4) 很明显，货物损坏是由于野蛮装卸造成的，请将此问题向保险公司提出。

(5) 很明显，这两箱货的严重损坏是在运输途中发生的，这是一个超出我们控制能力的问题。

Exercise 13-3

Direction: Write a reply letter according to the following information.

You have received a letter from one of your clients. He complained that 15 cases of the goods were in bad condition. After checking up, you found the shipping company should be responsible for the consequence.

9. Supplementary Reading

Tips for Delivering Customer Service

· Have a clear idea about how to manage unhappy customers

Have a clear idea about how your company manages unhappy customers. This way you can assure your agents that processes are being managed to avoid them having to deal with the same issues coming up again and again. This should also improve overall customer satisfaction as recurring issues will be addressed, preventing future customers from encountering the same problems.

· Always share the outputs of customer satisfaction surveys

Always share the outputs from any customer satisfaction surveys with every member of staff in the business. This will help to remind agents that their efforts are recognized, as well as steer them back in the right direction if they go off course.

· Equip your agents with EQ skills

We have now led our clients away from "transactional" and scripted customer service, and are seeing great results on developing agents' EQ (Emotional Quotient) skills. This helps agents in a short time to build early trust and rapport, stop weak words and phrases and ask powerful questions to get the full picture. It is especially useful for angry customers, and for passive customers, too.

· Encourage your agents to take ownership of problems

We encourage our operators to take ownership of problems and spend time dealing with the customer, rather than escalating or passing over the problem. This gives advisors a real sense of pride in their job and means they are taking their own action and really shows excellent customer service.

· Monitor the number of call-backs to ensure agents get it right first time

We analyze whether customers have to call back—if we can allow agents to get it right first time, the extra few minutes that might take means that the customer has had a resolution on the first attempt, so saves cost in the long run!

· Develop your agents and empower them with knowledge

Rewarding advisors with "time off the phones" gives a negative impression of the day-to-day work they do. Instead, reward them with individual projects which may or may not require calls. This aids advisor development, empowers them and gives them further knowledge of the business.

· Learn from your mistakes and always keep the customer informed

We aim to get it right first time every time. It doesn't always work, but when it doesn't, we take that as an opportunity to develop ourselves, so that we get it right from that point onwards. ALWAYS keep the customer up to date so they don't become frustrated by not knowing what's going on in the background.

· Link PR departments closely to Customer Service departments

Link your PR departments（公共关系部）closely to your Customer Service departments to ensure that you give customer service that differentiates you from the market and is aligned with the business's core values. Our customer service department "feels" like our brand. We have the same terminology, tone and behaviors aligned throughout our organization.

· Regularly carry out customer satisfaction surveys

Regularly carry out customer satisfaction surveys to ensure you are doing the best for your customers. Include the Net Promoter Score to act as a benchmark as to how you are scoring in comparison to the market and your competitors.

· Log all interactions in a customer database

Use a good CRM system（客户关系管理系统）to log any communication so everyone in the team can get to know your customers. This will make the customer feel you have a personal relationship. Taking the time to build personal and professional relationships will take you a long way and give you more loyal customers.

· Understand the root cause to prevent situations recurring

Make sure that data taken from customer services is fed back for root cause analysis to prevent situations recurring, and is also passed on to sales and development teams.

Chapter 14
Agency
代理

1. Learning Objectives

By the end of this chapter, you will be able to do the following:

· Get to know the key words and expressions related to agency.

· Have a general picture of agency.

· Know the useful sentence patterns in establishment of agency.

· Know how to write request and reply letters in respect of agency.

2. Case Study

Are you planning to sell your products abroad or looking for some information on what agents can do for you? Or if you are a licensed agent looking to promote your business, how would you establish an agency relationship with your ideal partners?

Or if you are an exporter of foodstuffs and you want to market your goods in India, when you read the following NOTICE on the Internet or newspaper, how will you establish your relationship with him?

Agency Wanted

We are looking for the distributorship of food products. We have empty space and good sales network. Prepared to invest Rs.5 lakhs initially and assure sales of Rs.10 lakhs. Interested companies can contact us with their product list and offer.

---

3. Introduction

Agency is defined in Longman Dictionary as a business that makes its money esp. by bring people into touch with others or the products of others, and agent as a person whose job is to represent another person, a company, etc. esp. one who brings people into touch with others or deals with the business affairs of a person or company. The establishment of Agency can help businesses to reduce their operation risks.

An agent is always authorized to act on behalf of another (called the principal) to create legal relations with a third party. Succinctly, it may be referred to as the equal relationship between a principal and an agent whereby the principal authorizes the agent to work under his or her control and on his or her behalf. The agent is, thus, required to negotiate on behalf of the principal or bring him or her and third parties into contractual relationship. So agents or sales representatives are an important part of manufacturers' and exporters' success. Exporters or manufacturers may appoint an agent to act on their behalf to collect information about the target market and sell commodities.

There are generally a few types of agents: general agents, sole agents and special agents. General agents hold a more limited authority to conduct a series of transactions over a continuous period of time and act under some instructions from his principals to sell or buy goods on the most favorable terms; Sole agents act for one principal with an exclusive agency right to sell certain commodities on a commission basis in certain area or region under an agreement or contract; and special agents are authorized to conduct either only a single transaction or a specified series of transactions over a limited period of time.

Agents spend much of their time traveling to and visiting with prospective buyers and current clients. During a sales call, they discuss the client's needs and suggest how their merchandise or services can meet those needs. They may show samples or catalogs that describe items their company stocks and inform customers about prices, availability, and ways in which their products can save money and boost productivity. Because a vast number of manufacturers and wholesalers sell similar products, sales representatives must emphasize any unique qualities of their products and services.

Manufacturers' agents or representatives might sell several complementary products made by different manufacturers and, thus, take a broad approach to their customers' business. Sales representatives may help install new equipment and train employees in its use. They also take orders and resolve any problems with or complaints about the merchandise.

An agent who acts within the scope of authority conferred by his or her principal binds the principal in the obligations he or she creates against third parties.

After the establishment of agency relationship between the principal and his agent, they should undertake reciprocating liabilities and duties.

Liability of Agent to Third Party

If the agent has actual or apparent authority, the agent will not be liable for acts performed within the scope of such authority, so long as the relationship of the agency and the identity of the principal have been disclosed. When the agency is undisclosed or partially disclosed, however, both the agent and the principal are liable. Where the principal is not bound because the agent has no actual or apparent authority, the purported agent is liable to the third party for breach of the implied warranty of authority.

Liability of Agent to Principal

If the agent has acted without actual authority, but the principal is nevertheless bound because the agent had apparent authority, the agent is liable to indemnify the principal for any resulting loss or damage.

Liability of Principal to Agent

If the agent has acted within the scope of the actual authority given, the principal must indemnify the agent for payments made during the course of the relationship whether the expenditure was expressly authorized or merely necessary in promoting the principal's business.

Duties

The principal must make a full disclosure of all information relevant to the transactions that the agent is authorized to negotiate.

In return, the agent should do the following duties:

- Undertake the tasks specified by the terms of the agency.
- Discharge his duties with care and due diligence.
- Not accept any new obligations that are inconsistent with the duties owed to the principal.
- Not represent the interests of more than one principal, conflicting or potentially conflicting, unless after full disclosure and consent of the principal.
- Not usurp an opportunity from the principal by taking it for himself or passing it on to a third party.

4. Specimen Letters

Specimen 1
Request for Marketing Agency

> Dear Sir,
>
> We have learned from *Qianjiang Evening News* that you are looking for a reliable firm with good connection in the foodstuff trade to represent you in India.
>
> Having had experience in marketing foodstuffs, we are familiar with customers' needs and are confident we would develop a good market for you in India. We have large and well-equipped showrooms and an experienced staff of sales representatives who could promote your business.
>
> We would be very pleased to learn that you are interested in our proposal and on what terms you would be willing to conclude an agency agreement.
>
> As for our credit standing, we suggest you refer to the following bank:
>
> The State Bank of India, Please call SBI's 24X7 helpline through Toll free 1800 11 2211, 1800 425 3800 or Toll number 080-26599990
>
> We are looking forward to your early reply.
>
> Yours faithfully,
> [Signature]

Specimen 2
Reply

Dear Sir,

We have carefully considered your letter dated Nov. 10 and would like to go further into your proposal for an agency in India. In view of your connections throughout that trade in India, we feel there is a lot you could do to expand our business there.

Our final decision would depend on your terms and conditions. As Mr. Gurrinder Singh Khanna from your firm will visit China in the next few days, we think it would be better to discuss this matter with him directly. Therefore, please let us know when we may expect Mr. Gurrinder Singh Khanna to call.

Yours faithfully,
[Signature]

Specimen 3
Identify an Agent

Dear Sir,

Our company manufactures a range of electronic devices that are used successfully by companies in over 30 countries and regions.

We are thinking to expand our business to new markets and we would appreciate your assistance. Particularly, we would like to identify the best agents who are presently serving the electronic industry in your region.

We are looking for firms that are conducting their business in a truly professional manner. They must have a comprehensive understanding of all the features of the lines they represent.

We would be very grateful if could take a few moments to send us the names of four or five companies that can match our requirements. We will then contact them to find the possibility of establishing a mutually acceptable business relationship.

Please kindly find enclosed herewith a copy of our product catalogue and specifications.

Thank you very much for your time and consideration in this matter.

Yours faithfully,
[Signature]

Specimen 4
Importer Asks for Sole Agency

Dear Sir,

We visited Guangzhou Fair recently held in China and were impressed by the high quality, attractive design and reasonable price of your digital printers. We have seen your full catalogue and are convinced that there is here in Karachi a promising market for your products. If you are not already represented here, we should be very interested in acting as your sole agent.

As leading importer and distributor of more than twenty years' standing in the printer trade we have a good knowledge of the Karachi market and, through our sales, good contacts with the leading retailers. We handle several other agencies, but in non-competing lines and, if our proposal interests you, we can supply first-class references from manufacturers in Europe.

We strongly believe that an agency for marketing your products in Karachi would be of considerable benefit to both of us and look forward to learning that your are interested in our proposal.

Yours faithfully,
[Signature]

Specimen 5
Appoint Agent

Dear Sir,

Further to our fax of Nov. 10 and following our discussion with Mr. Gurrinder Singh Khanna when he called on the 20th, we are quite willing to offer you an appointment on a del credere basis of 8% commission on the net value of all orders received through you, provided you are willing to lodge adequate security with our bankers here.

If security is deposited we shall be ready to protect your interests by entering into a formal agreement giving you the sole agency for a period of three years.

We shall be pleased to learn that you are willing to accept the agency on these terms.

Yours faithfully,
[Signature]

Specimen 6
Exporter Offers the Agency Terms and Conditions

Dear Sir,

We are pleased to learn from your fax dated July 20th that you are willing to act as our agent for marketing our digital printers in Karachi.

We believe you have good connections throughout the trade, and it seems to us a favorable opportunity to further develop our business in Pakistan.

We set out the main terms below to be covered in the agency agreement and should like you to confirm them before drafting the formal agreement.

1. The agency will be a sole agency for marketing our digital printers in Pakistan.

2. The agency will operate from August 20th, 2015 for a period of three years, subject to renewal.

3. All customers' orders will be sent to us immediately for prompt supply.

4. A commission of 8%, based on FOB values of all goods shipped to Karachi, whether on orders placed through you or not, payable at the end of each quarterly period.

5. Customers shall settle their accounts with us directly, and we shall send you a statement at the end of each month of all payments received by us. We shall be pleased if you will kindly confirm these terms. We will then arrange for a formal agreement to be drafted and

copies sent to you for signature.

Yours faithfully,
[Signature]

Specimen 7
Decline a Request for Sole Agency

Dear Sir,

We thank you for your letter dated Oct. 20th, 2014, offering your service as our agent in your region.

In reply, we would like to open an account with you at first as principal to principal. If, after the lapse of twelve months of business with you, our mutually profitable business relations have been established, we feel sure that an agency contract will be concluded on the following terms and conditions:

- Price: All prices shall be quoted on FOB Shanghai in US dollars.
- Commission: 5% of our invoice amount for each shipment shall be remitted to you as your commission only after the indentor's account has been fully settled.
- Payment: The terms of D/P at sight may be acceptable, through the payment under an Irrevocable and Confirmed L/C is preferable. The business on D/P terms shall be done if the amount does not exceed $1 000 or its equivalent.

We enclose price list covering all the products you are interested in and look forward to hearing from you soon.

Yours faithfully,
[Signature]

5. Writing Templates

Request for Marketing Agency

Dear Sir,

We have learned from _____ that you are looking for a reliable firm with good connection in the _____ trade to represent you in _____.

Having had experience in marketing _____, we are familiar with customers' needs and are confident we would develop a good market for you in _____. We have large and well-equipped showrooms and an experienced staff of sales representatives who could promote your business.

We would be very pleased to learn that you are interested in our proposal and on what terms you would be willing to conclude an agency agreement.

As for our credit standing, we suggest you refer to the following bank:

_____

We are looking forward to your early reply.

Yours faithfully,
[Signature]

Reply

Dear Sir,

    We have carefully considered your letter dated _____ and should like to go further into your proposal for an agency in _____. In view of your connections throughout that trade in _____, we feel there is a lot you could do to expand our business in _____.

    Our final decision would depend on your terms and conditions. As Mr. _____ from your firm will visit China in the next few days, we think it would be better to discuss this matter with him directly. Therefore, please let us know when we may expect Mr. _____ to call?

Yours faithfully,
[Signature]

Appoint Agent

Dear Sir,

    Further to our fax of _____ and following our discussion with Mr. _____ from your company when he called on the _____, we are quite willing to offer you an appointment on a del credere basis of _____% commission on the net value of all orders received through you, provided you are willing to lodge adequate security with our bankers here.

    If security is deposited we shall be ready to protect your interests by entering into a formal agreement giving you the sole agency for a period of _____.

    We shall be pleased to learn that you are willing to accept the agency on these terms.

Yours faithfully,
[Signature]

Decline a Request for Sole Agency

Dear Sir,

    We thank you for your letter dated _____, offering your service as our agent in your region.

    In reply, we would like to open an account with you at first as principal to principal. If, after the lapse of _____ months of business with you, our mutually profitable business relations have been established, we feel sure that an agency contract will be concluded on the following terms and conditions:

    Price: All prices shall be quoted on _____ in US dollars.

    Commission: _____% of our invoice amount for each shipment shall be _____.

    Payment: _____.

    We enclose price list covering all the products you are interested in and look forward to hearing from you soon.

Yours faithfully,
[Signature]

6. Key Words and Expressions

(1) agency　代理

(2) agent　代理商

(3) principal　委托人

(4) general agent　总代理人

(5) special agent　特定代理人

(6) sole agent　总代理，独家代理

(7) undertaking　承诺

(8) irrevocable and confirmed L/C　不可撤销的保兑的信用证

(9) FOB：Free on Board　船上交货价，离岸价

(10) D/P: Documents against Payment　付款交单

(11) at sight　即期，见票即付

(12) commission　佣金

(13) Note: Del Credere Agent　信用担保代理人

7. Useful Sentence Patterns

(1) We request/ask to be the sole agent for your ... in our territory. 我们要求成为贵司……在我方所在地的独家代理商。

(2) We would like to offer our service in the sale of your ... 我们愿意为销售贵方的……（产品）做出贡献。

(3) Thank you for your proposal of acting as our agent. 谢谢你方提出作为我方代理人的建议。

(4) We thank you for your letter dated ... offering your service as our agent in your region. 谢谢你方××号关于作为我方在你方所在地代理的来信。

(5) We shall be very much pleased to act as your sole agent in ... for your products. 我们非常乐意作为贵方在……（地区）的独家代理，销售贵方的产品。

(6) We have the ability to work as your sole agent because we have wide connections here. 我们有能力担当贵方的独家代理，因为我们在本地有广泛的人脉关系。

(7) If we have the honor to act as your sole agent in the sale of ... in our territory, we surely will try our best to expend our mutual trade. 如果我们有幸能成为贵方在本地区的独家代理，销售×××（产品），我们一定会尽力拓展我们双方的贸易。

(8) After careful and due consideration to your proposals and looking into your credit standing, we are ready to appoint you as our sole agent in the region. 经过对你方的提议及对你方资信的调查后，我们准备委托你方作为我们在该区域的独家代理。

(9) With your excellent connections, we believe it will be possible to promote the sale of our products in your region, and we hope your acting as our agent will be to our mutual benefit. 借助你方良好的人脉关系，我们相信在你方所在地区促销我们的产品是可能的，我们希望你方作为我方的代理实现我们双方的互惠互利。

(10) But we think it would be better to wait until business between us has developed to our mutual satisfaction. 但是我们认为最好先等一等，待我们之间的业务发展达到双方都满意为止。

(11) Referring to your request to act as our sole agent for … we may consider this matter seriously when business between us has been further extended. 有关你方希望作为我方××的独家代理一事，待我们双方之间的业务进一步发展之后，我方会认真考虑。

8. Exercises

Exercise 14-1

Direction: Put the following sentences into English.

(1) 有关独家代理之事，我方暂不予以考虑。一旦交易发展到能令我们双方均满意时，我们会立即考虑此事。

(2) 希望你方在了解我们的销售能力之后，会考虑给我们数码相机的独家经销权。

(3) 在调查了你们的业务情况之后，经过考虑你方的提议，我们决定根据以下条款委托你方在你方所提议的地区作为我们的独家代理。

(4) 你方9月20日有关建议担任家用亚麻制品独家代理的来信收悉。

(5) 奉上贵方感兴趣的所有产品价目单，盼尽快回复。

Exercise 14-2

Direction: Write a letter based upon the following particulars.

(1) S.H. Saifuddin Trading Co. is a Pakistani company, located at 103, A.H. Chamber, Shahrah-E-Liaquat, Karachi, Pakistan.

(2) Presently, S.H. Saifuddin Trading Co. is a sole agent specially for electrical household appliances.

(3)They have been doing business with Matsushita Electric Industrial Co., Japan for six years to mutual satisfaction.

(4) They give Matsushita Electric Industrial Co., Japan for references.

(5) They want to be a sole agent of Hangzhou Import and Export Co. for household digital products.

9. Supplementary Reading

Anatomy of an Agency Relationship

One of the most common legal relationships in business is that of agency. With many high-tech companies marketing, selling and licensing their products through third party channels of distribution, such as distributors, resellers and independent sales representatives, the contractual arrangement between these various entities becomes very critical and the agreement between the parties must be very clear, detailed and unambiguous.

The Agency Relationship

The two common agency relationships in business are: (1) employer/employee and (2) company and its third party channels for distributing product—the "Agent". When a third party deals with a company employee or a company third party (non-employee) agent, he is in fact dealing with the company itself as the principal. Agents have the legal power to commit the company to definite acts with respect to third parties and the company then is legally bound by these acts. An agency relationship encompasses two contracts; the contract of agency between the company and the agent and the contract which the agent makes with the third party for, and on behalf of, the company.

Classification of Agents

Agents are generally classified in terms of the extent of the business to be transacted by them as follows:

General Agents—are authorized by the principal to transact all of the affairs in connection with a particular kind of business or trade or to transact all of the company's business, these agents are generally employees of the company.

Special Agents—are authorized by the principal to transact a definite business affair or to do a specific act, these agents are generally third parties hired by the company under an agreement.

An agency relationship is legally created as follows:

· Authorization by Appointment

The usual method of creating an agency relationship is by express authorization; that is, a person is appointed to act for and on behalf of another. No particular form of language is necessary for the appointment of an agent. It is sufficient that the words used indicate that one person wishes another to represent him. In many instances, the authorization of the agent could be oral, or done by a Board of Directors Resolution. In addition to an agents express authority, an agent also has what is called "incidental/customary" authority to perform any act reasonably necessary to execute the express authority given to him and to do any act which, according to the custom of the trade, usually accompanies the transaction for which he is authorized to act as agent. Here is where many issues can arise if the agreement between the company and the channel partner is not clear regarding the partner's authority and limitations.

· Authorization by Principal's Conduct

Authorization by Principal's Conduct is also legally referred to as "Agency of Estoppel". An agent has apparent authority when the principal, by his words or conduct, reasonably leads a third party to believe that such a person has the authority to bind the principal. Any conduct, including words that gives the agent reason to believe the principal consents to his acting as agent is sufficient to create an agency. If a person knowingly and without objection permits another to act as his agent, the law will find in this conduct an expression of authorization to the agent, and the principal will not be permitted to deny that the agent was in fact authorized. In other words, the principal is "estopped" from denying the agency, thus protecting the third party who dealt with the agent in good faith.

Generally the law of agency is applicable in the same manner to the United States Government and state purchasing agencies as in the private sector. It should be noted, however, government contracting officers and state purchasing officers derive their power from the statutes which created their organizations. In most cases, the authority and limits of authority granted to federal and state contracting officers is expressly defined by these statutes. The important exception to this general statement, however, is the law dealing with apparent authority. Corporations, as principals, are bound to the extent of the power they have apparently given their agents, while the United States Government is bound only to the extent of the power it has actually or expressly given its agents, and unauthorized acts of such agents does not stop the Government from asserting their invalidity. Therefore, employees (agents) of the US Government possess only actual authority which includes both express and implied powers. It should also be noted that, while the scope of a contracting officer's authority is commonly limited by the statute conferring the authority, it is not unusual to find that the authority delegated may also be limited by regulations promulgated pursuant to statutes. These regulatory restrictions on the agents authority when published in the Federal Register are binding in transactions even though the other party did not have actual knowledge of the regulations. Therefore, he who deals with an agent of the government must look to his authority, which will not be presumed but must be established. He cannot rely upon the scope of dealing or apparent authority as in the case of a private agent. However, when the Government deals with employees (agents) of bidders or contractors, the Government may rely upon the apparent authority as well as the actual authority of the employee representing the contractor.

In summary, the law of agency is the consensual relationship between two parties (Principal-Agent) by virtue of which one of them is to act for and on behalf of the other. Business need to be aware of these relationships to ensure that their employees and agents do not commit the company to an unauthorized act which will legally and financially bind the company.

Chapter 15
Trade Show
会展

1. Learning Objectives

By the end of this chapter, you will be able to do the following:

· Acquire general knowledge about trade show.

· Learn how to write invitation and reply letters for participating in the trade shows.

· Learn to use the right words, expressions and sentence patterns in writing such letters.

2. Case Study

As a manufacturer or an exporter, when you read the following information or when you receive an invitation from the following company for attending the trade fair for construction materials, what actions will you take and how will you deal with such a case?

印度尼西亚雅加达国际建材展览会
展会时间：2015-06-03至2015-06-07
主办单位：印度尼西亚DEBINDO公司
举办周期：一年一届
首届举办：2002年
展会行业：建材/石材/照明/暖通—建材
举办地点：亚洲—印度尼西亚—雅加达
举办展馆：印尼雅加达国际会议中心
展会规模：10000~20000平方米
媒体宣传：www.showguide.cn

3. Introduction

Trade show has been increasingly becoming a rising industry, which integrates business, tourism and information, etc., into a whole. In order to introduce our trade shows to the world and bring the well-known world trade shows into our life, the employees shall have to acquire strong professional knowledge in this field.

Successful preparation will make the trade show a success, so when going to participate in a trade show, one must get to know something essential for the exhibition like trade show banner stands, conference rooms, portable flooring, trade show signs, truss systems, trade show exhibit counters, trade show display accessories, carrying case, trade show booth lights, literature rack, trade show displays, etc.

Trade Show Banner Stands are the perfect solution for fast and easy setup. It can be assembled just about anywhere within few seconds. Designed in a compact and lightweight model, it is easy to travel with, carry, and ship. With a dynamic graphic, trade show banner is an exceptional way to display. The smooth design leaves a lasting impression.

Conference Rooms are the heart of exhibit in any trade shows. It contains walls with panels to create a series of semi-private areas, which is used for demonstrations. Fabric graphics add to the impact on the visitors' mind. It is portable and is framed and deframed in seconds.

Portable Flooring is a rollable temporary flooring and pathway system providing access, surface protection and decorative enhancement to the trade shows. It snaps together on all sides. It is easy to install and can be stored and transported in sheets or rolled up form. It has drainage and ventilation holes to let the air, water and light flow.

Trade Show Signs are exciting way to make products, brands or logos make highly visible in many unique ways. It can be a hanging or standing on the floor or else fixed on the walls. It is lightweight, flexible, easy and quick to install. It creates a dynamic environment with its eye-catching appearance.

Truss Systems are functional and decorative element of any trade show booth. It is used to display graphics, products or projected images. Suspended monitors or lightings make a feel of wider booth space. It is a sure way of drawing attention to the booth. It gives a bold and provocative appearance to the design or pattern of the booth.

Trade Show Exhibit Counters are portable trade show cabinetry designed for easy setup, quick take-downs and effortless transporting. These podiums and counters or workstations save time and gives maximum space out of minimum in displaying product like books, CDs and more.

Trade Show Display Accessories are most important elements for trade show. It fulfills the customized demand of the exhibitor to display the brand as well as the product in a perfect eye-catching way. The accessories are portable and can be utilized for more than one purpose. They are portable and easily transportable.

Carrying Case is a portable container usually made of molded plastic to carry all the display and graphic system of trade shows. It is tough and especially designed to withstand the worst shipping conditions. It has wheels for easy transportation and internal foam linings for safety storage of lights like halogen.

Trade Show Booth Lights are used to draw attention to one's exhibit. It spotlights on brand as well as the products. It can be optional halogen lights, which throws light in the booth or it can also be banner halogen light. Banner halogen light is specially designed to make the rectangular banner glow up, exhibiting the product, brand or logo more emphatically.

Literature Rack is a foldable stand with racks to exhibit books, brochures, or journals in a rack. It is easy to assemble and transport. It has pockets in a series from floor frame to the customized height. It is easy to use and in seconds it transforms the appearance of a trade shows display.

Trade Show Displays are the ultimate to create a polished, professional image for one's business. There are different types of displays to serve the required demand of the exhibitor. All are portable, innovative, easy to carry and with quick setups and take downs attachments.

Besides, to an organizer or participant, the communication is the most important point, which is critical to the success of a trade show, so to learn to write and communicate in English is becoming an essential skill for employees in the field of international trade show.

4. Specimen Letters

Invitation and Reply
Specimen 1

Dear Sir,

We are pleased to introduce ourselves as the Indian Subsidiary office of Messe Frankfurt GMBH, one of the world's largest international trade fair organizers. We have been handling all aspects of Indian participation in all our fairs worldwide (which includes a wide spectrum of fairs covering textiles, consumer goods, technical and lifestyle fairs) for many years now and have been successfully promoting export business from India thus.

The Indian fairs organized by us include the much popular Heimtextil India which in its 7th year has already established itself as one of the leading trade fairs in home textiles and accessories in Asia. As an established and valuable sourcing point, Heimtextil India is the meeting pointing for the world of home fashion. Located in Mumbai, the business capital of the world's fastest growing free-market democracy, this exclusively and professionally organized fair attracts exhibitors both from India as well as overseas. The last show in 2005 attracted 273 exhibitors from 11 nations and registered 11,789 visitors from 106 countries.

We are also happy to announce the arrival of the world-famous international apparel textiles fair, "Texworld India" in Mumbai, to be premiered on the same dates as Heimtextile India, i.e. Oct. 10–13, 2006 at Bombay Exhibition Center, Mumbai. Held parallel to Heimtextil India, these fairs will constitute the "Textile Days in India", complete with fashion shows, seminars and trend shows.

We are keen to explore the possibilities of working together with you in order to increase the overseas participation from your region in our fairs in India. Our Regional Director for Asia Pacific region, Ms. Shammi Nagpal will be traveling to Hong Kong, China on March 22 and will be happy to meet you and initiate talks for mutual business growth. Kindly let us know a convenient date and time for the meeting. Incase you would also be visiting Interstoff-Spring (March 22-24, Hong Kong), kindly let us know so that we can organize the meeting during the fair days.

We are looking forward to hearing from you soon!

Best regards,
[Signature]

Specimen 2

Dear Sir,

Thank you for your letter dated 07 February, 2006 regarding the trade fair Heimtextil India. As it is well known, India is a fast-growing market in the world now, so I am very glad to have such a good chance to participate in the popular fair in India.

By the way, I am also going to Hong Kong, China in March to visit the Interstoff Asia – Spring (March 22-24, Hong Kong, China), and will be glad to meet your regional director for Asia Pacific region, Ms. Shammi Nagpal for further talk.

Yours faithfully,
[Signature]

Specimen 3

Dear Sir,

GLEE Exhibition–18th-20th September 2015
National Exhibition Center, Birmingham, U.K.

We are the organizers of the above mentioned trade exhibition and would like to officially invite the following named person to attend:

Name: Ms. Zhang Hui
Sex: Female
Date of Birth: 27.06.1982
Passport/ID No. G12008660
Company: Taizhou Haishui Brass Industry Co., Ltd.

Would you kindly supply the above named representative with the necessary Visa to enable her to attend this trade fair entirely at her own expense from 15th September until 1st October 2015.

If you require further information then please do not hesitate to contact me on direct dial telephone number +44(0)208 277 5811 or facsimile number +44(0)208 277 5894.

Yours faithfully,
[Signature]

Specimen 4

Dear Sir,

We are pleased to invite as follows:
Zhejiang Broad International Convention and Exhibition Co., Ltd.
All travel expenses and medical insurance incurred by them will be paid by themselves. We would be most grateful if you could issue Single Entry Permit to them in order to attend the exhibition on time.

Herein below is the itinerary for the duration of their stay:
15 September 2015: Departure from Shanghai to London
16 September 2015: Departure from London to Birmingham
17 September 2015: Supervise booth decoration, preparatory work
18-20 September 2015: Attend "GLEE"
21 September 2015: Supervise packing of exhibits and move-out show venue
22-23 September 2015: Visit Local Market
24 September 2015: Departure from Birmingham to Shanghai

Thank you for your assistance in advance.

Yours faithfully,
[Signature]

Specimen 5
Write to Embassy for Visa

Dear Ladies and Gentlemen,

As per request, we kindly ask for your support by granting a business visa for the following person, who would like to participate in the international trade fair Heimtextil 2015, which will take place from 11 January to 14 January 2015 in Frankfurt am Main, Germany.

Name	Passport/ID No.	Date of Birth
Mr. Luo Jianduo	G03571200	24 Oct. 1978

The duration of stay of the mentioned person will be from 9 January to 18 January 2015. His recommended schedule during his stay in Germany would be as follows:

9 January 2015   Leave China to Germany
10 January 2015   Prepare for display
11-14 January 2015   Duration of exhibition
15-17 January 2015   Stands dismantling; deal with exhibits
18 January 2015   Back to China

Yours faithfully,
[Signature]

Specimen 6

Dear Sir,

The visa applicant is an autonomous entrepreneur in the area of textile manufacture employed by the company Yitong Handiwork Co., Ltd Zhejiang and intends to participate in the international trade fair Heimtextil 2015 in Frankfurt am Main, Germany, due to professional/business interests. His address is as follows:

Company name: Yitong Handiwork Co., Ltd. Zhejiang
Address: Pujiang Economic Development Zone, Zhejiang
Tel: 0086-579-54178337
Fax: 0086-579-54178336
E-mail address: Salesman@yt-craft.com

All expense of his journey to/from Germany as well as hotel expenses and health insurance will be borne by his employer.

Please note that we will not assume legal or financial responsibilities in connection with this business trip.

We would be pleased to welcome the above mentioned person as a trade fair exhibitor to the international trade fair Heimtextil 2015 in Frankfurt am Main.

With best regards,
[Signature]

Specimen 7
Invitation to Visit Exhibition Booth

Dear Sir,

Many thanks for your letter and enclosures of 4 September. We were very interested to hear that you are looking for a UK distributor for your teaching aids. We would like to invite you to visit our booth, No. 6, at next month's London Toy Fair, at Earl's court, which starts on 2 October. If you would like to set up an appointment during non-exhibit hall hours please call me. I can then arrange for our senior staff to be present at the meeting. We are looking forward to hearing from you.

Yours faithfully,
[Signature]

5. Writing Templates

Invitation
Sample 1

Dear _____,

We are pleased to introduce ourselves as the _____, one of the world's largest international trade fair organizers. We have been handling _____ in all our fairs worldwide for many years and have been successfully promoting export business from _____ thus.

The _____ fairs organized by us include the much popular _____ has already established itself as one of the leading trade fairs in _____. The last show in _____ (year) attracted _____ exhibitors from _____ nations and registered _____ visitors from _____ countries.

We are also happy to announce the arrival of the world-famous international _____ fair _____ (date) at _____.

We are keen to explore the possibilities of working together with you in order to increase the overseas participation from your region in our fairs in _____ (country).

We are looking forward to hearing from you soon!

Yours faithfully,
[Signature]

Sample 2

Dear _____,

_____ (Date and Name of Trade Fair)

We are the organizers of the above mentioned trade exhibition and would like to officially invite the following named persons to attend:

Name   _____
Sex   _____
Date of Birth   27.06.1982
Passport/ID No.   _____
Company   _____

Would you kindly supply the above named representative with the necessary visa to enable him/her to attend this trade fair entirely at his/her own expense from _____ (date) until _____ (date).

If you require further information then please do not hesitate to contact me on direct dial telephone number _____ or facsimile number _____.

Yours faithfully,
[Signature]

Write to Embassy for Visa
Sample 3

Dear _____,

We are pleased to invite as follows:

_____ (Company Name)

All travel expenses and medical insurance incurred by them will be paid by themselves. We would be most grateful if you could issue Single Entry Permit to them in order to attend the exhibition on time.

Herein below is the itinerary for the duration of their stay:

_____ (date): Departure from _____ (Place) to _____ (Place)

```
_____ (date):   Supervise booth decoration, preparatory work
_____ (date):   Attend _____
_____ (date):   Supervise packing of exhibits and move-out show venue
_____ (date):   Visit Local Market
_____ (date):   Departure from _____ (Place) back to _____ (Place)
```

Thank you for your assistance in advance.

Yours faithfully,
[Signature]

Sample 4

Dear _____,

As per request, we kindly ask for your support by granting a business visa for the following person, who would like to participate in the international trade fair _____, which will take place from _____ to _____ in _____ (Place).

Name	Passport/ID No.	Date of Birth

The duration of stay of the mentioned person will be from _____ to _____. His recommended schedule during his stay in _____ (country) would be as follows:

```
_____ (date)   Leave China to _____
_____ (date)   Prepare for display
_____ (date)   Duration of exhibition
_____ (date)   Stands dismantling; deal with exhibits
_____ (date)   Back to China
```

Yours faithfully,
[Signature]

Sample 5

Dear _____,

The visa applicant is an autonomous entrepreneur in the area of _____ manufacture employed by the company _____ and intends to participate in the international trade fair _____ in _____, due to professional/business interests. His address is as follows:

Company name: _____
Address: _____
Tel: _____
Fax: _____

E-mail address: ＿＿＿＿＿＿＿＿＿

All expense of his journey to/from ＿＿＿＿ as well as hotel expenses and health insurance will be borne by his employer.

Please note that we will not assume legal or financial responsibilities in connection with this business trip.

We would be pleased to welcome the above mentioned person as a trade fair exhibitor to the international trade fair ＿＿＿＿.

With best regards,
[Signature]

Invitation to Visit Exhibition Booth
Sample 6

Dear ＿＿＿＿,

Many thanks for your letter and enclosures of ＿＿＿＿ (date). We were very interested to hear that you are looking for a UK distributor for ＿＿＿＿. We would like to invite you to visit our booth, No. ＿＿＿＿, at ＿＿＿＿ Fair, at ＿＿＿＿ (Place), which starts on ＿＿＿＿. If you would like to set up an appointment during non-exhibit hall hours please call me. I can then arrange for our senior staff to be present at the meeting. We are looking forward to hearing from you.

Yours faithfully,
[Signature]

6. Key Words and Expressions

(1) trade show　会展

(2) exhibition organizer　会展承办商

(3) meeting schedule　会议时间表

(4) location　场所

(5) booth　展位

(6) package booth　一揽子展台

(7) coordinate　协调，协作

(8) signing-up letter　注册信，报名信

(9) dismantle　拆卸，撤展

(10) stand　展台

(11) notice board　布告牌

(12) corner booth　角落展位

(13) pop-ups　展览品

(14) application form　申请表

(15) decorate　布展

(16) move in　接展

(17) move out　撤展

(18) call off　取消

(19) refund　退款

(20) trade show banner stands　会展张贴架

(21) conference rooms　会展室

(22) portable flooring　移动地板

(23) trade show signs　会展标志

(24) truss systems　会展构架

(25) trade show exhibit counters　会展展台

(26) trade show display accessories　会展附件

(27) carrying case　展品运输箱

(28) trade show booth lights　展位灯具

(29) literature rack　资料架

7. Useful Sentence Patterns

(1) If you send us your registration form and registration fees within two weeks, it is still possible for you to get one booth.　如果您递交注册表并在两周内缴纳注册费，还是有可能租到一个摊位的。

(2) Are you looking for a standard package booth or non-standard package booth?　您想寻找标准包价摊位还是非标准包价摊位呢？

(3) All center booths are booked up. We have only corner booths left.　所有的中心区摊位都订完了，我们只剩一些角落摊位。

(4) We'll send you a layout of the exhibition hall, and mark the available booth on it. 我们会给您发一份展厅的布局图，并把可预订的摊位标出来。

(5) I'm sorry, but we are all fully booked for those days as it is the peak season. 很抱歉，因为是旺季，那段时间的会议室都被订光了。

(6) Cancellation will only be accepted in writing before the stipulated deadline. 取消展位必须于截止日期前以书面形式提出。

(7) All cancelled orders will be subject to a 30% cancellation charge. 所取消的申请需缴付30%作取消手续费用。

(8) A written notification by the exhibitor is demanded for cancellation of exhibition space. 参展企业若取消参展或削减展出面积，应以书面形式通知。

(9) Only cancellation and refund requests made in writing will be accepted.　取消参展与申请退款必须以书面形式提出。

(10) All refunds will be processed after the event/exhibition. 所有退款需在本次活动/展览

结束之后方能办理。

(11) If you need more audiovisual equipment, you may order from our event's audiovisual vendor. 如果您还需要更多的视听设备，可以从我们的活动视频服务商那里预订。

8. Exercises

Exercise 15-1

Direction: Put the following sentences into English.

(1) 会展中心共有展览面积24000平方米，分上下两层：一层展厅16500平方米，二层展厅7500平方米，具有可提供各种展览服务的先进设施，包括宽带上网服务功能。

(2) 你可以电话报名，但是要等到你把注册费汇到我方账户后才能予以展位确认。

(3) 展位已经分配完。另外我正好有事和你协商。展览台数量太多，无法按岛形安排展位，因为岛形占据的空间较大。

(4) 因为展览是颇具竞争性的，参展商只有很短的时间来吸引参观者的注意力，并且了解参展商所想要传达的信息。

(5) 撤展时，所有东西都必须装箱，而且所有的事都必须在很短的时间内完成。大多数情况下，要求展馆腾空的时间要比允许安装的时间要短得多。

Exercise 15-2

Direction: Write a signing-up letter for a trade show according to the following information.

(1) Jerry is a sales clerk with Shanghai Galaxy Exhibition Company.

(2) Harney Robert, address: 254 Euclid Avenue, Bloomington, IN60698, USA; Phone number: 867-90-2475; E-mail address: wayne@bloomingtonauto.com.

(3) Harney Robert is looking for a standard package booth at the Auto Exhibition to be held on Oct. 25, 2015 in Shanghai.

(4) Harney Robert wants a center booth of 9 square meters.

9. Supplementary Reading

A Brief History of Exhibition

Where and when the first fair was held is not known, however, evidence points to the existence of fairs as early as 500BC scripture records in the book of Ezekiel: "Tarshish was the merchant by reason of the multitude of this kinds of riches with silver, iron, tin and lead, they traded in the fairs."

Fairs were commercial in character from the beginning. Merchants from distant countries would come together, bringing native wares to trade with one another, so it is reasonable to assume that "fair" was the name given to the place at which early trading between foreign merchants was conducted.

It is equally clear that religious activity was companion to the commerce. The Latin world "feria" meaning holy day, would appear the logical root of the word "fair". Each feria was a day when large numbers of people would assemble for worship. Worship in those early days was centered around temples in great cities, including Ninevah, Athens, Rome and Mecca. These cities were also respected as the great commercial centers of the world. Fields adjacent to these temples were staked out for traders and merchants.

During the early Christian era, the church took an active part in sponsoring fairs on feast days, and as a result, fairs came to be a source of revenue for the church. Possibly, our modern church bazaars possess some rudiments of these religious fairs.

Today, over 3200 fairs are held in North America each year. They provide industrial exhibits, demonstrations and competition aimed at the advancement of livestock, horticulture and agriculture with special emphasis placed on educational activities such as 4-H, FFA and similar youth development programs. While enjoying these high-minded pursuits, fair visitors are also able to see, hear, touch, smell and taste the richness and variety of what the world has to offer.

The World Exhibition is fundamentally different from ordinary exhibitions for trade and economic promotion, which is the highest-class exhibition in the world. It provides great opportunities for a country, through motivating the whole nation, to demonstrate its social, economic and cultural achievements and future prospects in a comprehensive way.

Chapter 16
Bid and Tender
招标与投标

1. Learning Objectives

By the end of this chapter, you will be able to do the following:

· Have a general view about biding.

· Get to know the general procedures of invitation for bids.

· Know how to write a No-Bid letter.

· Know how to write a cover letter

· Know how to write a contract award letter.

· Use the proper words and expressions and sentence patterns in writing letters in bidding and drafting bid documents.

2. Case Study

Open Bidding

> Republic of Ghana
> MINISTRY OF FOOD AND AGRICULTURE (MoFA)
> EXPORT MARKETING AND QUALITY AWARENESS PROJECT (EMQAP)
> INTERNATIONAL COMPETITIVE BIDDING FOR THE PROCUREMENT
> OF TEMPERATURE CONTROLLED VANS
>
> **Invitation for Bids**
> **Date: 9th April, 2014**
>
>   1. This Specific Procurement Notice follows the General Procurement Notice for this project that appeared in the UN Development Business No. 683 of 31st July 2012.
>   2. The Government of the Republic of Ghana has received a loan from the African Development Fund towards the Cost of the Export Marketing and Quality Awareness Project and intends to apply part of the funds to cover the eligible payments under the Contract for the Procurement of Temperature Controlled Vans.
>   3. The Project Division (Procurement) of the Ministry of Food and Agriculture acting on behalf of Export Marketing & Quality Awareness Project (EMQAP) now invites sealed bids from eligible bidders for the procurement of the under mentioned.
>   **<u>Bidders are to quote for complete Lot(s) and not items within the lot(s).</u>**

Brief Description of the Items to be Procured

Lot	Description	Quantity	Bid Security	Delivery Schedule
1	Temperature Controlled Van (24 tonner)	1	US$2000	120 days after
2	Temperature Controlled Van (10 tonner)	1	US$1500	contract signing

Bidders may bid for more than one (1) lot

Any delivery beyond 120 days will be considered non-responsive. Bidders quoting for an incomplete lot(s) will be considered non-responsive. The Bid Validity Period shall be 120 days after bid opening. The Bid Security shall be valid for twenty-eight (28) days beyond the end of the validity period of the bid.

4. Interested eligible bidders may obtain further information from and inspect the Bidding Documents at the office of the:

Projects Division (Procurement)
Ministry of Food and Agriculture.
P. O. Box M.37, Accra, Ghana.
Tel.: +233-21-66 82 48/67 7138
Fax: +233-21-66 82 48
Rooms: 3, 4, 5 and 8
Location: near the GHANA RED CROSS SOCIETY NATIONAL HEADQUARTERS in the vicinity of MDPI and RIVIERA BEACH HOTEL, ACCRA.

5. A complete set of Bidding Documents may be purchased by interested bidders on the submission of a written application to the above and upon payment of a non-refundable fee of **one hundred Ghana Cedis (GH¢100.00) or its equivalent in any freely convertible currency.**

6. Bids must be delivered to **Conference Room of the MOFA Information Resource Centre (Library), Accra** in the vicinity of Aglow Agric Products Ltd. and the Greater-Accra Regional MoFA Offices on or before 10.00am on May 20, 2014 and must be accompanied by a bid security as stated above.

7. Bids will be opened in the presence of bidders' representatives who choose to attend at **10.00 hrs. GMT on Tuesday, May 20, 2014, at Conference Room of the MOFA Information Resource Centre** (Library), Accra in the vicinity of Aglow Agric Products Ltd. and the Greater-Accra Regional MoFA Offices.

3. Introduction

A call for bids, call for tenders, or invitation to tender is a special procedure for generating competing offers from different bidders looking to obtain an award of business activity in works, supply, or service contracts. Many international organizations and governments in the world now require that almost all the large deals, projects or services with a loan up to a certain amount must be done through open tendering for which contractors or suppliers are often requested to send their quotations on specified conditions within a period of time. The successful bidder will be awarded part or whole of the bid. In accordance with the international practice, all the bidding documents and specifications are often worked out in English.

International Bidding Methods

(1) International Competitive Bidding (ICB)

With such a bidding method, the tenderee will invite a number of selected and prequalified tenderers to take part in the competition and make the best selection of winners. In the International Competitive Bidding, there are another two methods, and one is open bidding, and the other is selected bidding.

Open bidding, also called open calls for tenders, or advertised tenders, are open to all vendors or contractors who can guarantee performance, while selected bidding, which is limited competitive bidding, also called restricted tenders, restricted calls for tenders, or invited tenders, are only open to selected prequalified vendors or contractors, and it may be a two-stage process, of which the first stage produces a short list of suitable vendors and then the second stage is for the suitable vendors to compete for bidding.

(2) Negotiated Bidding

Negotiated Bidding is a non-competitive bidding. It is only open to a few particular contractors for negation for a deal. In this method the price to be paid for the work is negotiated with a single contractor. This, obviously, does not provide the owner with a comparative price. The cost of a work may be higher in this method, but the owner expects some advantages from employing a particular contractor whose policies and practices are known and who has in the past proved capable of fulfilling his obligations. The higher cost may be offset by better quality.

(3) Two-stage Bidding

This is a mixed method of unlimited competitive bidding and limited competitive bidding, in which the open bidding is first offered and then the selected bidding method is used in two-stage process.

In an open bid or tender system, a double envelope system may be used. The double envelope system separates the technical proposal from the financing or cost proposal in the form of two separate and sealed envelopes. During the tender evaluation, the technical proposal would be opened and evaluated first followed by the financing proposal. The objective of this system is to ensure a fair evaluation of the proposal. The technical proposal would be evaluated purely on its technical merits and its ability to meet the requirements set forth in the Invitation without being unduly skewed by the financial proposal.

In the process of invitation for bids or tendering, a tender box will be set. A tender box is a mailbox that is used to receive the physical tender or bid documents. When a tender or bid is being called, a tender or bid number is usually issued as a reference number for the tender box. The tender box would be open for interested parties to submit their proposals for the duration of the bid or tender. Once the duration is over, the tender box is closed and sealed and can only be opened by either the tender or bid evaluation committee or a member of the procurement department with one witness.

Registered contractors are usually required to furnish a bond for a certain amount as security or earnest money deposit to be adjusted against work done, normally in the form of Bank Guarantee or Surety.

While compiling your tender response, the most important thing is to do exactly as the Buyer asks, and if you are unsure of anything—ask them. Always think about what the Buyer is looking for when writing a tender, and write your response within that context. Keep the following points in mind:

1) Write a tender response in a simple but professional style.
2) Address exactly what the Buyer asks for, and ONLY what the Buyer asks for!
3) Use a consistent writing style.
4) Be professional in the format and presentation of the response.

If there is additional information that you think is relevant and you would like to include this detail, put it in an Added Value or Additional Products/Services section.

Documents should be presented in a way that makes it as simple as possible for the Buyer to evaluate—if you get too sophisticated or try to be different, this often will not impress the evaluation team. Don't forget the evaluation team is specifically asking for all proposals to be presented in a consistent way to make the evaluation process easier and quicker for them to complete.

Last but certainly not least is the Format and Presentation. The overall design of the proposal document makes a statement to the Buyer about the professional ability of your organization. A simple design with a header and footer which makes the document look professional, and perhaps might include your company name or brand in the header, will make your proposal more memorable during evaluation. The footer should contain the page number and proposal title. The document should be divided into clear sections, either as specified by the Buyer or created to provide a clear and logical presentation of the proposal content.

Tendering and Bidding Procedure

(1) Invitation for Bids

The tenderees need to do the following:

1) Issue the bidding documents.
2) Accept the tendering documents.
3) Open, evaluate and award the bid.
4) Publish the bidding results and notify the bid winners.
5) Establish contract with the bidders.

(2) Bidding procedures

Bidders need to take the following steps:

1) Obtain bidding documents
2) Analyze bidding documents (including technical requirements, cost, competitors etc.)
3) Prepare and submit tendering documents as per the stipulated time

4) Pay close attention to bid opening

5) Accept bid-winning notice

6) Establish contract with the tenderee

A prospective Bidder requiring any clarification of the Bidding Document shall contact the tenderee in writing at the tenderee's address indicated in the Bidding Documents or raise his enquiries during the pre-bid meeting. The tenderee will respond to any request for clarification, provided that such request is received prior to the deadline for submission of bids, within the number of days specified in the Bidding Documents. The tenderee's response shall be in writing with copies to all Bidders who have acquired the Bidding Document including a description of the inquiry but without identifying its source.

4. Specimen Letters

Specimen 1
Application Letter

Dear Sir,

We have learnt through your Specific Procurement Notice dated 9th April, 2014 that you are procuring two Models of Vans: Temperature Controlled Van (24 tonner) and Temperature Controlled Van (10 tonner). As an exporter, we believe that we are quite competitive in supplying you the products.

It is hereby to write this letter to apply for a complete set of Bidding Documents for the TWO lots of vans.

Thank you for your time and consideration.

Sincerely,
[Signature]

Specimen 2
Letter of Intent

Dear Sir,

I would like to indicate our interest in the above Invitation for Bids (IFD) and to be notified for any updates and amendments to the IFD.

Sincerely,
[Signature]

Specimen 3
Selected Bidding

African Development Bank Group
South SUDAN Country Office

tender@afdb.org

Date: July 29, 2013

REQUEST FOR PROPOSALS (RFP)
CLEANING AND TEA SERVICES AT THE AFRICAN DEVELOPMENT
BANK SOUTH SUDAN COUNTRY OFFICE
ADB/NCB/SSFO/ 2013/0100
(Please quote this reference on all communications pertaining to this bid)

LETTER OF INITIATION

Name of the Bidder_____

Dear Sir/ Madam,

1. The African Development Bank (hereinafter referred to as "AFDB" or the "Bank") requests for a quotation for cleaning and tea services at its South Sudan Country Offices situated, Juba, South Sudan. The successful Bidder shall enter into a contract with the Bank and will be expected to commence the duties on the 1st December 2013.
2. Only Companies having offices in Juba shall bid for this cleaning services contract. Your proposal should be received on or before 29th, August, 2013 at 15,00 hrs through postal mail, courier or by hand-delivery at the address given below:
    The Resident Representative
    The African Development Bank,
    South Sudan Country Office (SSFO),
    UNDP Compound, Ministries Road
    P.O.Box.622,
    Juba, South Sudan
3. Qualification of Bidder
    3.1 All bidders shall provide in Section II—Qualification Information, a preliminary description of the proposed work method and schedule, including drawings and charts, as necessary, including the people who will be involved in the works.
    3.2 To qualify for award of the contract, bidders shall meet the minimum qualifying criteria specified in the ITB.
4. This bid dossier includes the letter of invitation together with the annexes and the appendices, which are as follows:
    Annex I: Terms of Reference
    Annex 2: Contents of the Proposal to be submitted + Appendix A, B, C
    Annex 3: Evaluation Criteria
    Annex 4: List of the Member Countries of the Bank
    Annex 5: General Terms and Conditions of Purchase
    Annex 6: Sample Contract

5. Bidders should ensure that technical and financial proposals are sealed in two separate envelopes and both envelopes are enclosed in one big envelope (both the Technical and the Financial Proposal in separate sealed envelopes) and the big envelope should be sealed addressed to the African Development Bank Representation, tender delivery address given above.

6. Each bidder will submit their proposals in ONE original copy and FOUR duplicate copies: the original proposal must carry the mention "ORIGIONAL" and each of the four copies the mention "COPY". The technical proposal (one original + 4 copies) and the financial proposal (one original + 4 copies) will each be placed in two separate sealed envelopes (the "internal envelopes").

The following mention should appear on each internal envelope:

a) the purpose of the Present bid;

b) the mention "Technical Proposal" or "Financial Proposal" as the case may be;

c) the name and address of the bidder.

The two internal envelopes should be placed together in a large single sealed envelope called "external envelope", which must be anonymous and, **carry only the following label which should be photocopied and placed on the external envelope:**

> The Resident Representative
> South Sudan Country Office (SSFO),
> UNDP Compound, Ministries Road
> P. O. Box. 622
> Juba, South Sudan
> REQTTEST FOR PROPOSALS — DO NOT OPEN UNTIL ON BID OPENING DAY
> REFERENCE:ADBAICB/SSFO/20 13/0 100
> BID Closing Date and Time: 29th August, 2013, 15.30 hrs.
> The Opening shall be on the same date at 15.30 hrs bid shall be opened publicly.

7. It is the sole responsibility of the bidders to ensure that the sealed envelope containing the proposal reaches the above address before the time and date indicated in Article 4 above. When delivered by hand, the proposals must be delivered at the above delivery address during the South Sudan government working hours from 08h00 to 12h00 and from 14h00 to 16h00, Monday through Wednesday except for holidays observed by the South Sudan government. Delivery to any other office of the African Development Bank will be at the risk of the bidder and will not constitute any delivery to this bid.

8. Proposals received after the submission date and times shall be rejected. There shall be a public opening bid immediately after the closure of the bid.

9. At any time before the submission of proposals, the Bank may, for any reason, whether at its own initiative or in response to a clarification requested by the Bidder, amend the bid. The amendment shall be sent in writing by telefax or email to all invited firms and will be binding on them. The Bank may at its sole discretion extend the deadline for the submission of proposals. Proposals must be submitted in the English language in One Original + Four Copies (any attachments or appendices and annexes thereto must also be submitted in One

Original + Four Copies). The Technical Proposal must include information in sufficient detail to allow the Bank to consider whether your company has the necessary capability, experience, knowledge, expertise, and the required capacity to perform satisfactorily the services specified along with any other information that may be requested by Annex 2 of this BID. In accordance with the provisions of Annex 3, the technical proposal must include :

· the statement of conformity (Appendix A);

· project plan for the management of the contract;

· a description of your relevant experience on this particular field, supported with an example of similar services provided;

· the audited financial statements for the last three (3) fiscal years;

· qualifications and level of competency of each key staff to be assigned to the execution of the contract (use format as described in Appendix C);

· insurance certificate for professional liability of the bidder.

10. You are advised to separate the envelope for financial proposal from the envelope for technical proposal. It is mandatory for the bidders to submit the Financial Proposal by using the bid submission form, attached as Appendix B of this BID, including a description of the proposed services. Any deviation from the requested requirements (see TOR on Annex 1) shall be highlighted and explained. Please note that the Bank will only consider those deviations that have an effect of improving the services requested.

11. The evaluation method of the proposal is described in detail in under Evaluation Criteria. For this procurement, evaluation will be based on combined technical and financial proposals. Only bidders, whose technical proposal meet or exceed the minimum qualification points, will be considered for financial evaluation.

12. By submitting the proposal, the bidders confirm that they have taken into account all the documents of this BID including the addenda (if any), all the annexes and as the case may be, the appendices to annexes. The Bank is not bound by any other terms and conditions unless agreed in writing by the Bank.

13. The prices quoted shall be net free and clear of all applicable taxes including withholding tax duties, fees, levies or indirect taxes including customs duties. Surcharges imposed by, or pursuant to the laws, statutes or regulations of any governmental agency or authority as the Bank, its property, other assets, income and its operations and transactions are exempt from any obligation relating to the payment, withholding, or collection of any tax or duty, by virtue of article 57 of the Agreement establishing the Bank.

14. By submitting their bids, each bidder also warrants that they are legally authorized to perform the services and that they are not in default with the Tax and Social Security obligations in their country. The Bank may, at its sole discretion, ask any bidder to provide documentary evidence establishing the same.

15. Proposals should remain valid for a period of not less than sixty (90) days after the deadline date specified for submission.

16. The Bank will award the contract to the bidder whose technical proposal has been determined to be substantially responsive and who has offered the lowest financial proposal in accordance with the evaluation criteria given in under Evaluation Criteria. Responsiveness will be judged by conformance to all the terms, conditions and specifications of the BID.

17. The Contract shall be governed by the Terms of References, and the General terms and Conditions. Any such contract will require compliance with all factual statements and

representations made in the proposal.

18. Unless otherwise specified in this BID, the rates quoted should be fixed for the duration of the contract and should not be subject to adjustment on any account.

19. Notwithstanding the above, the Bank reserves the right to amend the content of this BID and to accept or reject any or all proposals and to cancel the bidding process at any time prior to the award of the contract without incurring any liability to any bidder.

20. Please note that it is the policy of the Bank that bidders, observe the highest standard of ethics during the procurement process and execution of such contracts. In pursuance of this policy, the Bank will reject a bid if it determines that the Bidder has engaged in corrupt or fraudulent practices in competing for the contract in question. In terms of clarity, corrupt or fraudulent practices are:
    · corrupt practice is the offering, giving, receiving, or soliciting, directly or indirectly, anything of value to influence improperly the actions of another party;
    · fraudulent practice is any act or omission, including a misrepresentation, that knowingly or recklessly misleads, or attempts to mislead, a party to obtain a financial or other benefit or to avoid an obligation;
    · coercive practice is an act or omission that impairs or harms, or threatens to impair or harm, directly or indirectly, any party or the property of the party to improperly influence the actions of a party;
    · collusive practice is an arrangement between two or more parties designed to achieve an improper purpose, including influencing improperly the actions of another party.
    · An unethical practice: conduct of behavior that is contrary to the provisions or other published requirements of doing business with the Bank pertaining to the conflict of interest, gifts and hospitality, post-employment, etc.

21. Bidders are specifically directed Not to contact any of the Bank's officers involved in procurement and contract management, or its consultants for meetings, conferences, discussions etc that are specifically related to this bid at any-time prior to any award and execution of a contract.

22. Bidders are advised to enquire for clarity through tender@afdb.org, citing the bid reference number. Unauthorized contact with any personnel of the Bank stipulated on Article 19 above may cause for rejection of the bidder's bid.

23. We look forward to receiving your proposal and thank you for your interest in the African Development Bank.

[Signature]
Resident Representative, SSFO

Specimen 4
RFP Cover Letter

Dear Sir,

You are invited to submit a proposal for our [Project title] project in accordance with the requirements set forth in the attached request for proposal (RFP), which is also available on-line at http://www.afdb.org.

The African Development Bank (AfDB) is a multilateral development finance institution established to contribute to the economic development and social progress of African countries and its mission is to fight poverty and improve living conditions on the continent through promoting the investment of public and private capital in projects and programs that are likely to contribute to the economic and social development of the region.

The AfDB is controlled by a Board of Executive Directors, made up of representatives of its member countries. Member governments are officially represented at the AfDB by their Minister of Finance, Planning or Cooperation who sits on the AfDB Board of Governors. Day-to-day decisions about which loans and grants should be approved and what policies should guide the AfDB's work are taken by the Board of Executive Directors. We now request for a quotation for cleaning and tea services at its South Sudan Country Offices situated, Juba, South Sudan.

I will hold a non-mandatory pre-proposal meeting for prospective providers at 9:30 a.m. on 10th August, 2013 until 12:00 a.m the same day at its South Sudan Country Offices situated, Juba, South Sudan. Should you plan to attend the conference, you must RSVP by 30th July, 2013. Questions must be received prior to the conference no later than 12:00 a.m. on 1st August, 2013. Both the RSVP and questions can be submitted to me in writing, by fax, or, preferably, by e-mail. Questions, answers, and modifications to the RFP will be posted on the web at http://www.afdb.org. and will be debated publicly during the conference.

If you intend to respond to the RFP, a letter of intent, which is not binding but will greatly assist me in planning for proposal evaluation must be submitted to me in writing, by fax or, preferably, by e-mail, and be received no later than 9:00 a.m. on 1st August, 2013. I will not accept your proposal if you do not complete the letter of intent within the specified time period.

The original, four copies, and an electronic version of your proposal must be received not later than 12:00hrs on 5th August, 2013 or your proposal will otherwise be disqualified. At the conference, you will receive pre-printed labels to insure proper delivery and identification of your proposal.

I anticipate that the provider whose proposal is the best solution for our project will be selected on 25th August, 2013. We will notify all providers, whether they are disqualified, rejected, or unsuccessful although responsive.

I will be the single point of contact for all inquiries and correspondences.

I thank you for your time, effort, and interest in our cleaning and tea services project.

Sincerely,
[Signature]
_____
[Name and title of the person responsible for handling proposals]
[Complete address]
[Phone and fax]
[E-mail address, an alias or distribution list dedicated to the RFP process]

Attachment:　　RFP #[RFP identification number]
cc:　　　　　　[List of persons copied]

Specimen 5
No-Bid Letter

Dear Sir,

Thank you for considering our service for your cleaning and tea services project.

We have carefully determined, as follows, the reasons that hamper us from considering a bid/proposal appropriate at this time:

Our company is an exporter with good reputation of construction machinery in the international market. However, we have no experience in dealing with the cleaning and tea services so far, but we are interested in this field and hope to have chances to cooperate with you in the future.

Having read with interest your invitation to bid, we have also learned more about your organization, and received confirmation that your organization benefits from a well-established reputation in the banking industry.

Again, I want to thank you for your interest in our export service. I am also excited about the prospect of soon submitting offers regarding projects for which the unique combination of our service and our dedicated staff will ensure a superior outcome.

Sincerely,
[Signature]

Specimen 6
Bid Cover Letter

Dear Sir,

The following represents HEPEC Inc.'s item by item response to IFB Dated July 29, 2013. The response documents consist of the following:
1. Bidding documents
    1) Bid Letter
    2) Copy of Bid Bond
    3) Priced Bill of Quantity
    4) Response to Bidding Requirements, terms and conditions, and technical specification.
2. Qualification Documents
3. Item-priced Bill

HEPEC Inc. is pleased to participate in this bid and is desirous to supply its superior product to you for the cleaning and tea services.

We look forward to your positive response to this proposal.

Sincerely yours,
[Signature]

Specimen 7
Contract Award Letter

Dear Sir,

I thank you for your time, effort and interest in our cleaning and tea services project.

Furthermore, I am pleased to announce that your proposal is the best apparent successful solution relative to our project.

Upon termination of the required protest period of 30 business days after the closing date of 29th August, 2013, I will be contacting you in order to execute a formal Professional Service Agreement (PSA).

Sincerely,
[Signature]

5. Writing Templates

RFP Cover Letter

The request for proposal (RFP) cover letter should accompany the RFP questionnaire. Beyond being polite and presenting your project, the RFP cover letter gives you a unique opportunity to emphasize the timeline of your state-of-the-art RFP-based selection process, particularly the dates on which different documents are due.

Dear [Contact name]:

You are invited to submit a proposal for our [Project title] project in accordance with the requirements set forth in the attached request for proposal (RFP), which is also available on-line at [Site URL].

[Brief description of the company]

[Brief description of your existing systems and proposed project]

I will hold a [non-] mandatory pre-proposal meeting for prospective providers on [Date, start time] until [End time] at [Location]. Should you plan to attend the conference, you must [should] RSVP by [Date]. Questions must be received prior to the conference no later than [Date and time]. Both the RSVP and questions can be submitted to me in writing, by fax, or, preferably, by e-mail. Questions, answers, and modifications to the RFP will be posted on the web at [Site URL] and will be debated publicly during the conference (see section [X] of the RFP).

If you intend to respond to the RFP, a letter of intent, [which is not binding but will greatly assist me in planning for proposal evaluation, should] must [should] be submitted to me in writing, by fax or, preferably, by e-mail, and be received no later than [Date and time] (see section [X] of the RFP). [I will not accept your proposal if you do not complete the letter of intent within the specified time period.]

The original, [X] copies, and an electronic [Format] version of your proposal must be received not later than [Date and time] or your proposal will otherwise be disqualified. At the conference, you will receive pre-printed labels to insure proper delivery and identification of your proposal (see section [X] of the RFP).

I anticipate that the provider whose proposal is the best solution for our project will be selected on [Date]. We will notify all providers, whether they are disqualified, rejected, or unsuccessful although responsive (see section [X] of the RFP).

I will be the single point of contact for all inquiries and correspondences.

I thank you for your time, effort, and interest in our [Project title] project.

Sincerely,
[Signature]
[Name and title of the person responsible for handling proposals]
[Complete address]
[Phone and fax]
[E-mail address, an alias or distribution list dedicated to the RFP process]

Attachment:　　RFP #[RFP identification number]
cc:　　　　　　[List of persons copied]

No-Bid Letter

A no-bid letter is a letter to the organization that invited you to bid or submit a proposal, notifying them that you will not do so. To remain potentially involved in future opportunities, the provider should state in the no-bid notice the reasons for declining such an invitation.

Dear [Contact name]:

Thank you for considering our [solution/service] for your [project title] project.

We have carefully determined, as follows, the reasons that hamper us from considering a [bid/proposal] appropriate at this time:

    1. [Reason 1]
      [Detail]
    2. [Reason 2]
      [Detail]
  ...

Having read with interest your [RFP/invitation to bid], we have also learned more about your organization, and received confirmation that your organization benefits from a [very strong/well-established] reputation in the [Industry] industry.

Again, [Contact First Name], I want to thank you for your interest in our [solution/service]. I am also excited about the prospect of soon submitting offers regarding projects for which the unique combination of our [solution/service] and our dedicated people will ensure a superior outcome.

Sincerely,
[Signature]

Bid Cover Letter

The bid cover letter should accompany the tendering documents. The letter should be written in a polite tone and enclosed with the bidding documents.

Dear Sir,

The following represents [Company Name]'s item by item response to IFB Dated _____.

The response documents consist of the following:

  1. Bidding documents
    1) Bid Letter
    2) Copy of Bid Bond
    3) Priced Bill of Quantity
    4) Response to Bidding Requirements, terms and conditions, and technical specification.
  2. Qualification Documents
  3. Item-priced Bill
  ...

[Company Name] is pleased to participate in this bid and is desirous to supply its superior product to you for the cleaning and tea services.

We look forward to your positive response to this proposal.

Sincerely yours,
[Signature]

Contract Award Letter

The contract award letter is sent to the provider which solution, for the best value, fully satisfies or the best addresses the requirements defined in the request for proposal (RFP).

Dear [Contact name]:

    I thank you for your time, effort and interest in our [Project title] project.

    Furthermore, I am pleased to announce that your proposal is the best apparent successful solution relative to our project.

    Upon termination of the required protest period of [] (X) business days after the closing date of [Closing date and time], I will be contacting you in order to execute a formal Professional Service Agreement (PSA).

Sincerely,
[Signature]
(Name and title of the person responsible for handling disqualifications)
(Address)

---

6. Key Words and Expressions

(1) tenderee　招标人，招标方

(2) tender　投标; 标书

(3) bid　投标

(4) contractor　承包人/商

(5) base price limit on bids　标底

(6) call for bid　招标通告

(7) tender notice　招标通知

(8) tenderee　招标方

(9) bidder /tenderer　投标方，投标商

(10) eligible bidder　合格的投标人

(11) bid quotation　报标

(12) tender discussion　议标

(13) tender decision　决标

(14) bid opening　开标

(15) date of the closing of tender　招标截止日期

(16) submission of bid/tender　投标书的提交

(17) validity of bid　投标书有效期

(18) bid letter　投标函

(19) qualifications of bidders　投标人资质

(20) limited tendering　局限性招标

(21) bid bond　投标押金，押标金

(22) bid/tender security　投标保证金

(23) open tender　公开招标

(24) bidding/tendering document　招/投标文件

(25) bidding/tendering conditions　招标条件

(26) bidding process　招标步骤

(27) bidding procedure　招标程序

(28) instruction to bidders/tenderers　投标人须知

(29) invitation for bids, invitation to tenders　投标邀请

(30) call for bid　招标通知

(31) tender notice　招标通告

(32) procurement notice　采购公告

(33) two-stage bidding　两步法招标

(34) response to bidding documents　应标

(35) withdrawal of bid　撤标

(36) work out tender documents　做标，编标

(37) Form of Tender　投标书

(38) evaluation criteria　评标标准

(39) prequalification　资格预审

(40) evaluation of tender/bid　评标

(41) requests of clarification　澄清要求

(42) late bid　迟到的标书

(43) bid/tender opening　开标

(44) sealing of bid　封标

(45) place of bid opening　开标地点

(46) examination of bid　核标

(47) award of bid　中标

(48) Letter of Acceptance　中标函

(49) notification of award, award of tender　中标通知

(50) has/have won the bidding in …　中标

(51) the winning/successful bidder, the successful tenderer　中标者

(52) the unsuccessful tenderer　未中标者

(53) award of contract　授予合同

(54) international competitive bidding　竞争性招标, 指招标人邀请几个乃至几十个投标人参加投标，通过多数投标人竞争，选择其中对招标人最有利的投标人成交，它属于兑卖的方式

(55) open bidding　公开投标, 是一种无限竞争性招标，招标人要在国内外主要 报刊上刊登招标广告，凡对该项招标内容有兴趣的人均有机会购买招标资料进行投标

(56) selected bidding　选择性招标，又称邀请招标，是有限竞争性招标（limited competitive bidding），招标人不在报刊上刊登广告，而是根据自己具体的业务关系

和情报资料由招标人对客商进行邀请，进行资格预审后，再由他们进行投标。

(57) negotiated bidding　谈判招标，又称议标，是非公开的一种非竞争性的招标。这种招标由招标人物色几家客商直接进行合同谈判，谈判成功，交易达成。

(58) two-stage bidding　两段招标，是指无限竞争招标和有限竞争招标的综合方式，采用此类方式时，则是用公开招标，再用选择招标分两段进行。

7. Useful Sentence Patterns

(1) We wish to tender for...　我们拟参加……的投标。

(2) ...is pleased to participate in this bid and is desirous to supply our superior product to you.　……乐于参加此次投标，并渴望向贵方提供我方的优等产品。

(3) We look forward to your positive response to this proposal.　盼望对该投标给予正面回应。

(4) We agree to abide by the conditions or Tender specified above.　我方同意遵守以上所规定的投标条款。

(5) Interested eligible bidders may obtain further information from and inspect the Bidding Documents at the office of...　有兴趣的合格投标方可以到……索取详细资料，查阅招标文件。

(6) A complete set of Bidding Documents may be purchased by interested bidders on the submission of a written application to the above and upon payment of a non - refundable fee of...　感兴趣的投标方可以向……书面申请购买整套标书，缴纳的招标文件费用概不退还。

(7) Bids must be delivered to ... on or before ... and must be accompanied by a bid security as stated above.　投标文件必须在……之前送达……　并按上述要求附投标保函。

(8) We have carefully determined, as follows, the reasons that hamper us from considering a [bid/proposal] appropriate at this time.　基于以下原因，我们慎重地决定现阶段投标不合适。

8. Exercises

Exercise 16-1

Direction: Put the following sentences into English.

(1) 修改文件将以书面形式通知所有购买招标文件的投标人。投标人应立即以书面形式确认已收到该修改文件。

(2) 应通知投标人，如果他在正式的提交日之前递交、邮寄或发送了他的投标书，他有权对其做出修改或更正，但投标人必须使雇主/工程师在规定的投标书提交日期之前收到书面文本。

(3) 招标中心可以请投标人澄清其投标内容。提出澄清的要求与答复均应是书面的，但不得要求改动价格或对投标内容进行实质性修改。

(4) 如果评定的报价最低的投标书在澄清后仍包含有不能接受的偏差，则应通知投标人，给予其书面撤回此类偏差的机会。只有在投标人书面确认撤回偏差，并不对标价做出

　　修改，他才真的撤回了偏差。

(5) 所有投标书须于规定的开标日当天上午10点之前送达下列规定的地址并被有效地接受。所有投标书将于北京时间2014年10月20日11:30被启封。

Exercise 16-2

Direction: Work out a draft of International Competitive Bid for the Project in accordance with the given particulars.

(1) 国际竞争招标项目。

(2) 招标工程为乌干达共和国卫生部改善穆拉戈医院及坎帕拉市卫生服务工程，项目编号为PROJECT No. P-UG-IB0-006，贷款号为LOAN No. : 2100150025094，招标文件标号为 IFB No.: MOH/SUPLS-MKCCA/2013-14/00599。

(3) 此招标项目为2014年10月11日网上公布的联合国发展商业项目（UNDB）No. AfDB299-809/11及非洲发展银行集团网站上公布的有关项目的一般性采购通告。

(4) 乌干达政府从非洲发展基金（ADF）和尼日利亚信托基金获得改善穆拉戈医院及坎帕拉市卫生服务工程的融资，按合同要求，打算把该贷款的部分款项为坎帕拉大城区购买10辆救护车。

(5) 乌干达卫生部(MoH)现向合格的投标方征求密封投标，提供10辆救护车。

(6) 有兴趣且符合条件的投标方均可通过下面的办公地点了解详细信息和查看投标文件。

　　The Project Coordinator,

　　MKCCA Project,

　　P.O. Box 8096, Kampala, Uganda

　　Tel.: +256 414 534025/533481

　　Fax: +256 414 530701

　　Email: hsrp@imul.com

(7) 投标说明和合同的一般条款见"货物采购非洲发展银行标准招标文件"。

(8) 有兴趣的投标方均可书面申请索取招标文件，附31000美元投标保函。

(9) 投标方代表应于2015年3月25日上午11:30（东非标准时间）到下列地址参加开标。

　　The Head of Procurement and Disposal Unit,

　　Ministry of Health Headquarters,

　　Plot 6, Lourdel Road, Room C308

　　P.O. Box 52372, Kampala-Uganda

9. Supplementary Readings

Instruction to Bidders

Vendor Questions

All questions regarding the contents of this solicitation, and solicitation process (including requests for ADA accommodations), shall be directed solely to the Purchasing Manager. Questions should be submitted in writing via letter, fax or email. Questions received less than seven (7) calendar days prior to the due date and time may be answered at the discretion of the City.

Addenda/Clarifications

Any changes to the specifications will be in the form of an addendum. Addenda are posted on the City website and mailed to those who register on the City website when downloading solicitations no less than seven (7) days prior to the Due Date. Vendors are cautioned to check the Purchasing Website for addenda and clarifications prior to submitting their bid. The City cannot be held responsible if a vendor fails to receive any addenda issued. The City shall not be responsible for any oral changes to these specifications made by any employees or officer of the City. Failure to acknowledge receipt of an addendum may result in disqualification of a bid.

The City will open all bids properly and timely submitted, and will record the names and other information specified by law and rule. All bids become the property of the City and will not be returned except in the case of a late submission. Respondent names, as read at the bid opening, will be posted on the City website. Once a notice of intent to award is posted or 30 days from day of opening elapses, whichever occurs earlier, bids are available for inspection by contacting Purchasing.

Bid shall remain firm and unaltered after opening for the number of days shown above. The City may accept the bid, subject to successful contract negotiations, at any time during this time.

Bids will be received at this address. Bidders may mail or hand-deliver bids. E-mail or fax submissions will not be accepted. No responsibility will attach to the City of Clearwater, its employees or agents for premature opening of a bid that is not properly addressed and identified.

Late Bids

The bidder assumes responsibility for having the bid delivered on time at the place specified. All bids received after the date and time specified shall not be considered and will be returned unopened to the bidder. The bidder assumes the risk of any delay in the mail or in handling of the mail by employees of the City of Clearwater, or any private courier, regardless whether sent by mail or by means of personal delivery. You must allow adequate time to accommodate all registration and security screenings at the delivery site. A valid photo ID may be required. It shall not be sufficient to show that you mailed or commenced delivery before the due date and time.

All times are Clearwater, Florida local times. The bidder agrees to accept the time stamp in the City Purchasing Office as the official time.

Lobbying Prohibition

Any communication regarding this solicitation for the purpose of influencing the process or the award, between any person or affiliates seeking an award from this solicitation and the City, including but not limited to the City Council, employees, and consultants hired to assist in the solicitation, is prohibited.

This prohibition is imposed from the time of the first public notice of the solicitation until the City cancels the solicitation, rejects all responses, awards a contract or otherwise takes action which ends the solicitation process. This section shall not prohibit public comment at any City Council meeting, study session or Council committee meeting.

This prohibition shall not apply to vendor-initiated communication with the contact(s) identified in the solicitation or City-initiated communications for the purposes of conducting the procurement including but not limited to pre-bid conferences, clarification of responses, presentations if provided in the solicitation, requests for Best and Final Proposals, contract negotiations, protest/appeal resolution, or surveying non-responsive vendors. Violations of this provision shall be reported to the Purchasing Manager. Persons violating this prohibition may be subject to a warning letter or rejection of their response depending on the nature of the violation, and/or debarment of the bidder as provided in Clearwater's Purchasing Policy and Procedures.

Commencement of Work

If bidder begins any billable work prior to the City's final approval and execution of the contract, bidder does so at its own risk.

Responsibility to Read and Uunderstand

Failure to read, examine and understand the solicitation will not excuse any failure to comply with the requirements of the solicitation or any resulting contract, nor shall such failure be a basis for claiming additional compensation. If a vendor suspects an error, omission or discrepancy in this solicitation, the vendor must immediately and in any case not later than seven (7) business days in advance of the due date notify the contact on page one (1). The City is not responsible for and will not pay any costs associated with the preparation and submission of the bid. Bidders are cautioned to verify their bids before submission, as amendments to or withdrawal of bids submitted after time specified for opening of bids may not be considered. The City will not be responsible for any bidder errors or omissions.

Form and Content of Bids

Unless otherwise instructed or allowed, bids shall be submitted on the forms provided.

An original and the designated number of copies of each bid are required. Bids, including modifications, must be submitted in ink, typed, or printed form and signed by an authorized representative. Please line through and initial rather than erase changes. If the bid is not properly signed or if any changes are not initialed, it may be considered non-responsive. In the event of a disparity between the unit price and the extended price, the unit price shall prevail unless obviously in error, as determined by the City. The City may require that an electronic copy of the bid be submitted. The bid must provide all information requested and must address all points. The City does not encourage exceptions. The City is not required to grant exceptions and depending on the exception, the City may reject the bid.

Specifications

Technical specifications define the minimum acceptable standard. When the specification calls for "Brand Name or Equal," the brand name product is acceptable. Alternates will be considered upon demonstrating the other product meets stated specifications and is equivalent to the brand product in terms of quality, performance and desired characteristics. Minor differences that do not affect the suitability of the supply or service for the City's needs may be accepted. Burden of proof that the product meets the minimum standards or is equal to the brand name, product, is on the bidder. The City reserves the right to reject bids that the City deems unacceptable.

Modification / Withdrawal of Bid

Written requests to modify or withdraw the bid received by the City prior to the scheduled opening time will be accepted and will be corrected after opening. No oral requests will be allowed. Requests must be addressed and labeled in the same manner as the bid and marked as a MODIFICATION or WITHDRAWAL of the bid.

Requests for withdrawal after the bid opening will only be granted upon proof of undue hardship and may result in the forfeiture of any bid security. Any withdrawal after the bid opening shall be allowed solely at the City's discretion.

Chapter 17
Entering Into a Contract
签订合同

1. Learning Objectives

By the end of this chapter, you will be able to do the following:

· Get to know the key words and expressions used in commercial contracts.

· Know the useful sentence patterns in working out contracts.

· Know the linguistic characteristics of contracts.

· have a rough idea about LOI, MOU, contract.

· Know the structure of commercial contract.

2. Case Study

Sale of walnut meat with following particulars:

Sellers: China National Foodstuffs Import & Export Co. Ltd.

Buyers: Vancouver Foodstuffs Co. Ltd.

(1) lowest price offer for walnut meat of first grade at US$13,500 per metric ton on CIF Vancouver basis.

(2) an order for 120 M / T of walnut meat of first grade at the price quoted.

Pack the goods in sacks of 100 kgs each and ship the order in three shipments of 40 tons each month, commencing from October.

Open an irrevocable L/C by sight draft in seller's favor after receipt of the Sales Contract.

The goods will be insured against ALL RISKS and WAR RISK for 110% of the invoice value.

Suppose you were a clerk working in China National Foodstuffs Import & Export Co. Ltd., how would you work out a draft of contract with the Buyer Vancouver Foodstuffs Co. Ltd.

3. Introduction

Most of English legal documents will be marked on the cover page with descriptions as "Business Plan", "Investment Proposal", "Investment Proposal", "Minutes of Board", "License Agreement" , "Know-how Transfer Agreement", "Share Purchase Agreement", "Joint Venture

Agreement", "Loan Agreement", "Distribution Agreement" etc. to indicate the function of the documents.

A contract is the offer and acceptance of a legal promise between two or more parties to ensure that all parties are protected. It enables all parties to conduct business with mutual advantage. An accurate understanding of the principles of offer and acceptance will enable the involved parties to identify the precise moment at which a contract comes into existence.

In order for a contract to be formed, the parties must reach mutual assent. This is typically reached through offer and an acceptance. If a purported acceptance does vary the terms of an offer, it is not an acceptance but a counteroffer and, therefore, simultaneously a rejection of the original offer.

If a contract is in a written form, and somebody signs it, then the signer is typically bound by its terms regardless of whether they have actually read it provided the document is contractual in nature. However, affirmative defenses such as duress or unconscionability may enable the signer to avoid the obligation. Further, reasonable notice of a contract's terms must be given to the other party prior to their entry into the contract.

In international trade, a contract is usually made to specify the rights and obligations of concerning parties. Should any conflict between the two parties involved arise later, reference is then made to the contract in an effort to resolve the misunderstanding.

A contract may be formal or informal. Sale or purchase contract is formal written contract, and sometimes a purchase contract may be in the form of a purchase order when countersigned by the seller, or of a sales confirmation when countersigned by the buyer. A written contract can be simply a handwritten note, a printed statement, a typewritten letter of intent, or any other memorandum containing the terms of the agreement, so long as it is signed by the parties who wish to be bound by the contract. However, for large and complicated sales, a detailed contract must be carefully worked out and signed by parties involved.

Breach of contract is a legal cause of action in which the binding terms and conditions agreed are not honored by one or more of the parties to the contract by non-performance or interference with the other party's performance.

The remedy for breach of contract can be "damages" in the form of compensation of money or any other specific performance enforced through an injunction. Both of these remedies award the party at loss the "benefit of the bargain" or expectation damages, which are greater than mere reliance damages, as in promissory estoppel.

A letter of intent (LOI) outlines the intent of one party toward another with regard to an agreement, and may only be signed by the party expressing that intent. Such agreements may be Asset Purchase Agreements, Share Purchase Agreements, Joint-Venture Agreements, Lease Agreements, and overall all Agreements which aim at closing a financially large deal.

LOIs are similar to written contracts, but are usually not binding on the parties in their entirety. Many LOIs, however, contain provisions that are binding, such as non-disclosure agreements. An LOI may sometimes be interpreted by a court of law as binding the parties to it, if it too-closely resembles a formal contract.

A letter of intent may be presented by one party to another party and subsequently negotiated before execution (or signature). If carefully negotiated, a LOI may serve to protect both parties to a transaction.

The most common purposes of an LOI are:

· To clarify the key points of a complex transaction for the convenience of the parties.
· To declare officially that the parties are currently negotiating.
· To provide safeguards in case a deal collapses during negotiation.
· To verify certain issues regarding payments done for someone else.

Many different reasons can make it necessary to provide a letter of intent, such as business partnership, professional and personal purposes. A successful letter of intent will be informative, scholarly or professional, and persuasive, but it is important to keep the end goal in mind.

While drafting a Letter of Intent, keep in mind the following tips:

· Keep the style of the letter direct and to the point. Avoid gimmicks, flowery prose or redundancy. Use an active voice, and be precise and concise.
· A letter of intent can also be referred to as a letter of interest, personal statement, or statement of purpose.

A Memorandum of Understanding

MOU describes a bilateral or multilateral agreement between two or more parties. It expresses a convergence of will between the parties, indicating an intended common line of action and must be signed by all parties to be a valid outline of an agreement. It is often used in cases where parties either do not imply a legal commitment or in situations where the parties cannot create a legally enforceable agreement. It is a more formal alternative to a gentlemen's agreement.

Whether or not a document constitutes a binding contract depends only on the presence or absence of well-defined legal elements in the text proper of the document (the so-called "four corners"). The required elements are: offer and acceptance, consideration, and intention to be legally bound.

One advantage of MOUs over more formal instruments is that, because obligations under international law may be avoided, they can be put into effect in most countries without requiring parliamentary approval. Hence, MOUs are often used to modify and adapt existing treaties, in which case these MOUs have factual treaty status. The decision concerning ratification, however, is determined by the parties' internal law and depends to a large degree on the subject agreed upon. MOUs that are kept confidential (i.e. not registered with the UN) cannot be enforced before any UN organ, and it may be concluded that no obligations under international law have been created.

4. Specimens

Specimen 1
Letter of Intent

Letter of Intent for Business

Much 25, 2015
Sara Davis
Kate's Pizza, Inc.

Dear Ms. Davis,

We welcome the opportunity to submit a proposal to acquire the business of Kate's Pizza, Inc. and related companies (collectively the "Company" or "Seller") operating approximately 20 retail stores in New York selling baked goods (the "Business"). We understand the desire to proceed expeditiously with a sale of the Business. We are prepared to move quickly on the transaction and believe we are well suited to do so. This letter summarizes our proposal.

1. Purchase Price

An entity newly formed by Robert ("Buyer") would purchase substantially all of the operating assets, including all tangible and intangible assets, equipment, leases, contract rights, and intellectual property used in the Business for a purchase price of two million dollars ($2,000,000). Buyer will not assume any liabilities of the Business of the Company other than liabilities accruing after the closing under contracts or leases assumed by Buyer.

2. Definitive Agreement

The closing will be subject to the negotiation and execution of definitive transaction documents that will include, among other things, customary representations, warranties, covenants, and indemnities by the Seller and their principals regarding the business, operations, and financial condition of the Business.

3. Closing Date

The parties acknowledge that time is of importance and that they will work towards closing the transaction as quickly as possible.

4. Conditions to Closing

The consummation of the Transaction will be subject to the satisfaction of customary conditions, including, without limitation, the following:

● The negotiation, execution, and delivery of definitive agreements satisfactory to each of the parties, including retail leases, and securing of any required governmental or third-party approvals, waivers, or consents.

● Maintenance of the Company's business in the ordinary course, and the absence of any material adverse change in the Company's business of financial condition or material changed in the conduct of its business as of the date of this Letter of Intent.

● The Company not seeking or requesting any type of bankruptcy protection or bankruptcy procedure.

5. Binding Agreement

Other than this paragraph 5, which is intended to be and is legally binding, this letter is nonbinding and constitutes an indication of intent only and creates no liability or obligation of any nature whatsoever among the parties hereto with respect to any contemplated transaction or any other matter or action described or referred to herein. Legally binding obligations with respect to the contemplated transaction will only arise upon execution of a definitive agreement and related agreements with respect to the transaction.

If the foregoing is satisfactory, please indicate your agreement with the foregoing by countersigning a copy of this letter and returning it to our attention. We look forward to proceeding together on this transaction.

_____

Bill Steveson
Managing Director
Bstevmdor@gmail.com

Specimen 2
Memorandum of Understanding

MEMORANDUM OF UNDERSTANDING
BETWEEN
THE GENERAL ADMINISTRATION OF CUSTOMS OF
THE PEOPLE'S REPUBLIC OF CHINA
AND
THE AUSTRALIAN CUSTOMS SERVICE OF
THE COMMONWEALTH OF AUSTRALIA
ON CUSTOMS CO-OPERATION AND MUTUAL
ADMINISTRATIVE ASSISTANCE
IN CUSTOMS MATTERS

General Administration of Customs, the People's Republic of China and the Customs Administrations of the Commonwealth of Australia, are the parties to this Memorandum of Understanding (MOU).

CONSIDERING the importance of accurate assessment of customs duties and other taxes collected at importation or exportation and of ensuring proper enforcement of specific measures of prohibition, restriction and control;

CONSIDERING that offences against customs law are prejudicial to their economic, commercial, fiscal, social, health, and cultural interests;

RECOGNISING the need for international co-operation to ensure the proper application and enforcement of their customs law;

RECOGNISING the importance of customs cooperation in counter-terrorism and fighting transnational crime;

CONVINCED that action against customs offences can be made more effective by close co-operation between their Customs Administrations;

The two parties here of have mutually decided as follows:

Clause 1 For the purposes of this MOU:

(a) "Customs Administration" means the General Administration of Customs for the People's Republic of China, and the Australian Customs Service for the Commonwealth of.

(b) "Customs law" means the statutory and regulatory provisions relating to the importation, exportation, movement or storage of goods, the administration and enforcement of which are specifically charged to customs administrations, and any regulations made by customs administrations under their statutory powers.

(c) "Customs offence" means any violation or attempted violation of customs law;

(d) "Information" means any data, whether or not processed or analyzed, and documents, reports, and other communications in any format, including electronic, or certified or authenticated copies thereof;

(e) "Official" means any customs officer or other government agent designated by either Customs Administration;

(f) "Person" means both natural and legal persons;

(g) "Personal data" means information or data which relates to a person whose identity is disclosed in the information or data, or whose identity can be reasonably ascertained from the information or data;

(h) "Requesting Administration" means the Customs Administration which requests assistance; and

(i) "Requested Administration" means the Customs Administration from which assistance is requested.

Clause 2 Scope of the MOU

1. The Customs Administrations will afford each other administrative assistance under the terms set out in this MOU, for the proper application of customs law and for the prevention, investigation and combating of customs offences.

2. All assistance under this MOU by either Customs Administration will be afforded in accordance with its national legal and administrative provisions.

3. Assistance will be afforded within the limits of the Customs Administrations' competence and available resources.

4. This MOU covers mutual administrative assistance between the Customs Administrations and is not intended to impact on mutual legal assistance agreements between the People's Republic of China and the Commonwealth of Australia.

5. The provisions of this MOU will not give rise to a right on the part of any person to impede the execution of a request.

Clause 3 Scope of Assistance

Information for the Application and Enforcement of Customs Law:

1. The Customs Administrations will provide each other, either on request or on their own initiative, with information which helps to ensure proper application of customs law and the prevention, investigation and combating of customs offences. Such information may be in respect of, but is not limited to:

(a) new customs law enforcement techniques which have proved their effectiveness;

(b) new trends, means or methods of committing customs offences;

(c) goods known to be the subject of customs offences, as well as transport and storage methods used in respect of those goods; and

(d) mutual assistance and cooperation on customs related matters including customs best practice procedures and relevant international standards.

2. Assistance provided under this MOU will, on request, include the provision of information to ensure the correct determination of customs value, tariff classification, origin of products and the proper management of operational risks.

3. Either Customs Administration will, in making inquiries in its national territory on behalf of the other Customs Administration, use all means available to provide the requested assistance.

Clause 4 Special Instances of Assistance

Information Relating to Customs Offences:

1. The Customs Administrations will provide each other, either on request or on their own initiative, with information on transactions, planned, ongoing, or completed which constitute or appear to constitute a customs offence.

2. In serious cases that could involve substantial damage to the national interests such as the economy, public health or public security or any other vital interest of either Customs Administration, wherever possible, the Customs Administrations will supply such information on their own initiative without delay.

Clause 5 Particular Types of Information

1. On request, the Requested Administration will provide the Requesting Administration with information related to:

   (a) whether goods imported into the territory of the Requesting Administration have been lawfully exported from the territory of the Requested Administration and the customs procedures relevant to the exportation;

   (b) whether goods exported from the territory of the Requesting Administration have been lawfully imported into the territory of the Requested Administration and the customs procedures relevant to the importation; and

   (c) administrative penalties in relation to customs offences and their application.

2. Where a Customs Administration has evidence showing that:

   (a) a citizen of, or person residing in the territory of the other Customs Administration has attempted to bribe, or has bribed, one of its officers; or

   (b) a citizen of, or person residing in its territory has been requested by an official of the other Customs Administration to pay a bribe to that official, or has paid a bribe to him or her.

3. Paragraph 2 of Clause 5 does not cover requests for evidence suitable for admission in criminal proceedings. Such requests will be dealt with under legislation enacted for that purpose.

Clause 6 Surveillance and Information

On request, the Requested Administration will, within its territory, maintain surveillance over and provide information on:

   (a) goods either in transport or in storage known to have been used or suspected of being used to commit customs offences in the territory of the Requesting Administration;

   (b) means of transport known to have been used or suspected of being used to commit customs offences in the territory of the Requesting Administration;

   (c) premises known to have been used or suspected of being used to commit customs offences in the territory of the Requesting Administration;

   (d) persons known to have committed a customs offence in the territory of the Requesting Administration, or suspected of doing so, particularly those moving into and out of the territory of the Requested Administration.

Clause 7 Controlled Delivery

On request, the Customs Administrations may, by mutual arrangement, permit the movement of unlawful or suspect goods out of, through, or into their territories, with the knowledge and under the control of the competent authorities, with a view to investigating and combating customs offences. If granting such permission is not within the competence of the Customs Administration, that Administration may endeavor to initiate cooperation with national authorities with such competence.

Clause 8 Technical Assistance

The Customs Administrations recognize that well-designed and targeted capacity building investments focused on improving the efficiency and effectiveness of customs administrations can be beneficial. With this in mind, the Customs Administrations may provide technical assistance or training to each other, including in relation to the application of technology and container X-ray scanning equipment in particular, to improve the ability of carrying out their functions and implementing this MOU.

Clause 9 Information

1. Original information will only be requested in cases where certified or authenticated copies would be insufficient and will be returned at the earliest opportunity. The rights of the Requested Administration or third parties relating to the information will remain unaffected.

2. Any information to be exchanged under this MOU will be accompanied by information relevant to its interpretation and use.

Clause 10 Communication of Requests

1. Requests for assistance under this MOU will be addressed directly to the Customs Administration. Requests will be made in writing or electronically, and will be accompanied by any information deemed useful to comply with the request. The Requested Administration may require written confirmation of electronic requests. Where the circumstances so require, requests may be made orally. Oral requests will be confirmed in writing, including by facsimile and email, as soon as possible.

2. Requests made pursuant to Paragraph 1 of this Clause, will include the following details:
   (a) the name of the Administration making the request;
   (b) the name of the person authorized to make a request in accordance with Clause 10.4;
   (c) the customs matter at issue, type of assistance requested, and reason for the request;
   (d) a brief description of the case under review and its administrative and legal elements; and
   (e) the names, dates of birth and addresses of the persons to whom the request relates, if known.

3. Where the Requesting Administration requests that a certain procedure or methodology be followed, the Requested Administration will comply with such request subject to its national legal and administrative provisions.

4. The information referred to in this MOU will be communicated to officials who are specially designated for this purpose by either Customs Administration. Contact details of these officials and any changes to these details will be notified to the other Customs Administration in accordance with Clause 19 of this MOU.

5. All requests will be made in English.

Clause 11 Execution of Requests

Means of Obtaining Information:

1. If the Requested Administration does not have the information requested, it will initiate inquiries to obtain that information.

2. If the Requested Administration is not the appropriate authority to initiate inquiries to obtain the information requested, it may indicate the appropriate authority and provide the contact details of the appropriate authority.

Clause 12 Presence of Officials of the Requesting Administration at the Invitation of the Requested Administration

Where the Requested Administration considers it useful or necessary for an official of the Requesting Administration to be present when, pursuant to a request, measures of assistance are carried out, it will inform the Requesting Administration. Where such a request for assistance is made, the Requesting Administration will make all efforts to provide the assistance.

Clause 13 Presence of Officials Advisory Role

Officials designated by the Requesting Administration to be present in the territory of the Requested Administration, as provided for in Clause 12, will have a purely advisory role.

Clause 14 Arrangements for Visiting Officials

When officials of either Customs Administration are present in the territory of the other Customs Administration under the terms of this MOU, they must at all times be able to furnish proof of their official capacity.

Clause 15 Confidentiality of Information

1. Any information received under this MOU will be used or disclosed only by the Customs Administrations and solely for the purposes for which the information is provided, but will not be used as evidence in judicial proceedings, except in cases where the use or disclosure is:

    (a) required or authorized by the national law of the Requesting Administration;

    (b) authorized by the Requested Administration; and

    (c) conducted in strict accordance with such terms or conditions as may be laid down by the Requested Administration.

2. Any information received under this MOU will be treated as confidential and will at least be subject to the same protection and confidentiality as the same kind of information is subject to under the national law of the Requesting Administration.

Clause 16 Protection of Personal Data

1. Personal data exchange under this MOU will not begin until the Parties have mutually arranged, in accordance with Clause 19 of this MOU, that such data will be afforded a level of protection that is consistent with the national law of the providing Customs Administration.

2. In the context of this Clause, the Customs Administrations will provide each other with their relevant legislation concerning the protection of personal data.

Clause 17 Exemptions

1. Where assistance under this MOU might infringe upon the sovereignty, security, public policy or any other substantive national interest of a Customs Administration, or prejudice any legitimate commercial or professional interests, assistance may be refused or provided subject to such terms or conditions as the Requested Administration may require.

2. If in relation to a request, the Requesting Administration would be unable to reciprocate if a similar request were made to it by the Requested Administration, the Requesting Administration will draw attention to that fact in its request. Compliance with such a request will be at the discretion of the Requested Administration.

3. Assistance may be postponed if there are grounds to believe that it will interfere with an ongoing investigation, prosecution or proceeding. In such a case, the Requested Administration will consult with the Requesting Administration to determine if assistance can be given subject to such terms or conditions as the Requested Administration may require.

4. Where assistance is denied or postponed, reasons for the denial or postponement will be given.

Clause 18 Costs

1. Subject to paragraphs 2 of this Clause, the Customs Administrations will waive all claims for reimbursement of costs incurred in the execution of this MOU.

2. If costs of a substantial or extraordinary nature are or will be required to execute a request, the Customs Administrations will consult to determine the terms and conditions under which the request will be executed as well as the manner in which the costs will be borne.

Clause 19 Implementation and Application of the MOU

The Customs Administrations will jointly decide on detailed arrangements to facilitate the application of this MOU.

Clause 20 Settlement of Disputes

1. The Customs Administrations will endeavor to resolve disputes or other difficulties concerning the interpretation or application of this MOU by mutual accord.

2. The Customs Administrations will also endeavor to resolve any disputes or difficulties arising from or in relation to the application of their customs law by mutual accord.

3. Unresolved disputes or difficulties will be settled by diplomatic means.

Clause 21 Final Provisions

This MOU will come into effect 28 days after signature.

Clause 22 Duration and Termination

1. This MOU is intended to be of unlimited duration but either Customs Administration may terminate it at any time by notification in writing.

2. The termination will take effect three months from the date of the notification of termination to the other Customs Administration. Ongoing proceedings at the time of termination will nonetheless be completed in accordance with the provisions of this MOU.

Clause 23 Review

The Customs Administrations will meet in order to review this MOU on request or at the end of five years from the date of its coming into effect, unless they notify each other in writing that no such review is necessary.

IN WITNESS WHEREOF the undersigned, being duly authorized thereto, have signed this MOU.

SIGNED AT Beijing on April 19th , 2004, in duplicate in the Chinese and English languages, both texts being equally authentic.

_____　　　_____

[signature]　　　　　　　　　　　　[signature]

Specimen 3
Sales Contract

SALES CONTRACT

This contract is made by and between the China National Foodstuffs Import & Export Co. Ltd. (hereinafter referred to as the Seller) and Vancouver Foodstuffs Co. Ltd. (hereinafter referred to as the Buyer).

Whereby the Seller agrees to sell and the Buyer agrees to buy the undermentioned goods according to the terms and conditions stipulated below:

1. Names of commodity (ies) and specification(s): walnut meat of first grade.
2. Quantity: 120 M / T of walnut meat of first grade.
3. Unit price: US$13,500 per metric ton on CIF Vancouver basis.
4. Total Amount: US$1,620,000 (Say US dollars one million six hundred and twenty thousand only) .
5. Packing: The goods should be packed in sacks of 100 kgs each.
6. Port of Loading: Shanghai Port, P.R. China.
7. Port of Destination: Vancouver, Canada.
8. Shipping Marks: Marks shown as below in addition to the port of destination, package number, gross and net weights, measurements and other marks as the Buyer may require stencilled or marked conspicuously with fast and unfailing pigments on each package.
9. Time of Shipment: Within 15 days after receipt of L/C, allowing transshipment and partial shipment.
10. Terms of Payment:

By 100% Confirmed, Irrevocable and Sight Letter of Credit to remain valid for negotiation in China until the 15th day after shipment.

11. Insurance:
Covers all risks and war risks only as per the Clauses of the People's Insurance Company of China for 110% of the invoice value.
To be effected by the Buyer.

12. The Buyer shall establish the covering Letter of Credit before _____; failing which, the Seller reserves the right to rescind this Sales Contract without further notice, or to accept whole or any part of this Sales Contract, non-fulfilled by the Buyer, of to lodge claim for direct losses sustained, if any.

13. Documents: The Sellers shall present to the negotiating bank, Clean On Board Bill of Lading, Invoice, Quality Certificate issued by the China Commodity Inspection Bureau or the Manufacturers, Survey Report on Quantity/Weight issued by the China Commodity Inspection Bureau, and Transferable Insurance policy or Insurance Certificate when this contract is made on CIF basis.

14. For this contract signed on CIF basis, the premium should be 110% of invoice value. All risks insured should be included within this contract. If the Buyer asks to increase the insurance premium or scope of risks, he should get the permission of the Seller before time of loading, and all the charges thus incurred should be borne by the Buyer.

15. Quality/Quantity Discrepancy; In case of quality discrepancy, claim should be filed by the Buyer within 30 days after the arrival of the goods at port of destination; while for quantity discrepancy, claim should be filed by the Buyer within 15 days after the arrival of the goods at port of destination. It is understood that the Seller shall not be liable for any discrepancy of the goods shipped due to causes for which the Insurance Company, Shipping Company, other transportation organizations and/or Post Office are liable.

16. The Seller shall not be held liable for failure or delay in delivery of the entire lot or a portion of the goods under this Sales Contract in consequence of any Force Majeure incidents.

17. Arbitration

All disputes in connection with this contract or the execution thereof shall be settled friendly through negotiations. In case no settlement can be reached, the case may then be submitted for arbitration to China International Economic And Trade Arbitration Commission in accordance with the provisional Rules of Procedures promulgated by the said Arbitration Commission. The arbitration shall take place in Beijing and the decision of the Arbitration Commission shall be final and binding upon both parties; neither party shall seek recourse to a law court nor other authorities to appeal for revision of the decision. Arbitration fee shall be borne by the losing party. Or arbitration may be settled in the third country mutually agreed upon by both parties.

18. The Buyer is requested always to quote THE NUMBER OF THE SALES CONTRACT in the Letter of Credit to be opened in favor of the Seller.

19. Miscellaneous

The Seller: The Buyer:

5. Writing Templates

Template for LOI

LETTER OF INTENT

Possible Seller: _____

Possible Buyer: _____

Business: _____

Date: _____, 20_____

  This is a non-binding letter of intent that contains provisions that are being discussed for a possible sale of the Business named above from the possible Seller named above to the possible Buyer named above.

  This is neither a contract nor a legally binding agreement. This is merely an outline of possible contract terms for discussion purposes only. This is being signed in order to enable the Possible Buyer to apply for financing of the purchase price. This letter of intent is confidential and shall not be disclosed to anyone other than the parties and their employees, attorneys and accountants and the possible lenders of the Possible Buyer. The terms of the transaction being discussed are attached hereto, but the terms (and the possible sale itself) are not binding unless and until they are set forth in a written contract signed by Possible Seller and Possible Buyer. The word "shall" is used in the attached terms only as an example of how a contract might read, and it does not mean that the attached terms are or ever will be legally binding.

_____ _____

Witnesses

_____ _____

Witnesses

Template for MOU

DATED

[PARTY A NAME] AND [PARTY B NAME]

MEMORANDUM OF UNDERSTANDING

  This Memorandum of Understanding ("MOU") is entered into on [date] by and between [Party A name], [Party A entity form] established and existing under the laws of China, with its legal address at [address] (hereinafter referred to as "Party A"), and [Party B name], [Party B entity form] organized and existing under the laws of [Party B jurisdiction of incorporation] with its legal address at [address] (hereinafter referred to as "Party B"). Party A and Party B shall hereinafter be referred to individually as a "Party " and collectively as the "Parties".

  A. [Description of Party A].

  B. [Description of Party B].

  C. [Description of contemplated transaction]("Project").

  D. The Parties agree that before any implementation of the Project, the Parties are required to procure corporate approvals and to enter into formal binding contracts (the "Contracts"), the terms of which are to be discussed and agreed to between the Parties.

E. Subject to the subsequent negotiation and execution of the Contracts, the Parties wish to record in this MOU the current status of the Project.

THEREFORE, the Parties hereby agree as follows:
1. Matters on which the parties have reached preliminary understanding
   [Describe matters on which the parties have reached preliminary understanding]
2. Matters on which the parties intend to conduct further negotiation [Describe matters on which the parties intend to conduct further negotiation]
3. Steps to be taken by the parties after signing of the MOU
   3.1 The Parties will in good faith within the next _____ days following the signing of this MOU negotiate the terms and conditions of the Contracts.
4. Confidential Information
   4.1 From time to time prior to and during the term of this MOU either Party ("disclosing Party") has disclosed or may disclose to the other Party ("receiving Party") business, marketing, technical, scientific or other information which, at the time of disclosure, is designated as confidential (or like designation), is disclosed in circumstances of confidence, or would be understood by the Parties, exercising reasonable business judgment, to be confidential ("Confidential Information"). The receiving Party shall, during the term of this MOU and for _____ years thereafter:
   a. _____ maintain the confidentiality of Confidential Information;
   b._____ not to use Confidential Information for any purpose other than those specifically set out in this MOU; and
   c._____ not disclose any such Confidential Information to any person or entity, except to its employees or employees of its Affiliates, its agents, attorneys, accountants and other advisors who need to know such information to perform their responsibilities and who have signed written confidentiality contracts containing terms at least as stringent as the terms provided in this Article___.
   4.2 The provisions of Article___.1 above shall not apply to information that:
   a._____ can be shown to be known by the receiving Party by written records made prior to disclosure by the disclosing Party; b._____ is or becomes public knowledge otherwise than through the receiving Party's breach of this MOU; or
   c._____ was obtained by the receiving Party from a third party having no obligation of confidentiality with respect to such information.
   4.3 Upon the expiration or termination of this MOU, and in any event upon the disclosing Party's request at any time, the receiving Party shall (i) return to the other Party, or at the disclosing Party's direction destroy, all materials (including any copies thereof) embodying the other Party's Confidential information and (ii) certify in writing to the other Party, within ten days following the other Party's Confidential Information and (ii) certify in writing to the other Party, within ten days following the other Party's request, that all of such materials have been retuned or destroyed.
5. Public announcements
   Neither Party shall make any announcement or disclosure concerning the MOU without the other Party's prior written consent except as may be reasonably required by law.
6. Intellectual property rights
   Both Parties acknowledge that they do not acquire any right in or any intellectual property rights (including without limitation, copyright, trademark, trade secret, know-how) of the other Party under this MOU.
7. Amendment of MOU
   The terms and conditions of this MOU shall be amended only by mutual written consent between the Parties.

8. Binding/Non-binding clauses of MOU

   The Parties acknowledge that, other than Clauses___.4 through 13 (inclusive) which are binding on the Parties, this MOU does not constitute a binding or enforceable agreement or contract or create an obligation on the part of either Party to do any act either expressly referred to or contemplated by this MOU.

9. Assignability of MOU

   A party may not assign this MOU to any third party without the written consent of the other party.

10. Party responsible for its own costs

    Except as may be provided under this MOU, each Party is responsible for its own costs incurred in performing the activities contemplated by this MOU.

11. No consequential damages

    No Party is liable for any indirect, special or consequential loss or damage or any loss or damage due to loss of goodwill or loss of revenue or profit arising in connection with this MOU.

12. Effectiveness and termination of MOU

    This MOU shall come into force on signature by both Parties and shall continue in effect until the earliest to occur of:

    (a) the replacement of this MOU with a Contract or further agreement;

    (b) anytime without cause upon providing a one (1) month prior written notice of one Party to the other Party; or

    (c) ___days from the signing of this MOU. Clauses 4, 5, 9, 10, 11, 12 and 13 shall survive the termination of this MOU.

13. Governing Law and Arbitration

    This MOU shall be governed by the laws of ____. In the event that any dispute between the Parties arising in connection with this MOU cannot be resolved within a period of thirty (30) days on the basis of mutual consultation, then either of the Parties may refer such dispute to [arbitration institution] for arbitration in [language] under the [arbitration rules].

    IN WITNESS WHEREOF, each of the Parties hereto has caused this MOU to be executed by its duly authorized representative on the date first set forth above.

[Party A name]	[Party B name]
By:	By:
Name: [Party A rep name]	Name: [Party B rep name] Title:
[Party A rep position]	Title: [Party B rep position]
Nationality:[Chinese]	Nationality: [Party B rep]

Template for Contract

Contract No:
Date:
The Buyer:
The Seller:

   The Contract, made out, in Chinese and English, both version being equally authentic, by and between the Seller and the Buyer whereby the Seller agrees to sell and the Buyer agrees to buy the undermentioned goods subject to terms and conditions set forth hereinafter as follows:

SECTION 1
1. Name of Commodity and specification
2. Country of Origin & Manufacturer
3. Unit Price (packing charges included)
4. Quantity
5. Total Value
6. Packing (seaworthy)
7. Insurance (to be covered by the Buyer unless otherwise)
8. Time of Shipment
9. Port of Loading
10. Port of Destination
11. Marks shown as below in addition to the port of destination, package number, gross and net weights, measurements and other marks as the Buyer may require stencilled or marked conspicuously with fast and unfailing pigments on each package. In the case of dangerous and/or poisonous cargo(es), the Seller is obliged to take care to ensure that the nature and the generally adopted symbol shall be marked conspicuously on each package.
12. Terms of Payment:

   One month prior to the time of shipment the Buyer shall open with the Bank of _____ an irrevocable Letter of Credit in favor of the Seller payable at the issuing bank against presentation of documents as stipulated under Clause 18. A. of SECTION II, the Terms of Delivery of this Contract after departure of the carrying vessel. The said Letter of Credit shall remain in force till the 15th day after shipment.
13. Other Terms:

   Unless otherwise agreed and accepted by the Buyer, all other matters related to this contract shall be governed by Section II, the Terms of Delivery which shall form an integral part of this Contract. Any supplementary terms and conditions that may be attached to this Contract shall automatically prevail over the terms and conditions of this Contract if such supplementary terms and conditions come in conflict with terms and conditions herein and shall be binding upon both parties.

SECTION 2
14. FOB/FAS TERMS

   14.1 The shipping space for the contracted goods shall be booked by the Buyer or the Buyer's shipping agent _____.

   14.2 Under FOB terms, the Seller shall undertake to load the contracted goods on board the vessel nominated by the Buyer on any date notified by the Buyer, within the time of shipment as stipulated in Clause 8 of this Contract.

   14.3 Under FAS terms, the Seller shall undertake to deliver the contracted goods under the tackle of the vessel nominated by the Buyer on any date notified by the Buyer, within the time of shipment as stipulated in Clause 8 of this Contract.

   14.4 10-15 days prior to the date of shipment, the Buyer shall inform the Seller by cable or telex of the contract number, name of vessel, ETA of vessel, quantity to be loaded and the name of shipping agent, so as to enable the Seller to contact the shipping agent direct and arrange the shipment of the goods. The Seller shall advise by cable or telex in time the Buyer of the result thereof. Should, for certain reasons, it become necessary for the Buyer to replace the named vessel with another one, or should the named vessel arrive at the port of shipment earlier or later than the date of arrival as previously notified to the Seller, the Buyer or its shipping agent shall advise the Seller to this effect in due time. The Seller shall also keep in close contact with the agent or the Buyer.

   14.5 Should the Seller fail to load the goods on board or to deliver the goods under the tackle of the vessel booked by the Buyer. Within the time as notified by the Buyer, after its arrival at the port of shipment the Seller shall be fully liable to the Buyer and responsible for all losses and expenses such as dead freight, demurrage. Consequential losses incurred upon and/or suffered by the Buyer.

14.6 Should the vessel be withdrawn or replaced or delayed eventually or the cargo be shut out etc., and the Seller be not informed in good time to stop delivery of the cargo, the calculation of the loss in storage expenses and insurance premium thus sustained at the loading port shall be based on the loading date notified by the agent to the Seller (or based on the date of the arrival of the cargo at the loading port in case the cargo should arrive there later than the notified loading date). The above-mentioned loss to be calculated from the 16th day after expiry of the free storage time at the port should be borne by the Buyer with the exception of Force Majeure. However, the Seller shall still undertake to load the cargo immediately upon the carrying vessel's arrival at the loading port at its own risk and expenses. The payment of the afore-said expenses shall be effected against presentation of the original vouchers after the Buyer's verification.

15. C&F Terms

15.1 The Seller shall ship the goods within the time as stipulated in clause 8 of this Contract by a direct vessel sailing from the port of loading to China port. Transshipment on route is not allowed without the Buyer's prior consent. The goods shall not be carried by vessels flying flags of countries not acceptable to the Port Authorities of China.

15.2 The carrying vessel chartered by the Seller shall be seaworthy and cargoworthy. The Seller shall be obliged to act prudently and conscientiously when selecting the vessel and the carrier when chartering such vessel. The Buyer is justified in not accepting vessels chartered by the Seller that are not members of the PICLUB.

15.3 The carrying vessel chartered by the Seller shall sail and arrive at the port of destination within the normal and reasonable period of time. Any unreasonable aviation or delay is not allowed.

15.4 The age of the carrying vessel chartered by the Seller shall not exceed 15 years. In case her age exceeds 15 years, the extra average insurance premium thus incurred shall be borne by the Seller. Vessel over 20 years of age shall in no event be acceptable to the Buyer.

15.5 For cargo lots over 1,000 M/T each, or any other lots less than 1,000 metric tons but identified by the Buyer, the Seller shall, at least 10 days prior to the date of shipment, inform the Buyer by telex or cable of the following information: the contract number, the name of commodity, quantity, the name of the carrying vessel, the age, nationality, and particulars of the carrying vessel, the expected date of loading, the expected time of arrival at the port of destination, the name, telex and cable address of the carrier.

15.6 For cargo lots over 1,000 M/T each, or any other lots less than 1,000 metric tons but identified by the Buyer, the Master of the carrying vessel shall notify the Buyer respectively 7 (seven) days and 24 (twenty-four) hours prior to the arrival of the vessel at the port of destination, by telex or cable about its ETA (expected time of arrival), contract number, the name of commodity, and quantity.

15.7 If goods are to be shipped per liner vessel under liner Bill of Lading, the carrying vessel must be classified as the highest _____ or equivalent class as per the Institute Classification Clause and shall be so maintained throughout the duration of the relevant Bill of Lading. Nevertheless, the maximum age of the vessel shall not exceed 20 years at the date of loading. The seller shall bear the average insurance premium for liner vessel older than 20 years. Under no circumstances shall the Buyer accept vessel over 25 years of age.

15.8 For break bulk cargoes, if goods are shipped in containers by the Seller without prior consent of the Buyer, a compensation of a certain amount to be agreed upon by both parties shall be payable to the Buyer by the Seller.

15.9 The Seller shall maintain close contact with the carrying vessel and shall notify the Buyer by fastest means of communication about any and all accidents that may occur while the carrying vessel is on route. The Seller shall assume full responsibility and shall compensate the Buyer for all losses incurred for its failure to give timely advice or notification to the Buyer.

16. CIF Terms:

Under CIF terms, besides Clause 15 C&F Terms of this contract which shall be applied the Seller shall be responsible for covering the cargo with relevant insurance with irrespective percentage.

17. Advice of Shipment:

Within 48 hours immediately after completion of loading of goods on board the vessel the Seller shall advise the Buyer by cable or telex of the contract number, the name of goods, weight (net/gross) or quantity loaded, invoice value, name of vessel, port of loading, sailing date and expected time of arrival (ETA) at the port of destination. Should the Buyer be unable to arrange insurance in time owing to the Seller's failure to give the above mentioned advice of shipment by cable or telex, the Seller shall be held responsible for any and all damages and/or losses attributable to such failure.

18. Shipping Documents

18.1 The Seller shall present the following documents to the paying bank for negotiation of payment:

18.1.1 Full set of clean on board, "freight prepaid" for C&F/CIF Terms or "Freight to collect" for FOB/FAS Terms, Ocean Bills of Lading, made out to order and blank endorsed, notifying _____ at the port of destination.

18.1.2 Five copies of signed invoice, indicating contract number, L/C number, name of commodity, full specifications, and shipping mark, signed and issued by the Beneficiary of Letter of Credit.

18.1.3 Two copies of packing list and/or weight memo with indication of gross and net weight of each package and/or measurements issued by beneficiary of Letter of Credit.

18.1.4 Two copies each of the certificates of quality and quantity or weight issued by the manufacturer and/or a qualified independent surveyor at the loading port and must indicate full specifications of goods conforming to stipulations in Letter of Credit.

18.1.5 One duplicate copy of the cable or telex advice of shipment as stipulated in Clause 17 of the Terms of Delivery.

18.1.6 A letter attesting that extra copies of above-mentioned documents have been dispatched according to the Contract.

18.1.7 A letter attesting that the nationality of the carrying vessel has been approved by the Buyer.

18.1.8 The relevant insurance policy covering, but not limited to at least 110% of the invoice value against all and war risks if the insurance is covered by the Buyer.

18.2 Any original document(s) made by rephotographic system, automated or computerized system or carbon copies shall not be acceptable unless they are clearly marked as "ORIGINAL" and certified with signatures in hand writing by authorized officers of the issuing company or corporation.

18.3 Through Bill of Lading, Stale Bill of Lading, Short Form Bill of Lading, shall not be acceptable.

18.4 Third Party appointed by the Beneficiary as shipper shall not be acceptable unless such Third Party Bill of Lading is made out to the order of shipper and endorsed to the Beneficiary and blank endorsed by the Beneficiary.

18.5 Documents issued earlier than the opening date of Letter of Credit shall not be acceptable.

18.6 In the case of C&F/CIF shipments, Charter Party Bill of Lading shall not be acceptable unless Beneficiary provides one copy each of the Charter Party, Master's of Mate's receipt, shipping order and cargo or stowage plan and/or other documents called for in the Letter of Credit by the Buyer.

18.7 The seller shall dispatch, in care of the carrying vessel, two copies each of the duplicates of Bill of Lading. Invoice and Packing List to the Buyer's receiving agent, _____ at the port of destination.

18.8 Immediately after the departure of the carrying vessel, the Seller shall airmail one set of the duplicate documents to the Buyer and three sets of the same to _____ Transportation Corporation at the port of destination.

18.9 The Seller shall assume full responsibility and be liable to the Buyer and shall compensate the Buyer for all losses arising from going astray of and/or the delay in the dispatch of the above-mentioned documents.

18.10 Banking charges outside the People's Republic of China shall be for the Seller's account.

19. If the goods under this Contract are to be dispatched by air, all the terms and conditions of this Contract in connection with ocean transportation shall be governed by relevant air terms.

20. Instruction leaflets on dangerous cargo:
For dangerous and/or poisonous cargo, the Seller must provide instruction leaflets stating the hazardous or poisonous properties, transportation, storage and handling remarks, as well as precautionary and first-air measures and measures against fire. The Seller shall airmail, together with other shipping documents, three copies each of the same to the Buyer and_____ Transportation Corporation at the port of destination.

21. Inspection & claims:
In case the quality, quantity or weight of the goods be found not in conformity with those as stipulated in this Contract upon re-inspection by the China Commodity Import and Export inspection Bureau within 60 days after completion of the discharge of the goods at the port of destination or, if goods are shipped in containers, 60 days after the opening of such containers, the Buyer shall have the right to request the Seller to take back the goods or lodge claims against the Seller for compensation for losses upon the strength of the Inspection Certificate issued by the said Bureau, with the exception of those claims for which the insurers or owners of the carrying vessel are liable, all expenses including but not limited to inspection fees, interest, losses arising from the return of the goods or claims shall be borne by the Seller. In such a case, the Buyer may, if so requested, send a sample of the goods in question to the Seller, provided that sampling and sending of such sample is feasible.

22. Damages:
With the exception of late delivery or non-delivery due to "Force Majeure" causes, if the Seller fails to make delivery of the goods in accordance with the terms and conditions, jointly or severally, of this Contract, the Seller shall be liable to the Buyer and indemnify the Buyer for all losses, damages, including but not limited to, purchase price and/or

purchase price differentials, deadfreight, demurrage, and all consequential direct or indirect losses. The Buyer shall nevertheless have the right to cancel in part or in whole of the contract without prejudice to the Buyer's right to claim compensations.

23. Force Majeure:

Neither the Seller or the Buyer shall be held responsible for late delivery or nondelivery owing to generally recognized "Force Majeure" causes. However in such a case, the Seller shall immediately advise by cable or telex the Buyer of the accident and airmail to the Buyer within 15 days after the accident, a certificate of the accident issued by the competent government authority or the chamber of commerce which is located at the place where the accident occurs as evidence thereof. If the said "Force Majeure" cause lasts over 60 days, the Buyer shall have the right to cancel the whole or the undelivered part of the order for the goods as stipulated in Contract.

24. Arbitration:

Both parties agree to attempt to resolve all disputes between the parties with respect to the application or interpretation of any term hereof of transaction hereunder, through amicable negotiation. If a dispute cannot be resolved in this manner to the satisfaction of the Seller and the Buyer within a reasonable period of time, maximum not exceeding 90 days after the date of the notification of such dispute, the case under dispute shall be submitted to arbitration if the Buyer should decide not to take the case to court at a place of jurisdiction that the Buyer may deem appropriate. Unless otherwise agreed upon by both parties, such arbitration shall be held in _____, and shall be governed by the rules and procedures of arbitration stipulated by the Foreign Trade Arbitration Commission of the China Council for the Promotion of International Trade. The decision by such arbitration shall be accepted as final and binding upon both parties. The arbitration fees shall be borne by the losing party unless otherwise awarded.

The Buyer: The Seller:

6. Key Words and Expressions

(1) hereto   关于这个

(2) set forth herein   此中所阐明的

(3) Consignment Agreement   寄售协议

(4) sales level   销售量

(5) damage allowance   合理破损；破损免赔额

(6) Ocean Marine Cargo Clause   海洋货物保险条款

(7) Force Majeure   不可抗力

(8) on the merits of the claim   依据索赔法

(9) underwriter   保险商

(10) outstanding service   优质服务

(11) Free Trade Zone   自由贸易区

(12) export subsidy   出口补贴

(13) return of product tax   退税

(14) Import License   进口许可证

(15) technological barriers   技术壁垒

(16) place of origin　原产地

(17) exchange rate　兑换率

(18) sale by sample　凭样品买卖

(19) sale by specification　凭规格买卖

(20) sale by grade　凭等级买卖

(21) sale by standard　凭标准买卖

(22) sale by descriptions and illustrations　凭说明书和图样买卖

(23) sale by trade mark or brand　凭商标或牌号买卖

(24) sale by name of origin　凭产地名称买卖

(25) duplicate sample　复样

(26) for your reference only　仅供你方参考

(27) counter sample　对等样品

(28) return sample　回样

(29) representative sample　代表性样品

(30) reference sample　参考样品

(31) commercial inspection　商检

(32) FAQ: Fair Average Quality　良好平均品质(大路货)

(33) GMQ: Good Merchantable Quality　上好可销品质

(34) within the life of the quality assurance　在质保期内

(35) Disinfection Inspection Certificate　消毒检验证书

(36) Sanitary Inspection Certificate　卫生检验证书

(37) unless the contract stipulates otherwise　除非合同另有规定

(38) be entitled to claim compensation for losses or reject the goods　有权索赔或拒收货物

7. Useful Sentence Patterns

(1) This Contract is made and entered into this ＿＿ (day) of ＿＿ (Month), ＿＿ (Year) by and between X Corporation, a corporation organized and existing under the laws of ＿＿＿＿ (State) with its principal office at ＿＿＿(address) (hereinafter referred to as the "＿＿＿") , and Y Company Ltd., a company organized and existing under the laws of ＿＿＿(State) with its principal office at ＿＿＿ (address) (hereinafter referred to as the "＿＿＿") . 依照＿＿＿法律组建的X公司，位于＿＿＿（地址）（以下称"＿＿＿"），与依照＿＿＿法律组建的Y公司，位于＿＿＿（地址）（以下称"＿＿＿"），于＿年＿月＿日订立本协议。

(2) Both parties hereby agree that... 或By this agreement both parties agree that... 双方当事人在此同意……

(3) The Seller hereby waives the right of... 或By this agreement the Seller waives the right of... 卖方在此放弃……的权利。

(4) No change in or modification of this Agreement shall be valid unless the same is made in

writing. 本协议之修改应以书面形式，方可生效。

(5) This Agreement is written in the English language. In case of any discrepancy between the English version and any translation thereof, the English text shall govern. 本协议以英文订定，与其他语言之翻译版本解释上产生差异时，应以英文版本为准。

(6) To be packed in wooden cases, 30 pieces per case of 40 yd each. 木箱装，每箱装30匹，每匹40码。

(7) In iron drum of 25kg net each. 铁桶装，每桶净重25千克。

(8) To be packed in polypropylene woven bags, 50kg each, gross for net. 用聚丙烯编制包装袋，每包重50千克，以毛重作净重。

(9) The bags, should be fairy good in quality and suitable for ocean transportation, on which the name of the goods, weight, country of origin and package date should be written / marked in English. 包装袋质量良好，适于海运，包装袋上用英语写上品名、重量、原产国别和包装日期。

(10) For the purpose of this Agreement, "Products" means all types of the machineries manufactured by Manufacturer as are specified in Attachment A hereto. 本协议所称的"产品"，是指制造商所制造如附件A表所列之各种机器。

(11) "Written", in relation to a notice under this Agreement, includes those sent by telex or fax. 本协议之"书面"通知，包括以电报或传真所为之通知。

(12) All notice shall be written in _____ and served to both parties by fax/courier according to the following addresses. If any changes of the addresses occur, one party shall inform the other party of the change of address within ____ days after the change. 所有通知用_____文写成，并按照如下地址用传真/快件送达给各方。如果地址有变更，一方应在变更后____日内书面通知另一方。

(13) IN WITNESS WHEREOF, the parties hereto have caused this Agreement to be executed by duly authorized representatives& of both parties on the date and year first written above. 本协议由被授权人，于本协议序文所记载日期，代表双方当事人缔结，特此为证。

(14) This Contract is executed in two counterparts each in Chinese and English, each of which shall deemed equally authentic. This Contract is in _____copies, effective since being signed/sealed by both parties. 本合同用中英文两种文字写成，两种文字具有同等效力。本合同共____份，自双方代表签字（盖章）之日起生效。

8. Exercises

Exercise 17-1

Direction: Put the following sentences into English.

(1) 买方通过卖方可接受的银行在装运前一个月开立以卖方为抬头的保兑的不可撤销的信用证，有效期至装运后15天。

(2) 双方同意以装运港中国进出口商品检验局签发的品质及数量检验证书为最后依据，对双方具有约束力。

(3) 在交货前制造商应就订货的质量、规格、数量、性能进行全面的检验，并出具货物与本合同相符的检验证书。该证书为议付货款时向银行提交单据的一部分，但不得作为货物质量、规格、数量、性能的最后依据，制造商应将记载检验细节的书面报告附在品质检验书内。

(4) 买方对于装运货物的任何异议必须与装运货物的船只到达目的港后30天内提出，并须提供经卖方同意的公正机关出具的检验报告，如果货物已经加工，买方即丧失索赔权利。属于保险公司或轮船公司责任范围的索赔，卖方不予受理。

(5) 承包商同意对不符合图纸规格的工程部分进行返工，并保证工程进行，同意完工一年后对有证据证明因瑕疵材料或工艺造成的缺陷进行补救。

Exercise 17-2

Direction: Put the following passages into Chinese.

(1) A party is not liable for failure to perform the party's obligations if such failure is as a result of Acts of God (including fire, flood, earthquake, storm, hurricane or other natural disaster), war, invasion, act of foreign enemies, hostilities (regardless of whether war is declared), civil war, rebellion, revolution, insurrection, military or usurped power or confiscation, terrorist activities, nationalization, government sanction, blockage, embargo, labor dispute, strike, lockout or interruption or failure of electricity or telephone service. No party is entitled to terminate this Agreement under Clause 17 (Termination) in such circumstances. If a party asserts Force Majeure as an excuse for failure to perform the party's obligation, then the nonperforming party must prove that the party took reasonable steps to minimize delay or damages caused by foreseeable events, that the party substantially fulfilled all non-excused obligations, and that the other party was timely notified of the likelihood or actual occurrence of an event described in the Clause of Force Majeure.

(2) The Seller shall not be responsible for the delay of shipment or non-delivery of the goods due to Force Majeure, which might occur during the process of manufacturing or in the course of loading or transit. The Seller shall advise the Buyer immediately of the occurrence mentioned above and within_____ days thereafter the Seller shall send a notice by courier to the Buyer for their acceptance of a certificate of the accident issued by the competent Government Authorities under whose jurisdiction the accident occurs as evidence thereof. Under such circumstances the Seller, however, are still under the obligation to take all necessary measures to hasten the delivery of the goods. In case the accident lasts for more than _____days the Buyer shall have the right to cancel the Contract.

(3) Both parties agree to attempt to resolve all disputes between the parties with respect to the application or interpretation of any term hereof of transaction hereunder, through

amicable negotiation. If a dispute cannot be resolved in this manner to the satisfaction of the Seller and the Buyer within a reasonable period of time, maximum not exceeding 90 days after the date of the notification of such dispute, the case under dispute shall be submitted to arbitration if the Buyer should decide not to take the case to court at a place of jurisdiction that the Buyer may deem appropriate. Unless otherwise agreed upon by both parties, such arbitration shall be held in _____, and shall be governed by the rules and procedures of arbitration stipulated by the Foreign Trade Arbitration Commission of the China Council for the Promotion of International Trade. The decision by such arbitration shall be accepted as final and binding upon both parties. The arbitration fees shall be borne by the losing party unless otherwise awarded.

9. Supplementary Readings

About Contract

A contract, defined in the Article 2 of Law of Contract of the People's Republic of China, approved in the year of 1999, refers to an agreement establishing, modifying and terminating the civil rights and obligations between subjects of equal footing, that is, between natural persons, legal persons or other organizations. While in the "Law Dictionary" compiled by Steven H. Gifts, a contract is defined as "contract is a promise, or a set of promises, for breach of which the law gives remedy, or the performance of which the law in some way recognizes as a duty." Meanwhile, "A Dictionary of Law" by L.B Curzon defines that "Contract is a legally binding agreement". As such, we may conclude that "A contract is an agreement which binds the parties concerned", or "An agreement which is enforceable by law".

A contract is any legally-enforceable promise or set of promises made by one party to another and therefore, reflects the policies represented by freedom of contract. In the civil law, contracts are considered to be part of the general law of obligations.

A promise is a transaction between two persons whereby the first person undertakes in the future to render some service or gift to the second person or devotes something valuable now and here to his use. A notable type of promise is an election promise. Both an oath and an affirmation can be a promise. One special kind of promise is the vow.

Freedom of contract is the key public policy that underpins the law of contract and justifies a legally enforceable system of bargaining as a benefit to society.

The Law of Obligations is one of the component elements of the civil law system of law and encompasses contractual obligations, quasi-contractual obligations such as unjust enrichment and extra-contractual obligations. The Law of Obligations is one of the branches of the civil law which includes the Law of Property, the Law of Persons, the Law of the Family, the Law of Successions, the Law of Hypothecs, the Law of Prescription. The Law of Obligations finds its origins in Roman law.

The Law of Obligations seeks to organize and regulate the voluntary and semi-voluntary legal relations available between moral and natural persons under as (1) obligations under contracts, both innominate and nominate (for example: sales, gift, lease, carriage, mandate, association, deposit, loan, employment, insurance, gaming and arbitration); (2) in unjust enrichment; (3) management of the property of another; (4) the reception of the thing not due and (5) the various forms of extra-contractual responsibility between persons known as delicts and quasi-delicts.

Then, what is an agreement?

L.B. Curzon defines an agreement in his "A Dictionary of Law" as "A consensus of mind, or evidence of such consensus, in spoken or written form, relating to anything done or to be done." And Black in his "Law Dictionary" defines an agreement as "A concord of understanding and intention between two or more parties with respect to the effect upon their relative rights and duties, of certain past or future facts or performance" of the "consent of two or more persons concurring respecting the transmission of some property, right or benefits, with the view of contacting an obligation, a mutual obligation."

Are a contract and an agreement substitutable?

A contract, if to be established, generally should involve the following components according to L.B Curzon's "A Diction of Law":

· offer and absolute and unqualified acceptance （要约和绝对接受）
· consensus ad idem （意思表示一致，也叫meeting of minds）
· intention to create legal relations （建立合同关系的意愿）
· genuineness of consent （同意的真实性）
· contractual capacity of the parties （合同当事人的缔约能力）
· legality of object （标的物的合法性）
· possibility of performance （履行的可能性）
· certainty of terms （条款的确定性）
· valuable consideration （等价有偿）

Black in his "Law Dictionary" further explains that although often used as synonyms with "contract", agreement is a broader term, e.g. an agreement might lack an essential element of a contact.

In practice, an agreement may not be restrained by General Provisions, while a contract generally must contain the General Provisions. Article 12 of Law of Contract of the People's Republic of China, 1999, specifies eight General Provisions including：

· title or name and domicile of the parities （当事人的名称或姓名和住址）
· contract object （标的）
· quantity （数量）

· quality （质量）

· price or remuneration （价款或者报酬）

· time limit, place and method of performance （履行期限、地点和方式）

· liability for breach of contract （违约责任）

· methods to settle disputes （解决争议的方法）

Based upon the depiction above, we may find that contract （合同） and agreement （协议） are quite close in meanings, but different in scope of use, which means they are generally not substitutable. A contract is surely an important part of agreement, and all contracts are definitely agreements while an agreement is not necessarily a contract, that is to say, only those agreements which satisfy the requirements for establishment of a contract and are enforceable by law can be taken as contracts.

Chapter 18
E-Business
电子商务

1. Learning Objectives

By the end of this chapter, you will be able to do the following:

· Have a general view about e-business and e-mail.

· Know how to write an e-mail.

· Know the general abbreviations in e-mail.

2. Case Study

Nowadays, many companies would write emails to their business partners to promote sales. The sellers advertise their products in these emails in order to persuade the buyers into accepting the priced goods. Please read the following information and write an email for promotion.

QUZHOU STARHOME OUTDOOR CO.,LTD is located in Quzhou, Zhejiang, China, which is named as Quzhou Lezheng Outdoor Co., Ltd. before. Our company is established in 2005, with an area of 5000 square-meters, including cutting workshop and sewing workshop. We have more than 500 workers including technical persons. There are more than 350 high speed double needle Sartorius, and more than 30 other related high-tech facilities in our workshop. Our production capacity is more than 50000 sets/month.

We persist in new products development; strict quality control. Thanks to joint efforts that our products have won great reputation from design, performance and material sourcing.

Our main products are Camping Tents, Family Tents, Beach Tents, Beach Chairs, Sleeping Bags and other related outdoor products. Our products are very popular in over 20 countries and regions, such as UK, Germany, America, Argentina, South Africa etc. OEM Business is also welcome.

3. Introduction

E-business is the abbreviation of electronic business, referring to the conduct of business on the Internet. It involves business processes covering the entire value chain: electronic process of the supply chain management, processing orders electronically, handling customer service, and collaborating with business partners. Presently, e-business ranges from simple sites providing corporate information to sites offering goods and services for sale online. Innovative uses for new voice and video communication technologies include online language tutoring.

E-business is more than e-commerce in that e-business refers to doing business on the Internet, not only buying and selling but also servicing customers and cooperating with business partners, while e-commerce mainly focuses on the electronic process of purchasing and selling goods via electronic means. The scope of e-business is wider than e-commerce, actually e-commerce is included in e-business.

E-business has many incomparable advantages, such as convenience (it has saved lots of time and efforts compared with traditional business), richer information and reviews (it offers abundant information and reviews online for the customers' reference), wider selection (without geographical constrains and time limit, all customers can select satisfactory goods and business partners on the Internet) and lower costs (the costs of doing business via electronic means is much lower than the traditional business). However, e-business also has some problems like fraud and security concerns, privacy, more competition, and difficult customer relations compared with the traditional business mode.

One of the most commonly used contacting ways between buyers and sellers in e-business is writing e-mail, which is the short term for electronic mail. It is the modernest communication service which can send a message to a person in the world who has an e-mail address within a few seconds.

E-mail message can be seen as a letter with attachments, such as photos or formatted documents. You can also send music, video clip and software programs by e-mail.

Everyone who enters the Internet will have an e-mail address with the typical form like "professor@learnthenet.com". The part before @ is the user's name referring to the recipient's mailbox. The part coming after @ is called the domain name (usually the name of a company or organization), consisting of a dot (.) and three or more letters which indicate the type of organization or the country where the host server is located.

These domains are currently in use:

com—For businesses, commercial enterprises, or online services like America Online. Most companies use this extension.

edu—For educational institutions and universities.

gov—Reserved for United States government agencies.

net—For networks; usually reserved for organizations such as Internet service providers.

org—For non-commercial organizations.

For the contents of e-mail, there are usually two parts, the header and the body. The header contains the name and address of the recipient, the name and address of anyone who is being copied, and the subject of the message. Some e-mail programs also display your name and address and the date of the message. The body contains the message itself.

Comparatively speaking, e-mail has the following strong points:

· It can be as fast as telex and fax.

· It is cheaper than an international phone call, fax, and telex.

· The message and attachment can be sent easily.

· Some of e-mail address can be applied freely.

· It is 24-hour service and the message can be received unattended.

4. Specimen Letters

Specimen 1

Date: Wednesday, Feb. 25, 2015 17:55 PM
To: Adam@hotmail.com
From: Judy@yahoo.com
Subject: Quotation No. 02005

Dear Sir,

We are pleased to send you our Quotation No. 14009 covering the goods as outlined under your fax Inquiry NO. 14018.

The goods covered by this quotation is at our lowest price and is listed at FOB Shanghai. Thank you for you inquiry again and hope our cooperation will be fruitful and successful.

Contact us immediately if you have any questions.

Yours faithfully,
[Signature]

Specimen 2

Date: Friday, Feb. 27, 2015 14:35 PM
To: Sam@hotmail.com
From: Catherine@sina.com
Subject: Garden cart TC1840

Dear Sir,

Thank you for your e-mail message of Feb. 25, 2015 inquiring about our Garden cart TC1835. We appreciate your interest but we cannot supply it because the production has been discontinued. We believe our new product Garden cart TC1840 is an excellent replacement:

model	load	weight	size
TC1840	600kg	37kg	L1235 × W615 × H1035(mm)

The quality and performance are much improved and it is sold very well. We will send you a catalogue and price list immediately.

Thank your again for you inquiry and look forward to your favorable reply.

Yours faithfully,
[Signature]

5. General Smileys and Abbreviations in E-mail

Smileys

"Smileys" are something made up by users to compensate for the lack of facial and voice cues in e-mail. They are simple series of symbols that are pieced together to express the writer's feelings. Here are some examples.

:-)   smile (humor, happy, encouragement)

:-(sad (disapproved)

;-)   wink (light sarcasm)

:-{   angry

:-@   cursing, scream

:-D   shock or surprise

:~)   wondering

:-   indifference

:->   devilish grin (heavy sarcasm)

:-/   perplexed

:-P   wry smile

:-}   leer

:-O   yell

Abbreviations

While Smileys add personality to your messages, abbreviations save keystrokes. Some common ones include:

Abbreviations	Means	Abbreviations	Means
<BBN>	bye bye now	<HTH>	hope this helps
<BBL>	be back later	<IJWTK>	I just want to know
<BFN>	bye for now	<IJWTS>	I just want to say
<BRB>	be right back	<IMHO>	in my humble opinion
<BS>	big smile	<IYSS>	if you say so
<BTW>	by the way	<LTNS>	long time no see
<CUL>	see you later	<LOL>	laughing out loud
<CWYL>	chat with you later	<NOYB>	none of your business
<4 ever>	forever	<OTOH>	on the other hand
<FTTB>	for the time being	<ROTFL>	rolling on the floor laughing
<4U>	for you	<SUP>	What' up
<FWIW>	for what it's worth	<TNSTAAFL>	there's no such thing as a free lunch
<FYI>	for your information	<TCOY>	take care of yourself
<G>	grin	<TOY>	thinking of you
<GL>	good luck	<TTYL>	talk to you later

6. Exercises

Exercise 18-1

Directions: Rearrange the following information into an e-mail.

(1) Thank you again for your order and support of our business.

(2) That is: 25 metric tons for each.

(3) Thank you for your Letter of Credit No. 048 covering your Order No. 054 for 50 metric tons of Ore which we received this morning.

(4) When making our Offer No. 038 dated March 5, 2015, we state clearly that the parcel is to be divided into 2 lots.

(5) After examination of the Letter of Credit, we found that there is no stipulation of partial shipments being allowed in the relative L/C, so we can hardly manage to arrange this parcel.

(6) The first lot of the goods is ready for shipment at present, so we have to request you to amend the L/C accordingly as soon as possible.

Exercise 18-2

Direction: Write a letter according to the following information.

Please write an e-mail, asking the Buyer to apply for the irrevocable Letter of Credit.

7. Supplementary Reading

E-Mail Etiquette

Introduction

This document is intended to offer guidance to users of electronic mail (e-mail) systems.

This is not a "how-to" document, but rather a document that offers advice to make you more computer-worthy (probably more worthy than you desire) and to prevent you from embarrassing yourself at some point in the near future.

To, Cc and Bcc

With only three choices for addressing an e-mail, i.e. the "To", "Cc" and "Bcc" fields, you would think addressing would be trouble free. Unfortunately, that's not the case.

First, there are the users who have no idea that the "Cc" exists. Every address is listed in the "To" even if the email is only directed to one person. In cases such as this the receivers have no clue as to who should take action so either they all do something or they all do nothing.

Secondly, there are users who feel that every single e-mail should be copied to their entire address book whether it's relevant to those receiving it or not. These are the "cry for attention" crowd.

Lastly, there are users who never read the names of the people who receive a copy of an e-mail. They are the "Did you see this?" crowd. For example, person X sends an e-mail to persons A, B and C. C immediately forwards it to A and B with the question "Did you see this?" not bothering to see that X already sent A and B copies.

In summary, here's a rough guide on how to populate the address fields:

The addresses in the "To" are for the people you are directly addressing.

The addresses in the "Cc" are for the people you are indirectly addressing. They are the FYI-ers or CYA-ers. Don't over do it here. Copy only those who need to be copied; not your entire universe of contacts.

The addresses in the "Bcc" are like "Cc" except that the addresses in "To" and "Cc" do not know that the addresses in the "Bcc" are included in the conversation. The "To" and "Cc" addresses are blind to the "Bcc" addresses. As you can imagine, use of the "Bcc" is somewhat unethical and therefore its use is discouraged.

Reply to All

The "Reply to All" button is just a button, but it can generate tons of unnecessary e-mails. For example, if I send a dozen people an e-mail asking if they are available at a certain time for a meeting I should get a dozen replies and that's it. However, if each person hits the "Reply to All" button not only do I get a dozen replies, but so does everyone else for a total of 144 messages!

I'm not saying that the "Reply to All" button should not be used. I'm saying that it should be used with care.

Privacy, Are You Kidding?

Stop right where you are and set aside a couple of brain cells for the following statement: there is no such thing as a private e-mail. I don't care what anybody says, states, swears or whatever, there is just no such thing as private e-mail. The reason? Keep reading.

With some e-mail systems, the e-mail administrator has the ability to read any and all e-mail messages. If this is the case where you are located you better hope that there is an honest and respectable person in that position.

Some companies monitor employee e-mail (I consider this one of the worst forms of censorship). The reasons for this obtrusive behavior range from company management wanting to make sure users are not wasting time on frivolous messages to making sure that company secrets are not being leaked to unauthorized sources.

E-mail software is like all software in that occasionally things go wrong. If this happens, you may end up receiving e-mail meant for another person or your e-mail may get sent to the wrong person. Either way, what you thought was private is not private anymore.

Somewhere in the world there is a person (usually a hacker) who is able to read your e-mail if he/she tries hard enough. Of course "Tries hard enough" is the key. It's not that simple to read another person's e-mail (usually). There are (usually) security measures in place to prevent this from happening, but no security is one hundred percent hacker-proof. I have "usually" in parenthesis in the prior two sentences because I'm making the assumption that the person/persons who install and operate your e-mail system have taken the necessary precautions. Of course, the same must also be true for the person/persons on the receiving end of your e-mail.

So where does this leave us. First, let me reiterate the initial statement: there is no such thing as a private e-mail. Got it? Second, don't send anything by e-mail that you would not want posted on the company bulletin board. If it's safe enough for the bulletin board, it's safe enough for e-mail. Finally, if you are debating whether or not to send something personal by e-mail, either deliver it by hand or send it by snail mail.

A Blessing and A Curse

E-mail is a conversation that does not require an immediate response (like a telephone). If someone calls you on the telephone, you pick it up (unless you have an answering machine, voice mail or you are just plain rude) and the conversation begins. This is an interactive conversation.

With e-mail you send a message and then wait for a response. The response may come in five minutes or the response may come in five days. Either way it's not an interactive conversation.

If a hundred people send you e-mail in one day, so what? You didn't have to talk with all one hundred. Just think of all the hellos, good-byes and other unnecessary chit-chat you avoided. With e-mail you only deal with their messages (which usually omit hellos, good-byes and such) and you deal with them on your own time. That's the blessing.

Now for the curse.

Too many users assume that the minute someone receives an e-mail it, the person will read it. Bad assumption.

If you schedule a meeting for an hour from now and send an e-mail to each attendee, the chance that all the attendees will read that message within the hour will be pretty small. On the other hand, if you schedule the meeting for the next day, the chance that they will read the message will be pretty high. Remember, e-mail is not designed for immediacy (that's why you have a telephone), it's designed for convenience.

Some (not all) e-mail systems have features that try to combat this problem. These features (usually called "notification") will notify you when a person has received your e-mail and may also notify you when the person has read it (really all it can do is assume you that the person has looked at the first screen of the message—it has no way to know if the person has read the message word for word). Referring back to the example in the last paragraph, you could check to see who has checked their e-mail before the meeting and then telephone those who have not read it.

Appendix: Answers
附录：参考答案

✎ Answer to Exercise 1-1

Dear Sir,

We thank you for your letter of September 11 regarding Ammonium Sulphate, for which you have received inquiries from your customers in East Africa.

We wish we could have received your inquiry a little earlier.

On the only one day before it reached us, a contract was signed with Ethiopia for a total of 480000 tons.

Because of this, our Government has decided not to grant export licenses for the commodity for areas other than Ethiopia until December 31, 2014, expecting the shortage which may be caused in the domestic market.

Therefore, we shall be pleased to inform you in detail as soon as the circumstances become favorable for us to do business in this line.

Yours faithfully,
[Signature]

✎ Answer to Exercise 1-2

Dear Sir or Madam,

Digital Cameras

We are interested in your various types of digital cameras displayed at the Guangzhou Fair in April.

We introduce ourselves as one of the largest importers of electric goods in New York and have been in this line for over twenty years. We expect to establish business relations with you with keen interest.

At present we are enlarging our import business. Please send us a full range of illustrated catalogues and samples. We will appreciate it very much if you will quote us the lowest price CIF New York for the digital cameras that can be supplied from stock.

We look forward to your early reply.

Yours faithfully,
[Signature]

Answer to Exercise 2-1

> 尊敬的先生们，
>
> 　　贵方9月20日来函收悉，函中提到的公司是最负责任的纺织品经销商之一。
> 该公司成立于1968年，为我方公司提供品质产品已20余年。他们交货及时、
> 价格适中、质量上乘，一直是我们最满意的供货商。
> 　　我们认为他们可以算得上是A级公司，因此，贵方可以放心与之交易。当然，
> 这只是我们单方面的观点，对贵方所提议的商务谈判，我们不会承担任何责任。
> 　　我们希望上述答复能够令你们满意，并将协助你们做出恰当的判断。
> 　　致礼!
>
> 签名

Answer to Exercise 2-2

> Dear Sir,
>
> We are sorry to say that our experiences with the company which you inquired about in your letter of June 17 have been unsatisfactory.
>
> It is true we were in business relations with the firm of the last two years and on several occasions we have had lots of trouble in effecting settlements.
>
> The company still owes US$ 250,400 for purchase made over seven months ago. The account is now in the hand of our attorneys for collection.
>
> May we ask that you treat this information as strictly confidential without any responsibility on our part.
>
> Very truly yours,
> [Signature]

Answer to Exercise 3-1

(1) We have obtained your name and address from the Commercial Counselor's Office of the Embassy of Singapore in Beijing and understand that you would like to establish a business relation with us.

(2) We are given to understand that you are potential buyers of Architectural Pottery, which falls in the scope of our business activities.

(3) We are convinced that with joint efforts business between us will be developed to our mutual benefit.

(4) As the items falls within the scope of our business activities, we shall be pleased to enter into direct business relations with you.

(5) A booklet including a general introduction, the scope of business and other aspects is enclosed for your reference.

(6) We will write to inform you of our credit standing.

(7) We have learnt from the Chamber of Commerce that you are in the market for a large quantity of Black Tea. We are writing to you in the hope of establishing business relations with you and enclosing you a copy of our latest catalogue.

(8) Could you give us a general idea of the market price of textiles at your end.

(9) We take this opportunity to re-emphasize that we shall, at all times, do everything possible to give you whatever information you desire. We will appreciate your confidence and support.

(10) In compliance with your request in letter of September 3rd, we enclose our sample and brochure.

✒ Answer to Exercise 3-2

Dear Sir,

　　We were very pleased to receive your letter of May 2nd, in which you express the wish to cooperate with us in the line of electrical goods.

　　We have various types of electrical goods in stock and we shall be pleased to arrange for you to try any type you like. We enclose a copy of our catalogue for your reference and hope that you would contact us if you are satisfied with any item.

　　Looking forward to your specific inquiry.

Yours faithfully,
[Signature]

✒ Answer to Exercise 3-3

Dear Sir,

　　Having obtained your name and address from www.alibaba.com, we learned that you are handling the import and export of canned food. And now we are writing to you to establish long-term trade relations.

　　We have been importers of canned food for many years and enjoyed high reputation in China. At present, we are interested in Indonesian Canned Sardine and will appreciate it if you could send us your latest catalogue and quotations.

　　We will highly appreciate it if you could make an early reply.

Yours faithfully,
[Signature]

✎ Answer to Exercise 4-1

Dear Sir,

We have read your advertisement in newspaper. Our company is one of the largest health food importers in Liverpool. It is our goal to establish direct business relations with you in order to promote trade between our two countries.

We look forward to receiving your quotation CIF Liverpool inclusive of our commission of 5% at an early date. Please state the earliest shipment and quantity available as well.

We are ready to conclude substantial business with you if your quotation is attractive.

We look forward to your early reply.

Yours faithfully,
[Signature]

✎ Answer to Exercise 4-2

(1) We would appreciate so much if you could kindly send us as soon as possible your catalogues, sample books or even samples if possible.

(2) We hope this will be a good start for a long-term and profitable business relations.

(3) From the price list you can see that we have managed to give you the lowest quotation with the increasing price in recent months.

(4) Please note that the above information is provided without any responsibility on our part and should be treated strictly confidential.

(5) Its balanced sheets of recent years enclosed will show you that its business has been operated satisfactorily.

✎ Answer to Exercise 4-3

Dear Sir,

Thank you for your inquiry dated January 4 asking for an illustrated catalogue and samples.

We are enclosing our latest illustrated catalogue for all bags (ladies fashion bag, wallet, clutch). We are also sending you, under separate cover, some samples for your reference. We believe you will place an order before further rises in costs after you examine the samples.

We are one of the leading exporters of this area. Our products are very popular both home and abroad due to their superior quality and reasonable prices.

We are looking forward to your first order soon.

Yours faithfully,
[Signature]

✦ Answer to Exercise 5-1

Dear Sir,

Thank you for your e-mail of October 1, inquiring for Sunshine bicycles.
Based on your requirement, we are quoting as follows:
26" Men's style   US $ 40 per set
26" Women's style   US $ 40 per set
Payment term: Draft at 60 d/s under Irrevocable Letter of Credit
The above prices are understood to be on CIF Ningbo basis net. A discount of 15% may be allowed if the quantity for each specification is more than 1500 sets.
The above quotation is made without engagement and is subject to our final confirmation.
We look forward to your early reply.

Yours faithfully,
[Signature]

✦ Answer to Exercise 5-2

(1) The prices quoted are for orders of invoice value below $ 3000.

(2) For larger orders we offer an extra 5 percent discount.

(3) To popularize the products, all the catalogue prices are subject to a special discount of 15% during this month only.

(4) We are offering you the goods of the highest quality on the most generous terms and would welcome your earliest orders.

(5) In addition, we are offering very generous terms of payment.

✦ Answer to Exercise 5-3

Dear Sir,

We are glad to offer you firm, subject to your reply reaching here by August 25 as follows:
Article: Shoes
Quality: Breeze No. 2
Quantity: 200 pairs
Price: US $ 35 a pair CIF Liverpool
Shipment: September-October
Payment: by confirmed, irrevocable L/C payable by draft at sight to be opened 30 days before the date of shipment
We are looking forward to your early order.

Yours faithfully,
[Signature]

✎ Answer to Exercise 6-1

Dear Sir,

　　We are pleased to receive your offer of July 15, and satisfied with your product. However, we find that we can get a price of US $ 5.00 per dozen with another supplier. This is sixty cents per dozen lower than your price.

　　If you can find out the reason and cut down the price, we would be pleased to place a big order till the end of this year. That order would be one of our largest orders ever since.

　　Looking forward to your early reply.

Yours faithfully,
[Signature]

✎ Answer to Exercise 6-2

(1) In order to finalize the transaction, we suggest that you reduce the prices by 15%.

(2) But we want you to notice that the quality of the other suppliers does not measure up to that of our products.

(3) We believe our price is fixed at a reasonable level.

(4) Considering the fact that we have cooperated so well for these years, we would like to grant your request by reducing the price by 5%.

(5) We hope you take our suggestion into serious consideration and give us your reply as soon as possible.

✎ Answer to Exercise 6-3

Dear Sir,

Re: Beautiful greeting card for all occasions

　　Thank you for your offer of May 5 for the subject article. We are satisfied with the artistic design and high quality of your product.

　　However, since our customers are in urgent need of the goods, we sincerely hope you could shift the delivery time from "the end of October" to "on or before September 15". Otherwise we are afraid they will find other resources.

　　We hope we will receive your acceptance as soon as possible.

Yours faithfully,
[Signature]

✎ Answer to Exercise 7-1

(1) Enclosed we send you an order which please execute at your lowest prices. It is our first trial of your goods and we shall carefully examine their value.

(2) Enclosed pleased find a trial order for 300 bicycles. If the quality of your products proves to be satisfactory to us, we will place large orders in the future.

(3) We have received your letter of the 10th August, enclosing S/C No.90SP-5861 in duplicate against the order No.100 for 500 sets of sewing machines.

(4) As wages and prices of materials have risen considerably, we regret we are not in a position to book the order at the prices we quoted half a year ago.

(5) We are sorry to say that because orders for the item required have been booked up to the end of this year, we are unable to accept any fresh order for shipment within this year.

✦ Answer to Exercise 7-2

Dear Mr. Spear,

　　We are pleased to receive your order for our canned mushroom. We accept the order and are enclosing our Sales Confirmation No. A 786 in duplicate of which please sign and return one copy to us for our file.

　　The terms of payment you suggested, D/P at sight are quite acceptable to us. All the products you order are in stock and we will proceed with the shipment of the captioned products well before March. Special attention will be paid to its packing, which we feel confident. We believe that our products will prove satisfactory to your clients in every respect.

　　We hope that our handling of this order will lead to further business between us and to a happy and lasting association.

Yours faithfully,
[Signature]

✦ Answer to Exercise 7-3

Omitted.

✦ Answer to Exercise 8-1

(1) We believe that this arrangement should make little difference to you and help with our sales, we trust that you will agree to our request.

(2) We regret we cannot accept "cash against documents" on arrival of goods at destination.

(3) We suppose D/P or D/A should be adopted as the modes of payment this time.

(4) We do not think there is any difficulty for you to establish a confirmed irrevocable L/C in our favor to cover your present order, so that we may expect to receive the money at a definite time.

(5) We regret to have to decline your request for D/P terms. Payment by L/C is our usual method of financing trade in these traditional goods.

(6) Since it is a rather substantial order and the machine is to be manufactured to your own specifications, we can only accept your order on sight L/C basis.

(7) We very much regret that we cannot agree to make payment before shipment.

(8) For this transaction, we exceptionally agree to make payment by L/C. But for future transactions, we would ask for more favorable payment terms, i.e., D/P.

(9) It will be highly appreciated if you can kindly give priority to the consideration of the above request and give us an early favorable reply.

(10) We require payment by confirmed and irrevocable letter of credit.

✎ Answer to Exercise 8-2

> Dear Sir,
>
> We would like to place an official order with you for 200 sets of Haier refrigerators as a trial at your price of USD 1200 per set CIF New York for shipment during May/June.
> As this order involves a relatively small amount of money and we have only moderate cash at hand, we would like to pay by D/A at 30 days' sight. If the trial sale proves successful, we shall place large orders in future.
> We hope our proposal can meet with your agreement and look forward to your early reply.
>
> Yours faithfully,
> [Signature]

✎ Answer to Exercise 8-3

Omitted.

✎ Answer to Exercise 9-1

(1) Our cotton should be packed in wooden cases lined with kraft paper and water-proof paper.

(2) The eggs are packed in cartons lined with shake-proof paper board.

(3) Each shirt is packed in a polybag and 6 to a box.

(4) The goods should be packed in a manner that ensures safe and sound arrival of goods at the destination and facilitate handling during transshipment.

(5) The package for export goods should be strong enough to withstand roughest handling during transit.

(6) Garments packed in plastic-lined cartons are not so susceptible to damage by moisture as those packed in wooden cases.

(7) On the outer packing please mark our initials SCC in a diamond.

(8) Each package should have the marking "fragile".

(9) Our cartons for canned food are not only seaworthy but also strong enough to protect the goods from possible damage.

(10) Folding chairs are packed 2 pieces to a carton.

✒ Answer to Exercise 9-2

Dear Sir,

We refer to our S/C No.456WR covering 30" wide × 60" high cotton towel featuring Bottlenose Dolphins D149 with picture below at $15.99 per piece.

We write to you with intention to confirm the order and make the packing clear so as to enable you to carry out the order smoothly.

The goods are packed in a zip-lock style reusable clear plastic package, which a cardboard is inserted covering the front and back of the package, 12 dozen to a carton. The towel was neatly folded inside with the color visible.

When you make shipping marks, please see to it that gross weight, net weight, tare weight shall be put in a diamond with "Made in China" underneath. Contract Number (s) and Number of cartons shall also be stenciled on the packing as well.

Thanks for your cooperation.

Yours faithfully,
[Signature]

✒ Answer to Exercise 10-1

(1) We are sending you today by the American Railway Express, prepaid, the following books.

(2) The cargoes were discharged at San Francisco.

(3) Upon receipt of the L/C, please arrange shipment of the goods booked by us with the least possible delay.

(4) We are informed by the local shipping company that S.S. "Victory" is due to sail for Shanghai on or about the 10th this month.

(5) This consignment is on the S.S. "Princess", which departed from Shanghai on March 20th and is due to arrive in New York on April 5th.

(6) We regret to inform you that we cannot get the goods ready due to the delay by our suppliers at the place of origin.

(7) Shipment is to be made during May to July in three equal lots.

(8) Please let us know the method of transport you prefer for both these consignments.

(9) Since there is no direct steamer to your port from Shanghai, the goods have to be shipped via Hong Kong, China.

(10) Since the L/C has been amended as required and everything is now in order, we hope you will ship our order as early as possible.

✎ Answer to Exercise 10-2

> Dear Sir,
>
> We are glad to inform you that we have shipped the 200 sets of furniture under the Order No. 234 on board S.S. "Princess", which is due to reach your port on May 25.
>
> The goods were carefully checked before shipment, we hope that they will arrive at your end in sound condition and satisfy you.
>
> We sincerely hope that we can have more cooperation in the future.
>
> Yours faithfully,
> [Signature]

✎ Answer to Exercise 10-3

> Dear Sir,
>
> We are pleased to inform you that the goods under your order No. 3979 have now been dispatched.
>
> The coffee machines are packed in fifty separate cartons marked UMT IND MANILA and numbered 1 to 50.
>
> The consignment is on the MV "Mermaid", which left Shanghai on December 5th and is due to arrive in Manila on December 16th.
>
> We have presented to the Overseas Chinese Banking Corporation our draft for the amount of your L/C, together with a full set of shipping documents consisting of clean, shipped on board Bills of Lading in triplicate, Certificate of Insurance, Certificate of Origin and our invoice in triplicate.
>
> We hope that the coffee machines will prove suitable for your customers' needs and look forward to receiving your next order.
>
> Yours faithfully,
> [Signature]

✎ Answer to Exercise 11-1

(1) The Seller shall present the following documents to the paying bank for negotiation/ collection, or to the Buyer in case of payment by M/T.

(2) The full set of negotiable clean on board Bill of Lading marked with "FREIGHT TO COLLECT" and make out to order, blank endorsed, and notifying the China National Foreign Trade Transportation Corporation at the port of destination.

(3) Certificate of Quality/Quantity/Weight and Inspection Report, each in duplicate, issued by the manufacturers.

(4) Within 10 days after shipment is effected, the seller shall prepare three sets, each comprising one copy each of the above-mentioned documents with the exception of the cable shipping advice, one set to be airmailed to the Buyer and the other two sets to the

China National Foreign Trade Transportation Corporation at the port of destination.

Answers to Exercise 12-1

(1) In addition, it is stipulated in the Sales Contract that insurance is to be covered by the Sellers for 10% above the invoice value against All Risks and War Risk with the PICC.

(2) This insurance must be valid for a period of 60 days after the arrival of merchandise at inland destination.

(3) The insurance policy is in triplicate covering All Risks and War Risk including breakage.

(4) We can cover all the risks of ocean transportation.

(5) As our order was placed on CIF basis and you covered the insurance, we should be grateful if you would take the matter up for us with the insurers.

(6) If you desire, we can provide wider coverage, but the extra premium should be for your account.

(7) We hereby confirm the receipt of your letter dated August 8, requesting us to effect insurance on the goods ordered for 110% of the invoice value.

(8) We usually cover insurance against W.P.A. and War Risk in the absence of definite instructions from our clients.

(9) Regarding insurance, the coverage is for 130% of the invoice value up to the port of destination.

(10) The present premium of All Risks including War Risk for the above goods is 0.6%.

Answers to Exercise 12-2

Dear Sir,

Through the introduction of our business partner, we learn that you are a reliable insurance company and have provided satisfactory services to numerous customers in the world.

We have concluded a transaction with a supplier in Britain for 3,000 mobile phones. The goods will be shipped to us from port of London in October. In order to save cost, please issue an open policy for our order at the most favorable terms. For further information about the goods, please refer to the enclosed documents.

We are anticipating your reply.

Yours sincerely,
[Signature]

✎ Answers to Exercise 12-3

Dear Sir,

　　Hereby we acknowledge the receipt of your letter dated March 20, requesting us to cover insurance on 2,000 pairs of Women's shoes on your behalf.
　　We are glad to notify you that the goods have been insured against All Risks including War Risk for 110% of the invoice value, premium amounting to USD 3,200. The policy will be sent to you in two days together with our debit note for the premium.
　　For your information, the goods ordered will be shipped on April 30 by S.S "Princess" sailing from Wuhan to your port if everything goes smoothly.

Yours sincerely,
[Signature]

Answer to Exercise 13-1

Dear Sir,

　　We should like to draw your attention to the defective sewing machine. By the end of June 2014, the machine has broken down four times. The breakdown has led to the loss of more than 15 days' production time while we waited for your local agents' maintenance.
　　The machine is now out of order again. Although it is still on a one-year warranty, we really don't want to have it repaired again and again. Instead, we want you to replace it with a new one.
　　Please inform us when we can expect the delivery of a replacement for the machine under order No.20 on August 2nd.
　　We bought this machine on the basis of your company's reputation for quality and service. We believe that both of us will neither expect nor permit the interruptions caused by repeated breakdowns.
　　Thanks for your cooperation.

Yours faithfully,
[Signature]

✎ Answer to Exercise 13-2

(1) On examination, we found 15% of the packages were broken, which is clearly due to the improper packing.

(2) On examination, we have found that the quality of the products is too inferior to meet the requirement at our local market.

(3) We feel very regretful that a shortage in weight of the goods delivered was noticed after the inspection by China Commodity Inspection Bureau.

(4) The damage was clearly due to the rough handling by the shipping company, you should take up this matter with the insurance company.

(5) The two badly damaged packages have obviously occurred in the transit, and that is a matter over which we can exercise no control.

✎ Answer to Exercise 13-3

Dear Sir,

With reference to your letter regarding 15 cases of the goods delivered in bad conditions. After checking up, you found the shipping company should be responsible for the consequence.

We are very sorry to note your complaint, but we can assure you that the cases in question were in perfect order when they left here, hence the damage complained of must have occurred in the transit. Under such circumstances, we are apparently not liable for the damage and would advise you to claim on the shipping company who should be held responsible.

At any rate, we deeply regret to learn from you about this unfortunate incident and should it be necessary we shall be pleased to take the matter up on your behalf with the shipping company concerned.

Yours faithfully,
[Signature]

✎ Answer to Exercise 14-1

(1) We will not consider a sole agency for the time being, but we may consider this matter by the time when business between us has developed to our mutual satisfaction.

(2) We hope that you would consider appointing us as your sole agent for your digital camera products after knowing our marketing abilities.

(3) After considering your proposal and looking into your business standing, we have decided to entrust you as our sole agent in your specified region under the following terms and conditions.

(4) Thank you for your letter of September 20 proposing that we grant you a sole agency for our household linens.

(5) We enclose price lists covering all the products you are interested in and look forward to hearing from you soon.

✎ Answer to Exercise 14-2

Dear Sir,

We would like to inform you that we act on a sole agency of Matsushita Electric Industrial Co., Japan. We specialize in electrical household appliances for the Pakistani market: Our activities cover all types of household appliances. Until now, we have been working with Matsushita Electric Industrial Co., Japan for six years and our collaboration has proved to be mutually beneficial to mutual satisfaction. Please refer to them for any information regarding our company. We are very interested in an exclusive arrangement with your company for the promotion of your products in Pakistan. We look forward to your early reply.

Very Truly Yours,
[Signature]

Answer to Exercise 15-1

(1) The exhibition center, equipped with various exhibition facilities including broadband access, covers an area of 24000 m^2 with two storeys, of which the ground floor covers 16500 m^2 and the first floor 7500 m^2.

(2) You may call by phone to sign up, but your exhibition booth shall be confirmed only after you remit the registration charges to our account.

(3) All the exhibition stands have been assigned. By the way I have something to talk with you. There are too many exhibition stands and they can not be arranged in an Island because the island arrangement will take a larger space.

(4) The exhibition is quite competitive because all the exhibitors only have a very limited time to attract the visitors and make them understand the information to be conveyed.

(5) At the time of moving out, all the articles must be packed up within a quite short time. In most cases, the time remained for moving out of the exhibition hall will be much shorter than that for moving in.

Answer to Exercise 15-2

Dear Jerry,

I am very glad to hear that Shanghai Galaxy Exhibition Company is going to hold an Auto Exhibition on Oct. 25, 2015 in Shanghai. My company is a big car dealer registered at 254 Euclid Avenue, Bloomington, IN60698, USA and we know that China is a fast-growing car market, so we take great interest in having such a chance to participate in the exhibition.

By the way, I want to have a center booth of 9 square meters at the Auto Exhibition. My full address is as under:

254 Euclid Avenue, Bloomington, IN60698, USA

Phone number: 867-90-2475,

E-mail address: wayne@bloomingtonauto.com

Looking forward to your early.

Yours faithfully,

Harney Robert

Answer to Exercise 16-1

(1) The revised documents will be sent to all the bidding document purchasers, and the bidders should immediately confirm the receipt of the modified documents in written form.

(2) The bidder will be notified that he has the right to modify his Form of Tender submitted, sent or delivered before the official bidding time, but the bidder must assure the Employer/Engineer the receipt of the Bid in written form before the stipulated submission time.

(3) The tendering centre may ask the bidders to clarify their bidding contents, of which all the requests for clarification and reply should be made in written form, but it is not allowed to make any alteration of the quotation or any material alteration of the bid.

(4) If the bidder's tender evaluated as the lowest quotation, includes some unacceptable biases even after clarification, the bidder will be notified and granted with the right to withdraw such biases. Only when the bidder makes a written confirmation of withdrawal of such biases and make no alteration of the quoted prices, will he be considered to have withdrawn the biases.

(5) Bids must be delivered to the address below and accepted with validity before 10:00 am on bid opening date. Bids will be opened at 11:30 am (Beijing time) on 20 October 2014.

✎ Answer to Exercise 16-2

> INTERNATIONAL COMPETITIVE BIDDING
> THE REPUBLIC OF UGANDA
> MINISTRY OF HEALTH
> IMPROVEMENT OF HEALTH SERVICES AT MULAGO
> HOSPITAL AND THE CITY OF KAMPALA PROJECT (MKCCAP)
>
> PROJECT NO. P–UG–IB0–006
> LOAN NO: 2100150025094
> IFB No.: MOH/SUPLS–MKCCA/2013–14/00599
>
> 1. This Invitation for Bids follows the General Procurement Notice (GPN) for this project that appeared in the United Nations Development Business (UNDB) No. AfDB299–809/11 online 11 October 2014 and on the African Development Bank Group's Internet Website.
> 2. The Government of Uganda has received financing from the African Development Fund (ADF) and the Nigerian Trust Fund towards the cost of the Improvement of Health Services Delivery at Mulago Hospital and the City of Kampala Project. It is intended that part of the proceeds of this loan will be applied to eligible payments under the contract for Purchase of 10 ambulances for Kampala Metropolitan Area.
> 3. The Ministry of Health (MoH) now invites sealed bids from eligible bidders for the supply of 10 ambulances.
> 4. Interested and eligible bidders may obtain further information from and inspect the bidding documents at the office of:
>   The Project Coordinator,
>   MKCCA Project,
>   P.O. Box 8096, Kampala, Uganda
>   Tel.: +256 414 534025/533481
>   Fax: +256 414 530701
>   Email: hsrp@imul.com
> 5. A complete set of bidding documents may be obtained by interested bidders on submission of written application to the address below.
> 6. The provisions in the Instructions to Bidders and the General Conditions of Contract are the provisions of the African Development Bank Standard Bidding Document for Procurement of Goods.

7. Bids must be delivered to the address below on or before 11:00 am (East African Standard time) on 20 March 2015 accompanied by a bid security of USD 31000.
8. Bids will be opened in the presence of the bidders' representatives who choose to attend at 11:30 am (East African Standard Time) on 25 March 2015 at the offices of
    The Head of Procurement and Disposal Unit,
    Ministry of Health Headquarters,
    Plot 6, Lourdel Road, Room C308
    P.O. Box 52372, Kampala–Uganda

Key to Exercise 17-1

(1) The Buyer shall open a confirmation irrevocable L / C in favor of the Seller with / through the bank acceptable to the Seller, one month before the shipment.

(2) It is mutually agreed that the goods are subject to the Inspection Certificate of Quality and Inspection Certificate of Quantity issued by China Import and Export at the port of shipment. The Certificate shall be binding on both parties.

(3) Before delivery the manufacturer should make a precise and overall inspection of the goods regarding quality, quantity, specification and performance and issue the certificate indicating the goods in conformity with the stipulation of the contract. The certificates are one part of the documents presented to the bank for negotiation of the payment and should not be considered as final regarding quality, quantity, specification and performance. The manufacturer should include the inspection written report in the Inspection Certificate of Quality, stating the inspection particulars.

(4) Any discrepancy on the shipped goods should be put forward within 30 days after the arrival of the vessel carrying the goods at the port of destination and the Buyer should present the Survey Report issued by the Surveyor agreed by the Seller. If the goods have been processed the Buyer will loss the right to claim. The Seller shall not settle the claim within the responsibility of the Insurance Company or Ship Company.

(5) The contractor agree to redo the part of the project which are not conformed to the drawings' specification with the other projects performed/done meanwhile, remedy defects caused by/result from/arise from faulty materials and workmanship which are proved by evidence in one year after the completion of the project.

Key to Exercise 17-2

(1) 当事一方如因不可抗力原因（包括火灾、旱灾、地震、风灾、飓风或其他自然灾害），以及战争、入侵、外敌行为、敌对行动（无论是否宣战）、内战、动乱、革命、暴动、军事或篡权或征用、恐怖活动、国有化、政府制裁、封锁、禁运、劳资纠纷、罢工、因电力或电话服务中断而停工或生产中断等造成当事一方无法履行其责任义务。在此情况下，任何一方都无权按照该协议第17款（协议的终止）要求终止该协议。如果一方提出不可抗力作为其不履行其义务的理由，则未履行义务的一方必须证明其采取了合理的措施把可预测的事件所造成的延迟交货或损害降低至最小，且该当事一方已充分履行了所有免责义务，并及时将不可抗力条款中所列的事件发生的可能性或实际发生的情形通知另一方。

(2) 凡在制造或装船运输过程中，因不可抗力致使卖方推迟或不能交货时，卖方不负责任。在发生上述情况时，卖方应立即通知买方，并在____天内，给买方特快专递一份由政府主管当局签发的事故证明书。在此情况下，卖方仍有责任采取一切必要措施加快交货。如事故延续____天以上，买方有权撤销合同。

(3) 合同双方均同意，对有关该合同中所指交易的任意条款的适用或解释，双方将努力通过友好协商的方式，解决双方之间发生的一切纠纷。如果以该方式无法在合理的时间内（自告知该纠纷之日起最长不超过90天）解决纠纷，使买卖双方均达到满意，买房不将该事件上诉到买房认为合适的裁判管辖地法院，则该争议事项应当提交仲裁。除双方另有约定外，此仲裁应按照中国国际贸易促进会对外贸易仲裁委员会所规定的仲裁规则和程序进行仲裁，仲裁地点在_____（地点）。仲裁裁决是终局的，对双方均有约束力。仲裁费应当由败诉方承担，另有裁定者除外。

Answer to Exercise 18-1

Dear Mr. Smith,

Thank you for your Letter of Credit No. 048 covering your Order No. 054 for 50 metric tons of Ore which we received this morning.

After examination of the Letter of Credit, we found that there is no stipulation of partial shipments being allowed in the relative L/C, so we can hardly manage to arrange this parcel. When making our Offer No. 038 dated March 5, 2015, we state clearly that the parcel is to be divided into 2 lots. That is: 25 metric tons for each.

The first lot of the goods is ready for shipment at present, so we have to request you to amend the L/C accordingly as soon as possible.

Thank you again for your order and support of our business.

Yours faithfully,
[Signature]

Answer to Exercise 18-2

Dear Ms. Li,

Have you received the Pro forma Invoice No. 150323 covering the material required under your Order 000380 which we sent to you on April 7th? Please proceed to apply for the irrevocable Letter of Credit as outlined by the attached instruction sheet.

Thank you for your cooperation. Please feel free to contact us if you have any questions.

Yours faithfully,
[Signature]

References
参考文献

1. 蔡惠伟. 外经贸函电教程（第二版）. 上海：华东理工大学出版社，2012.

2. 綦颖，王菲，钱福东. 国际贸易函电. 北京：北京理工大学出版社，2009.

3. 范红，王朝晖，廖国强. 英文商务写作教程. 北京: 清华大学出版社, 2000.

4. 管春林，章汝雯. 新编商务英语函电教程. 北京：清华大学出版社，北京交通大学出版社，2013.

5. 胡英坤，车丽娟. 商务英语写作. 北京: 外语教学与研究出版社, 2005.

6. 兰天. 外贸英语函电. 大连：东北财经大学出版社，2004.

7. 李艳丽. 外贸英语函电. 山东：山东人民出版社，2009.

8. 李文彪，张丽红，鄢华平. 国际商务函电学习指导. 北京：北京理工大学出版社，2009

9. 廖瑛，肖曼君. 实用外贸英语函电——译文、练习答案及常见错误辨析. 武汉：华中科技大学出版社，2012.

10. 陆墨珠. 国际商务函电. 北京：中国商务出版社，2005.

11. 戚云方. 新编外经贸英语函电与谈判. 杭州：浙江大学出版社，2002.

12. 任素贞. 新编外贸英语教程. 北京：北京大学出版社，2012.

13. 谭燕. 外贸英文信函. 北京：人民邮电出版社，2013.

14. 王乃彦. 对外经贸英语函电（第五版）. 北京：对外经济贸易大学出版社，2013.

15. 王美玲. 外贸函电. 北京：机械工业出版社，2013.

16. 王妍，刘亚卓. 外贸函电. 北京：北京大学出版社，2013.

17. 王宗湖，李细平，郭天宇. 商务英语写作. 北京: 对外经济贸易大学出版社, 2006.

18. 朱纪伟. 入世商务英语写作. 合肥: 安徽科学技术出版社, 2002.

19. 蒋磊. 国际商务英语函电. 北京：对外经济贸易大学出版社，2014.

20. 梁树新. 外贸函电情景实训. 北京：清华大学出版社，2014.

21. 滕美荣，许楠. 外贸英语函电. 北京：首都经济贸易大学出版社，2005.

22. 王传见. 国际货代物流实务英语手册. 上海：华东理工大学出版社，2011.

23. 王慧敏. 外贸函电. 北京：北京大学出版社，2005.

24. 吴云. 会展交际英语. 上海：立信会计出版社，2004.

25. 张占军，张宝敏，张宏杰. 北京：中国商务出版社，2005.

26. 尹小莹. 外贸英语函电——商务英语应用文写作（第3版）. 西安：西安交通大学出版

社，2004.

27.（美）辛克曼（E. G. Hinkelman）. 国际支付. 上海：上海外语教育出版社，2000.

28.（美）希皮（K. C. Shippey）. 国际商务合同. 上海：上海外语教育出版社，2000.

29. 查尔斯·W. L. 希尔（Charles W. L. Hill）. 国际商务. 北京：中国人民大学出版社，2005.

30.（美）迈克尔 R. 钦科陶 (Michael R. Czinkota). 国际商务. 北京：机械工业出版社，2003.

31.（美）迪马特奥（L. A. DiMatteo）. 国际商法. 北京：北京大学出版社，2004.

32. 张亦辉，（美）赫德（Bruce Hird）. 点石成金——英语商函写作实务. 北京：外语教学与研究出版社，2002.

33.（英）埃里斯（M. Ellis），（英）约翰逊（C. Johnson）. 商务英语教学. 上海：上海外语教育出版社，2002.

34.（美）萨宾（W. A. Sabin）. 最新英文商务写作手册. 北京：机械工业出版社，2003.

35.（美）托马斯. A. 普格（Thomas A. Pugel）. 国际贸易. 北京：中国人民大学出版社，2005.

36.（美）莱曼 （C. M. Lehman），(美) 达弗林（D. D. DuFrene）. 商务沟通. 大连：东北财经大学出版社，2005.

37.（美）简·耶格尔（Jan Yager）. 美国商务写作. 北京：中国长安出版社，2004.

38. http://smallbusiness.chron.com

39. http://writingcenter.unc.edu/handouts/business-letters/

40. http://china.findlaw.cn/gongsifalv/zixindiaocha/zxdctj/.

41. http://en.wikipedia.org/wiki/Commercial_credit_reporting.

42. http://wenku.baidu.com.

43. http://www.fobshanghai.com.

44. http://www.doc88.com.

45. http://www.alibaba.com.

46. http://course.baidu.com.

47. http://fanyi.baidu.com.

48. http:// www.ehow.com.

49. http://www.docin.com.

50. http://www.en8848.com.cn.

51. http://www.gedu.org.

52. http://en.wikipedia.org.

53. http://www.proceq.com.

54. http://www.answers.com.

55. http://metc.gdut.edu.cn/trade/index.htm.

56. http://www.callcentrehelper.com.

57. http://www.nanosft.com/igc/AnatomyofAnAgencyRelationship.html.

58. http://www.expo2010china.com.

59. http://www.fairsandexpos.com.

60. http://secure.investni.com/static/library.

61. https://search.yahoo.com/search.

62. http://construction.about.com/od/Bidding–Process.

63. http://www.afdb.org/fileadmin/uploads/afdb/Documents/Procurement.

64. http://www.jianshe99.com/upload/html.

65. http://rfptemplates.technologyevaluation.com/rfp–letter–of–intent.html.

66. http://www.clearwater–fl.com.

67. http://www.66us.com.cn.

68. http://www.66law.cn/lawarticle/1055.aspx.